BLOODLINE

BLOODLINE

THE CELTIC KINGS OF ROMAN BRITAIN

MILES RUSSELL

AMBERLEY

For Bill Putnam
Without whom there would be no Bournemouth University
Without whom there would be no Wessex Archaeology
Without whom our understanding of Roman Britain would be so much the
poorer

First published 2010

Amberley Publishing Plc
Cirencester Road, Chalford,
Stroud, Gloucestershire, GL6 8PE

www.amberley-books.com

Copyright © Miles Russell 2010

The right of Miles Russell to be identified as
the Author of this work has been asserted in
accordance with the Copyrights, Designs and
Patents Act 1988.

ISBN 978 1 84868 238 2

British Library Cataloguing in Publication Data.
A catalogue record for this book is available from
the British Library.

Typeset in 10pt on 12pt Sabon.
Typesetting and Origination by FONTHILLDESIGN.
Printed in the UK.

CONTENTS

Acknowledgements 7

Introduction 9

1. Background: a blood-spattered curse on our land 15
2. Cassivellaunos and Caesar: the circus of death 33
3. Tasciovanus and Augustus: someone with a grudge 50
4. Cunobelinus and Rome: the currency of pain 68
5. Amminus and Caligula: the dignity of labour 83
6. Caratacus and Claudius: the ones who make a stand 91
7. Boudicca and the Catuvellauni: blind revenge on a blameless victim 116
8. Togidubnus and Nero: the path of least resistance 140
9. Agricola and the North: you can carry on your slaughter 147
10. Lucullus and Domitian: empire state human 161
11. Aftermath: a trail of the dead 178

Further Reading 187
Index 191

'The one duty we owe to history is to rewrite it'

Oscar Wilde The Critic as Artist 1891

ACKNOWLEDGEMENTS

This book developed from my teaching of a unit entitled 'The Archaeology of Roman Britain' to undergraduate students at Bournemouth University between 1995 and 2009. Over the years, as I delivered this unit, I began to realise that there was an increasing disparity between what I believed and what I was being asked to teach. Not only was the archaeological evidence often apparently at odds with the historical sources but also our understanding of 'what really happened' seemed to be based on little more than a series of plausible, if ultimately ungrounded fictions, something that the students themselves were only too aware. That it has taken something close to six years to finally write down my concerns, is as much an admission of guilt as it is a statement of honesty. I could of course blame the lack of study leave at my own particular institution, but this is an ever increasing problem in many of Britain's universities, most of which no longer seem to value research, making the pursuit of study leave an increasingly thankless task. Instead of apologising, therefore, I will acknowledge that the 72 months spent 'mulling things over' during the course of my work, have indeed proved useful. Archaeology relies upon the continual discovery of new sites and artefacts and the generation of alternative theories and ideas. When conducted properly, it is a subject that is constantly self-renewing and is therefore an ideal area in which to work. I am grateful that, in those seventy two months I have had the opportunity to discuss, debate and argue with a truly unique collection of staff and students, colleagues and friends, all of whom have made my time at Bournemouth interesting, exciting and enjoyable. I would particularly like to thank all those undergraduates who have studied my year three unit on Roman Britain, especially those who took the maxim 'question everything' to beyond its logical extreme. You know who you are.

In the actual writing of this book, I am supremely grateful to those who shared their knowledge, ideas and thoughts, particularly Guy de la Bedoyere, Paul Cheetham, Mark Corney, Tim Darvill, Neil Faulkner, John Gale, Ellen Hambleton, Mark Hassall, Iain Hewitt, Neil Holbrook, Stuart Laycock, Mark Maltby, Dave McOmish, Richard Reece and Bronwen Russell. A big thank you also to all the institutions, organisations and individuals who generously allowed me to quote from their works or use their images within this book: I have acknowledged these where they occur. I am further indebted to Jane Russell for compiling and creating all the line drawings and plans in the present work, often at very short notice and without any useful (or coherent) instruction from myself and to Glynis Laughlin for proof reading the final text. Any mistakes or errors that remain are entirely my fault and relate to last minute changes for which she had no control.

Special thanks must also go to all at Amberley Publishing, in particular Peter Kemmis Betty and Tom Vivian for commissioning, overseeing and believing.

Book writing is an addiction and as with all addictions it is those closest to the addict who suffer the most and so in this respect I would like to thank Bronwen, Megan and Macsen for their continued support and for helping me get through this particular endeavour one day at a time. It has been a long haul, but at least the dining room can once more be used for its original purpose, rather than acting as a store for unread books, unused photocopies and countless notepads. I would also like to thank all those students who, since 1993, have passed through BSc Archaeology, BSc Heritage, BSc Field Archaeology, BSc Marine Archaeology, FdSC Field Archaeology, HND Archaeology, BA Archaeology and Prehistory and, of course, BA Roman Archaeology. You have sat through my lectures, hiked through my fieldtrips and hacked through my trenches – I hope now that it all makes sense.

Finally I would like to acknowledge a huge debt of gratitude to Bill Putnam who reignited my interest in Roman archaeology when I first came to Bournemouth. Bill was an extraordinary man blessed with an inexhaustible enthusiasm for Roman archaeology. A student of Sir Mortimer Wheeler, Bill was appointed lecturer in archaeology at Weymouth College Dorset in 1967, where he swiftly became Head of History and Archaeology. He was chairman of the Dorset Archaeological Committee in the 1970s and 80s, at a time when both the pace of development was increasing and as archaeology iteslf was first becoming a serious and profession. He was also Chairman of Wessex Archaeology from 1977 to 1999, guiding the organisation as it became one of Britain's leading archaeological companies. The basis of Weymouth College transformed (and moved) becoming first the Dorset Institute of Higher Education and then Bournemouth Polytechnic. Its final evolution into Bournemouth University in 1992 was thanks primarily to the core science programmes undertaken there, the most important of which was the HND in Archaeology. Throughout this time, Bill continued both his research into Roman Dorset, particularly at the Dorchester aqueduct and Dewlish villa, and his teaching, inspiring many generations of archaeologists with his energy, knowledge and irrepressible sense of humour.

It is to his memory that this book is respectfully dedicated.

INTRODUCTION

There have been so many books on Roman Britain, and one needs some
justification for adding yet another
(Cottrell 1956, ii)

Some will pick up this volume with a feeling of 'oh, not another book about
Roman Britain'. I have great sympathy with this view as there are too many
books with little new to say
(Millett 1990, xv)

A new book on Roman Britain requires explanation and perhaps justification,
since the island has been the subject of many a book already
(Braund 1996, ii)

The story of Roman Britain has been written many times; indeed perhaps too
often ...
(Mattingly 2002, xi)

Yet another book on Roman Britain perhaps deserves some explanation
(Creighton 2006, ix)

There is a curious sense of self-flagellation apparent in most books detailing life
in Roman Britain. It is a strange phenomenon, one that I cannot detect within
any other period or historical genre. Not even the biographers of Henry VIII, a
British monarch studied in more obsessive detail than any other person in British
history, feel the need to abase themselves for producing 'yet another' work on
the monarch. However much is said about the bloated, corrupt and thoroughly
unpleasant king, there always seems to be something new to say; some new angle
to examine. The same is ultimately true of Roman Britain.

SAME OLD STORY?

As long ago as 1982, Richard Reece noted that:

> text books on Roman Britain to date make the subject appear like a nice sandpit in which toddlers can safely be left to play. I am thankful that it is instead a wild, overgrown garden in which anything may happen
> (Reece 1982, 456)

Despite Reece's warning, the need to 'ask other things' in order to question models of complacent orthodoxy has been absent within academic circles for some time now. Comparatively few archaeologists have dared raise their heads above the parapets of complacency for fear of either being savagely mauled by their colleagues or being branded 'pseudo', 'alternative' or 'fringe'. There has been, within the past half a century or so, no archaeo-reboot for Roman Britain, involving a dramatic and all-embracing shift in perspective and understanding.

The problem with archaeology, of course, is that new discoveries generate paradoxes which, if they contradict existing belief-systems, can easily be ignored or overlooked. The perceived failure of the archaeological community to engage in alternative discourse about the past has meant that the 'baton of creativity' is frequently clasped by those beyond the walls of academia. As a result, this means that there are often two versions of history in existence: the safe, ordered sand pit of orthodoxy and the disordered bear-pit of those unconstrained by academic respectability. It is easy for those protecting the establishment perspective to criticise, deride or ignore the alternative standpoint, although it is interesting, and perhaps rather sobering, to note that the most pertinent and refreshing questions and perspectives have often been generated from the world of the 'fringe' rather than the 'mainstream'.

I am not, of course, saying that everything that has been said about Roman Britain in the past is wrong; far from it. It is my firm belief that Sheppard Frere's book *Britannia*, first published in 1967 (and reprinted countless times thereafter) is the greatest book ever written about the province (if not one of the greatest books on any period in British history). Frere's writing is so convincing, his arguments so masterful, that *Britannia* has created a template for Roman Britain that is by turns totally believable and also wholly unassailable. My problem is, that in the words of television marketing today, the consumer should be aware that 'other products are also available'. The archaeological and historical evidence for Roman Britain, such as it is, has in the last three decades, frequently been presented as a single and largely coherent story. Unfortunately, the evidence itself, when one looks at it closely, is easily capable of supporting multiple, alternative versions of 'the truth'.

ESTABLISHED FACTS

Any study of Roman Britain is riddled with Established Facts. I capitalise deliberately here (and indeed throughout the book), not only to draw attention to these key issues, but also to highlight those areas where supposition has become a theory, where theory has then become the basis for a model and where the model has, before long, become a 'Fact'. 'Facts', once established in print become almost impossible to disprove or otherwise argue against. They are the large immovable objects, the great certainties of historic discourse. They are also frequently unprovable, if not completely wrong.

There are many examples of Established Fact littered throughout this present work and, where they occur, I have tried either to question them, pointing out their sometimes inherent ridiculousness; at others to present alternative theories based upon the same evidence. Examples where the supposition has become the unquestionable fact with regard to Roman Britain include such examples as:

The Roman invasion army of AD 43 comprised four legions, the II, IX, XIV and the XX.

Who says? Certainly not the only surviving Roman historical account of the event, written by one Dio Cassius in the third century AD. He provides no numbers and no idea of combat strength for the initial invasion force. In short, anything that you read about the units involved in the 'Great Invasion' is a modern fiction.

The Invasion army first landed at Richborough in Kent.

Really? Were you there? No one has any idea where this mystery strength army landed in AD 43. It may have been Richborough, it may not. There is no firm evidence one way or another. Anyone who tells you differently is lying.

The Catuvellauni tribe were Rome's chief opponent in the early stages of the British campaign.

You don't say. That presumably is why they were so well treated immediately after the conquest whilst Rome's apparent allies (at least according to Established Fact), the Trinovantes, were treated like a defeated enemy.

The Druids co-ordinated British resistance against Rome.

I bow to your greater knowledge in this respect for, as far as I'm aware, no Roman historian ever comments upon either the organisational ability of the Druids or whether they possessed any influence beyond the island of Anglesey (where the Roman army finally caught up with them in AD 60). I assume that you must have good evidence from an alternative source?

Boudicca's revolt against Rome was confined to Essex and Hertfordshire and did not extend south of the river Thames.

And we know this because…? If Queen Boudicca and her people only destroyed the towns of Colchester, London and St Albans, then why is there evidence of extensive burning in Silchester and Winchester at the same date? Did these cities also fall prey to the horde or were the good citizens of these two towns simply careless with candles?

Fishbourne Roman palace was the residence of king Togidubnus.

Sorry, I must have missed something. Have we found his nameplate or calling card with address? No, didn't think so – just a guess then.

Of course, I am not, in any of these examples, saying that 'I am right' or at least pretending that I know any of the answers: I'm not and I don't. Neither am I pointing accusingly at those that have made the initial suppositions or dared to put forward any of the theories. Their view is just as valid as mine or anyone else's. I do hope, however, to show that certain key Established Facts about Roman Britain require a little more discussion and debate than they normally receive. I am also pleading for more open and questioning minds when it comes to both historic and archaeological 'evidence'. There is ultimately very little in the way of black and white fact about the province of Britannia, but there are multiple shades of grey. The discovery of such grey areas/errors/possible alternative interpretations within the accepted history of Roman Britain may, perhaps, seem small and rather insignificant in the 'big scheme of things'; but it is not. Our entire perception of what being Roman meant, to whom, when and for how long is challenged by their identification. Our understanding of how Britain became Roman and whether or not this was a success is fundamentally altered as well.

This book is permeated throughout by the principle known as 'Occam's Razor', a medieval maxim, often (perhaps erroneously) attributed to the Franciscan William of Ockham. The basis for the principle is one of economy whereby in attempting to explain a phenomenon an observer should work from the evidence supplied and, whilst taking all the circumstances into account, make as few assumptions as possible. In other words, 'why go for a difficult explanation when a simple one will do?' It is the simple answer that, however 'unpleasant', is often the more preferable. History and archaeology are difficult enough to interpret without needless over complication. *Bloodline* is therefore presented to you as an attempt to provide an alternative history for early Roman Britain. It may not go as far as I (or others) would like, but at least it's a start. That essential points of the established narrative for *Britannia* will certainly change as new sites are excavated and new discoveries made (and ultimately new theories are generated) is exactly as it should be, for that is the joy of archaeology.

The majority of books on Roman Britain treat the early history of the province as a straightforward move from prehistory to history, AD 43 being the critical point at which the island became a province. Given the surviving evidence, however, I would prefer to view the transition from Britain to *Britannia* as a gradual evolution, one that comprised three main periods of time. Before 55 BC, southern Britain was, beyond the harbours and coastal trading centres, largely untroubled by the world of Rome. Between 55 BC and AD 96, the tribes of central-southern and south-eastern Britain developed into a series of client states, supported and (at least nominally) protected by Rome. In this, the pivotal date of AD 43 is nothing of the sort, merely representing an acceleration of the process in which the south was becoming 'Roman' (with tribes and their rulers being recognised and permitted to continue in power) rather than a sudden change in leadership accompanied by a military crackdown (as happened in AD 1066). After AD 96 Britain becomes a province of the empire, just like everywhere else, the client states having been formally dissolved. This transition is, it is usually believed, thought to have been due to the direct involvement of two distinct and powerful families, both Roman: the Julio-Claudians (who treated Britain as their play-thing) and the Flavians (who moulded it into a proper working province). There was a third family however, one who, although firmly based in Britain, possessed a curiously distinctive Roman outlook. The account that follows is essentially their story.

1

BACKGROUND: A BLOOD-SPATTERED CURSE ON OUR LAND

The Britons were formerly governed by kings, but at present they are divided in factions and parties among their chiefs; and this want of union for concerting some general plan is the most favourable circumstance to us, in our designs against so powerful a people. It is seldom that two or three communities concur in repelling the common danger; and thus, while they engage singly, they are all subdued (Tacitus *Agricola*, 12)

Modern maps of 'Late Iron Age Britain' make everything appear well ordered and organised: the island divided into neat, discrete tribal zones (*1*). Each identified tribe must (we presume) have had its own peculiar language, dress code, gods and ways of doing things. Each tribe (we can further presume) must have had its own leaders, political centre and road infrastructure, created for the purposes of war, trade and tax collection. Every tribe must (by implication) have had a clear idea of which land was theirs, where the frontiers were and where their own distinctive brand of civilisation came to an end. It is worth pointing out, however, that, given the evidence available, such a view is entirely without foundation.

Our understanding of Late Iron Age tribal structure is poor to say the least. Ultimately we do not possess any clear understanding of what a tribe was within Iron Age society, nor what the term actually meant in the context of prehistoric Britain. Classical writers, such as Caesar, Tacitus and Dio Cassius, all talked in fairly generalised terms about tribes, tribal groups and tribal leaders (princes, kings, queens and other aristocrats), but none provided specific information as to the nature of authority and social organisation in Britain. Indigenous political structure was almost certainly more complex and intractable than the average Roman mind could deal with. A Mediterranean readership, having been brought up within a system of 'the Senate and People' guided by 'the first citizen', or emperor, were happy in the knowledge that more 'primitive' social systems existed: tribes with one leader (or one city state with one king). Anything else could safely be filed under 'curious', 'barbaric' or just plain 'weird'.

1 The neat ordering of tribal zones as set out in most modern maps claiming to depict the political reality of Later Iron Age Britain.

THE PEOPLE OF BRITAIN

In the year 55 BC, the Roman general Gaius Julius Caesar, fresh from slaughtering his way across Gaul (modern day France), set his sights upon a distant goal: the island of Britain. As he butchered his way through Gallic society, Caesar had cleverly documented the unfolding events in a collected series of dispatches from the front line. Together these commentaries are referred to as the *Gallic Wars* and they are an invaluable source of information: first hand observations made, not only by someone who was there, but by someone who was making the events happen. Written entirely in the third person, as if Caesar were describing the exploits of another (a literary masterstroke, making the text appear less egocentric and slightly more objective), the *Gallic Wars* provide a unique and totally Roman perspective upon the population of Gaul, Germany and Britain. They are, however, wholly subjective and totally biased; a bigoted take on an unjust and unwarranted war and one in which the hero (Caesar himself) is shown in the best possible light whilst the 'enemy' are simultaneously denigrated and demonised.

A Roman audience, eagerly lapping up Caesar's account of his experiences in alien lands would probably not have cared too much for the political landscape of Britain, nor would they have needed much in the way of specific geographical detail. Such information, although vital to a modern researcher trying to understand Roman strategy, would only have slowed the pace of Caesar's account. In fact, the only time the general pauses from the main action, is to provide lurid detail surrounding the customs, appearance, culture and sexual proclivities of the average savage Briton and not to provide a description of either the political climate or the topography. Hence, we are told by Caesar that:

> The interior portion of Britain is inhabited by those of whom they say that it is handed down by tradition that they were born in the island itself: the maritime portion by those who had passed over from the country of the Belgae for the purpose of plunder and making war
> (*Gallic Wars* 5, 12)

The Britons are, in this account, therefore both warlike and highly mobile; a dangerous combination. Direct military intervention in Britain therefore seems to makes sound strategic sense.

> The number of the people is countless, and their buildings exceedingly numerous
> (*Gallic Wars* 5, 12)

In other words 'there are worryingly large quantities of them'.

> The number of cattle is great. They use either brass or iron rings, determined at a certain weight, as their money. Tin is produced in the midland regions; in the maritime, iron; but the quantity of it is small: they employ brass, which is imported. There, as in Gaul, is timber of every description, except beech and fir
> (*Gallic Wars* 5, 12)

They are, from both and agricultural and mineralogical perspective, extremely wealthy. Invasion would also therefore make sound economic sense.

> They do not regard it lawful to eat the hare, and the cock, and the goose; they, however, breed them for amusement and pleasure
> (*Gallic Wars* 5, 12)

They are odd, let's face it.

> The climate is more temperate than in Gaul, the colds being less severe
> (*Gallic Wars* 5, 12)

Even their surroundings are strange.

> Most of the inland inhabitants do not sow corn, but live on milk and flesh, and are clad with skins
> (*Gallic Wars* 5, 14)

Compared to us Romans, they lead a rather simple, primitive existence.

> All the Britons, indeed, dye themselves with woad, which occasions a bluish colour, and thereby have a more terrible appearance in fight. They wear their hair long, and have every part of their body shaved except their head and upper lip
> (*Gallic Wars* 5, 14)

They also look like nothing on earth (2).

> Ten and even twelve have wives common to them, and particularly brothers among brothers, and parents among their children; but if there be any issue by these wives, they are reputed to be the children of those by whom respectively each was first espoused when a virgin

And they're filthy.

It is the more extreme elements in Caesar's account that strike a chord with his contemporary Mediterranean audience. Strabo, a Greek philosopher and geographer writing in the late first century BC for his multi-volume *Geographica* (*The Geography*), borrows heavily from Caesar's book, adding a little something of his own when he notes that Britain:

> bears grain, cattle, gold, silver, and iron. These things, accordingly, are exported from the island, as also hides, and slaves, and dogs that are by nature suited to the purposes of the chase; the Celti, however, use both these and the native dogs for the purposes of war too.

2 A rare contemporary depiction of an Iron Age face from the time of Julius Caesar. The bronze, from Welwyn, Hertfordshire, reflects Caesar's concerns that the British males shaved 'every part of their body ... except their head and upper lip'. Originally one of a series of decorative elements accompanying a cremation burial dating to between 50 and 20 BC. © *Trustees of the British Museum*

The economic wealth of the Island, especially in those things the Roman State desired, namely food, metals and slaves, are cited by Strabo almost in the same way one would compile a shopping list. Then, having dealt with the financial side of Britain, Strabo goes on to describe the people:

> The men of Britain are taller than the Celti, and not so yellow-haired, although their bodies are of looser build. The following is an indication of their size: I myself, in Rome, saw mere lads towering as much as half a foot above the tallest people in the city, although they were bandy-legged and presented no fair lines anywhere else in their figure. Their habits are in part like those of the Celti, but in part more simple and barbaric, so much so that, on account of their inexperience, some of them, although well supplied with milk, make no cheese; and they have no experience in gardening or other agricultural pursuits.

Their physical characteristics are, therefore, not to be admired (especially when compared to the average Roman), for they are tall but gangly (and ugly). It is their utter lack of any civilising features, their simple way of life, drinking milk and eating meat under the stars, with no concept of best agricultural practice, that marks the Britons out as mere children; savages to be patronised and pitied.

> And they have powerful chieftains in their country. For the purposes of war they use chariots for the most part, just as some of the Celti do. The forests are their cities; for they fence in a spacious circular enclosure with trees which they have felled, and in that enclosure make huts for themselves and also pen up their cattle – not, however, with the purpose of staying a long time. Their weather is more rainy than snowy; and on the days of clear sky fog prevails so long a time that throughout a whole day the sun is to be seen for only three or four hours round about midday
> (Strabo *The Geography* IV, 5, 2)

But, unlike children, they are to be feared: their warlike and hardy traits, derived from the harsh environments they inhabit, making them a formidable foe. All these barbarian characteristics take more obvious form when Strabo turns his attention to Ireland. Here, concerning the inhabitants, he observes that they:

> are more savage than the Britons, since they are man-eaters as well as heavy eaters, and since, further, they count it an honourable thing, when their fathers die, to devour them, and openly to have intercourse, not only with the other women, but also with their mothers and sisters
> (*The Geography* IV, 5, 4)

… adding, rather tellingly, 'but I am saying this only with the understanding that I have no trustworthy witnesses for it'. Quite.

Such descriptive interludes tell us more about the Roman mindset, and the need to belittle and demonise a foe, than the archaeological reality of Iron Age life across Britain and Ireland. Caesar and Strabo were not the ancient equivalents of modern anthropologists, hiding within unobtrusive dens or bravely trying 'fit in' in order to objectively record the native; their observations were purely designed to both horrify and amuse their 'civilised' audience.

THE TRIBES OF CAESAR

When it comes to indigenous political structure, Caesar records the presence of only six tribes in southern Britain (3), the area in which he conducted his campaign of systematic terror and violence: The Cenimagni, the Trinobantes, the Ancalites, the Bibroci, the Cassi and the Segontiaci.

The Trinobantes may be dealt with first for, led by their king Mandubracius, they appear to have been Caesar's chief allies in Britain, All later sources seem to suggest that the tribe occupying the area around modern Essex, whose capital centre may have been at Camulodunum (Colchester), at the time of the Claudian invasion of AD 43 were the Trinovantes, hence Trino*bantes* in the Gallic Wars is a later scribal error, b replacing the more correct v form. In this the name Trinovantes may be broken down into two elements: Novantae, perhaps meaning 'lively or vigorous', coupled with the prefix Tri, creating 'most lively or most vigorous'. All well and good and it is clear that b is sometimes used instead of v in personal Celtic names appearing in

3 British politics in 54 BC according to Julius Caesar. Caesar names only six tribes in southern Britain, the Cenimagni, Trinobantes, Ancalites, Bibroci, Cassi and Segontiaci, whilst confirming the presence of at least another five. Only the Trinobantes and Cenimagni seem to have survived into the mid first century AD.

Latin or Greek texts (hence Berikos for Verica), but it is worth noting that, of the forms provided for the tribe in a variety of ancient sources we have: Trinobantes in Caesar's *Gallic War*, Trinobantes in Tacitus (*Annals* xiv, 31), Τρινοαντες (Trinoantes) in Ptolemy (*Geography* II, 3, 11) and Trinobantum in Orosius (*History against the Pagans*, vi, 9). If we humour these normally (reasonably) authoritative sources, we should note that 'Bantes' could derive from the British banno / banna and the Gallic benno meaning a geographical peak, horn or promontory, possibly a notable feature in the Essex coastline. Could it be that Caesar, Tacitus and Orosius were all right and the tribe were never called the Trino*vantes* at all?

Of the other tribes in Caesar's *Gallic Wars*, the Cenimagni are, quite plausibly, the Iceni or Eceni *Magni* – the Great Eceni, a tribe later identified under Claudius and Nero as occupying the area around Norfolk and northern Suffolk. None of the remaining tribes, the Cassi, Ancalites, Bibroci and Segontiaci are ever mentioned again (either by Caesar or by any later source) and, rather frustratingly, Caesar provides no geographical placement for any of them. As his attack upon Britain seems to have been restricted solely to south-eastern England (Kent, Essex, Hertfordshire), we might expect the four tribes to have existed within this general region. The Cassi are perhaps the most intriguing, given that the British war leader fighting against Caesar in the campaign of 54 BC was Cassi-Vellaunos. Caesar neglects (or forgets) to provide this Cassivellaunos with a particular tribal affiliation. As we shall see later, however, it is possible that the Cassi, a name perhaps meaning 'the excellent ones', later evolved into the Catuvellauni, one of the key tribal players during Claudius' invasion of AD 43. It is also possible, given that Vellaunos is a perfectly acceptable British name (meaning 'excellent'), that the leader of the resistance against Caesar was actually 'Velaunos of the Cassi' and somehow this was mistranscribed (or misunderstood) becoming Cassi-Vellaunos in the process.

The remaining three tribes, the Ancalites, Bibroci and Segontiaci may originally represented discrete clans within the people of Cantium. Cantium (from which the modern term 'Kent' is derived), appears to represent a geographical name, possibly meaning 'corner land' (which could relate to the promontory of Kent rather than as a distinct ethnic group). Caesar mentions 'four kings of that region, Cingetorix, Carvilius, Taximagulus and Segovax' (Gallic War V, 22) whom the British war leader Cassivellaunos requests make an attack on Caesar's naval base. Unfortunately for us, he ascribes them no tribal affiliation. It is possible that the four may have ruled over any of the three remaining tribes mentioned in the *Gallic War*, although in Caesar's text, reference to the four kings and their planned attack comes *after* the surrender of the Ancalites, Bibroci and Segontiaci. Bibroci, if taken literally, could have meant 'Beaver Men', the Ancalites possibly 'Very Tough'. Segontiaci are perhaps the most elusive of all as their moniker may have derived from a personal name, possibly the 'people of Segontios' or something similar. Considering that one of Caesar's four kings of Cantium was called Segovax, it could be that these were his people.

With the exception of the Trinobantes and possibly the Cenimagni, none of the tribal names supplied by Caesar survive beyond AD 43. Perhaps they were after all only a series of small clan groups that, by the time of Claudius' invasion, had either ceased to exist or were considered too insignificant to receive official recognition by the Roman state.

ALTERNATIVE PERSPECTIVES

There are, other than the writings of Roman historians such as Caesar himself, a number of alternative textual sources that are often drawn upon to provide evidence for the tribes and tribal groupings of Britain. Best known and mostly widely used are the apparently official documents known as the *Tabula Peutingeriana* (the Peutinger Table) and the *Itinerarium Provinciarum Antonini Augusti* (the Antonine Itinerary). The Antonine Itinerary represents a collection of some 225 routes along the major highways of the Roman world, citing all major stopping-off points (towns, rest-stations and the like). Although the document is named after, or at least credited to, Marcus Aurelius Antoninus ('Caracalla'), sole emperor of Rome between AD 211 and 17, it is clear that the final version of the itinerary is not all of one date or origin. The best that can be said is that the text, as it survives today, was probably compiled between the reigns of the emperors Trajan (AD 98-117) and Diocletian (AD 284-305).

The Peutinger Table, so named because in the early sixteenth century it was in the possession of one Konrad Peutinger, comprises a map of the Roman Empire and those areas immediately bordering it, from Britain to the western coast of India. The Table appears to represent a road map for the *Cursus publicus*, the State run courier service of Rome used to transport all official mail, messages, documents, tax details, tax revenue and representatives of the emperor from Rome across all the provinces. The version that survives today was transcribed in north-eastern France during the thirteenth century, although the original source may have been compiled and revised at some point between the third and early fifth centuries AD. Unfortunately its usefulness for Britain is somewhat limited by the fact that only the southern and eastern coastal districts survive, the remainder of Britain together with virtually all of Spain and North Africa having been lost before the creation of the medieval copy. Comparison with the Antonine Itinerary, furthermore, demonstrates a considerable amount of name-corruption and mis-identification of distance, both presumably generated during the transmission procedure.

Two further useful sources in the identification of people and places in Roman Britain are provided by the mathematician, astronomer and geographer Claudius Ptolemaeus (Ptolemy) and the anonymous author of a work known as the *Ravenna Cosmography*. Ptolemy was writing in the city of Alexandria in Egypt during the early second century AD. His magnum opus, the *Geography*, probably compiled somewhere between AD 140-150, was designed to present a 'graphic representation of the known world as a whole' (*Geography* I, 1). The 'known world' was divided into eight separate books, with book II containing the full description of places within the British Isles. Not all settlements were cited by Ptolemy, only those he judged to be of specific importance. A number of forts and small roadside settlements, known from archaeological evidence to have been in use at the time of the book's compilation, are therefore absent from the finished text. Unfortunately, as with so many other texts from the ancient world, we do not possess a complete and unadulterated *original* version of Book II, what has come down to the present day having been repeatedly transcribed by a variety of medieval copyists, sometimes becoming irretrievably garbled in the process.

The *Cosmography* was compiled by a cleric (or clerics) working in the Italian town of Ravenna at or shortly after AD 700. Although this version of the text was therefore set down some significant time after the collapse of Roman rule in Britain, it evidently borrowed heavily from a variety of earlier sources. Modern historians have been cautious of using the Cosmography too closely for, although the work is comprehensive, there are a great many errors contained within it, as if the compiler (or copying scribe) was unfamiliar with the source material. Despite the corruption of place names and the sometimes strange order of citation, which often ignores the true geographic sequence, the *Cosmography* is a valuable source, as long as one is careful about how the information contained within it is used.

THE TRIBES OF CLAUDIUS

The official, state sanctioned verdict on the Claudian invasion of Britain was set in stone above the Arch of Claudius in Rome in AD 51. The Arch itself has now vanished, a victim of the countless periods of alteration, collapse and demolition prevalent in any great city, but fragments still survive and the full textual content of the main inscription was recorded and may be restored:

> To Tiberius Claudius Caesar Augustus Germanicus, son of Drusus, Pontifex Maximus, in the 11th year of his holding Tribunician Power, 5 times Consul, 22 times saluted Imperator, Censor, Father of his Country, the Senate and Roman People dedicate this because he received the surrender of 11 British kings, defeated without any reverse, and was the first to bring the barbarian tribes beyond Ocean under Roman sway

It is a powerful piece of spin: one which glamorises the military achievements of the fourth emperor of Rome, whilst effectively consigning those of his illustrious ancestor, Gaius Julius Caesar, to oblivion. Caesar may have been the first to cross 'Ocean', the legendary expanse of water separating Europe from the unknown, but it was Claudius who could proclaim a lasting victory. It is Claudius who is acknowledged as being *the first* Roman to bring justice to the Briton. Annoyingly we possess no information as to the identity of the '11 British kings' cited in the inscription, but 11 kings presumably implies 11 tribes. 'Defeated without reverse' sounds like pure propaganda, for other sources tell us that fighting between Britons and the invader was at times fierce; or it could simply refer to the fact that the 11 cited were not actively engaged in armed resistance. In other words, they capitulated without a fight.

It is not known whether the 'Essex 11' (the treaty between Rome and the Britons was probably signed at either Colchester or Chelmsford) represented major players in the Iron Age political scene, or whether they were bit-part actors, 'puppets', small-scale businessmen with an appetite for change or leaders of local militia with an over inflated sense of their own worth. Intriguingly, perhaps there are 11 main tribes within the area of central-southern Britain that, in the years immediately following the events of AD 43, appear to have received Roman recognition, whether they wanted it or not.

The early Roman provincial government of Britain created (or at least respected) a series of tribal groups, each centred upon a brand new *civitas* capital, or tribal market (4). *Civitates* were not only designed to provide discrete groups with a sense that their identity and status were being retained; they were also provided in order to maintain a reliable form of state control and initiate more efficient forms of tax collection. Ultimately, we have no idea whether these *civitates* in anyway reflected the real nature of political authority in pre-Roman society, but their existence tells us much about how Rome viewed the Britons and how their complex political networks were understood within the context of a Mediterranean superpower.

Although the Roman State was to preserve and fossilise particular British tribal names (such as the Atrebates, Iceni, Cantiaci etc.) within their new tribal

4 The Iron Age 'tribes' of Britain as preserved within the system of *civitates*, urban centres designed to increase state control whilst maintaining the fiction of political continuity. We have no way of knowing whether such Roman organisation in anyway reflected the real nature of tribal authority in pre-Roman society. Note that the boundaries provided for each political group are a modern fiction.

5 The 11 major Iron Age tribes of central-southern Britain. The tribal names, whilst plausible, represent modern creations.

6 An alternative reading of the tribal names based on archaeological and historic information.

centres (*Calleva Atrebatum*, *Venta Icenorum* and *Durovernum Cantiacorum*), it is highly probable that in establishing this new framework, they recognised only the larger political groupings. There could, for example, have been other, far less significant (at least to Rome) political groups or clans that were not legitimised within the new order. Other groups could have been conflated for greater efficiency in government whilst wholly artificial 'tribes' may have been generated so that some form of control mechanism could be established within a particularly troublesome area. As these *Civitates* were in effect created by Rome, it is debatable whether the people of a specific farming community in a particular geographic zone would have recognised the new names or indeed possessed any affinity to a 'tribe' or to the leaders of that tribe.

The real political map of Iron Age Britain and the Britons was modified and, no doubt, simplified by Roman government, an organisation that was altogether happier with the concept of single tribes occupying single areas under the rule of individual leaders. Much easier to deal with. The names given to such tribes could, therefore, merely reflect the names of a particular ruling dynasty or aristocratic lineage (as may be the case with Cassivellaunos and the Catuvellauni), at the time of first contact with Rome, rather than a discrete ethnic group. A 'tribe' could therefore have simply comprised those who owed allegiance to a particular political or economic leader, in much the same way as perhaps a medieval baron or post-medieval landowner.

We must also be wary of the 'tribal' names themselves. The Established Facts are pretty clear on the matter: we know the names of the most important tribes in the Iron Age and we know where each tribe was based (5). The problem is, that although a series of plausible tribal names, such as the Iceni, the Durotriges, the Cantiaci, the Atrebates, the Trinovantes and the Catuvellauni, are regularly cited and discussed in most modern texts on Roman Britain, such names are essentially modern creations. In all cases they represent an attempt by modern linguists and historians to create a 'best fit' from a diverse mass of stone inscriptions, coin legends and thoroughly corrupted (or mistranscribed) Latin texts.

A good example of this is a tribe that, up until fairly recently in historical literature, was always referred to as the Coritani. The Coritani were thought to have occupied an area established around the *Civitas* of Leicester, possibly extending as far as Nottinghamshire, Derbyshire, Lincolnshire and Northamptonshire. The Roman name for Leicester is recorded by Ptolemy as Κοριτανοι (*Coritani*) and in the Ravenna Cosmography as *Rate Corion*, itself generally transcribed in full as *Ratae Coritanorum*. The recent archaeological discovery of a self-named, self-stamped tribal tile, however, has demonstrated that the more correct form of the ethnic name was 'Corieltauvi', the administrative district presumably having been the Civitas *Corieltauvorum*. Corieltauvi has since formed the new orthodoxy, whilst 'Coritani' has been consigned to the waste-bin of history (6).

Unfortunately this rule of 'new discovery / new interpretation / new theory taking precedence' has not been consistently applied to the tribal groups of

7 An Iron Age gold stater of CORIO depicting a stylised horse and a possible tree. It is not known whether CORIO was a personal name (perhaps Corionos?) or a mint mark (*Corinium* being the later Romanised name for Cirencester). *Images of ancient British coins provided by dealer Chris Rudd. Cat. No. 1895*

Later Iron Age Britain. The Iceni, for example, probably the most famous of British tribes thanks to the events which later surrounded their queen, Boudicca, were based within what is today Norfolk. Their distinctive coin series, however, clearly possess the name (or partial name) Ecen, Eceni, Ec, Ecn or Ece. Some academics have gone to extraordinary lengths to demonstrate that Ecen, Eceni, Ec, Ecn and Ece was a garbled or abbreviated name of a particular aristocrat or discrete place within the area of the clan group. To me this seems like special pleading. True, the clan group in question were writing (and thinking) in Latin, rather than attempting to transcribe something directly in their own language (whatever that was) but the presence of an 'E' on the coins cannot be disputed. It is there. Critically we never get 'Icen, Iceni, Ic, Icn or Ice' on the coin series, despite the fact that the Ravenna Cosmography calls their capital (at Caistor) *Venta Cenomum*. The spelling 'Iceni' that you get in most works detailing the province of *Britannia* is a piece of modern interpretation: a fiction.

Similarly the 'established' tribal name 'Dobunni', a group credited with occupying an area centred upon modern day Cirencester is by no means certain, despite appearing in pretty much every book on Roman Britain. 'Dobunni' as a name is of unknown derivation – it is certainly not Celtic and possesses no known parallel anywhere within the Roman world – and yet the name persists. Proof of the 'correct form' is, it is often claimed, derived from the *Ravenna Cosmography* which records the Roman name for Cirencester as *Cironium Dobunorum*, the market town of the Dobunni, and yet the Cosmography is not an infallible source, most authorities agreeing that the correct form for Cirencester was *Corinium*, not *Cironium*. Intriguingly the name CORIO appears on a small number of coins from this area and may therefore indicate a mint mark, rather than the name of a specific ruler (7). Further evidence for the Dobunnic name is claimed from a milestone found at Kenchester, Herefordshire, the inscription on which ends with the abbreviation RPCD, usually expanded to read R[es] P[ublica] C[ivitatis] D[obunnorum] (the Canton of the Dobunni). Problem is, the final letter is clearly not a 'D', although it could plausibly be a 'B', making 'Dobunni' seem rather unlikely in this instance. A military diploma (retirement record) of one Lucco, son of Trenus, serving with the cohors I Britannica (first cohort of Britons) on the Danube cites his origin as being DOBUNN, although it is fair to say that there remains significant debate as to the exact nature of this particular tribal or ethnic affiliation.

8 Gold stater of BODVOC, possibly a personal name (Bodouc / Bodoucus?) of a ruler operating in the pre-Roman Cotswolds. The coin seems to indicate that the tribal name 'Bodunni' ('the victorious ones') is more likely than the traditional accepted form 'Dobunni'. *Images of ancient British coins provided by dealer Chris Rudd. Cat. No. 1886*

The solution may lie with Dio Cassius, who in his account of the events of AD 43, refers to a tribe in southern Britain called the Bodunni (Βοδυννι). Dio Cassius, it is fair to say, is normally assumed by modern writers to have got the D and B in the wrong order, or was subsequently mis-transcribed, the correct form (once again) being Dobunni. Few have ever considered the fact that Dio Cassius may actually have got it right. Coins minted in the area of Cirencester just prior to the Roman invasion contain the name BODVOC (8), which, if assumed to be a personal (and not a tribal) name, may conceivably have been 'Boduocus'. The important thing to note is that there are comparatively large numbers of names, both personal and tribal, in the so-called Celtic territories of the West that possess the *boud* or *bod* prefix. *Boud* may be translated as meaning 'victorious', the name of the British leader of a revolt against Rome in AD 60, Boudicca, being perhaps the most famous. The 'Bodunni' could plausibly be the tribe / people or followers of Bodvoc / Boduocus, assuming of course that the name appearing on the coins was not tribal, as per the ECE / ECEN coins of Norfolk. Either way, the established name Dobunni possesses no legitimacy other than its repeated use in modern literature. All things considered, Bodunni seems far more plausible.

South of the Bodunni lie the Durotriges, a tribe generally ascribed to an area of central south-western Britain roughly corresponding with modern Dorset. The Durotriges are one of the more famous of Iron Age tribal units, given that they are traditionally viewed as strenuous resistors to Roman influence in the months immediately following AD 43. The reasons for believing this are both archaeological and historical (with, it is fair to say, a smattering of modern interpretation thrown in for good measure). Culturally speaking, the Later Iron Age of Dorset / western Hampshire / southern Wiltshire / southern Somerset appears markedly distinct from those areas to the immediate north and east. Crudely speaking, hillforts seem to dominate the settlement dataset within the 'Durotrigian' zone, whilst their defended counterparts in western Hampshire, Sussex, Essex, Kent, Hertfordshire etc, are largely defunct by the first century AD, being replaced by the more expansive forms of enclosure known as *oppida*. Artefactually, there are also far fewer items originating from the Mediterranean-based world of Rome in circulation in Dorset at this time, whilst the coinage, comprising bronze issues with curiously stylised designs, is in marked contrast to the more ordered, Roman-image heavy issues of their eastern neighbours.

9 Maiden Castle, an Iron Age hillfort in Dorset that may well have been both active and battle-ready in AD 43. *Author*

From a historical perspective, support for theory that the Durotriges were markedly anti-Roman may be derived from a short passage in Suetonius' *Lives of the Twelve Caesars* where, in briefly describing the emperor Vespanian's early career, the author notes that the then general:

> reduced to submission two powerful tribes, more than twenty towns, and the Island of Vectis which is very close to Britain, this partly under the command of Aulus Plautius, the Consular Governor, and partly under the command of Claudius himself
> (*Vespasian* 4)

We shall return to examine this particular section in detail later, but it is worth noting that the description of events provided by Suetonius is vague to say the least. Mention of *Vectis*, the traditional form for the Isle of *Wight*, at least provides some geographic placement, although it would perhaps be unwise to automatically assume that that either the 'two powerful tribes' or the 'twenty towns' reduced to submission were in anyway associated with Vespasian's action there. Mention of the emperor Claudius, whose stay in Britain was very brief and seems to have centred upon Colchester in Essex, may indicate that one (or both) of the powerful tribes mentioned were, in reality, based in eastern Britain, whilst the twenty towns, either hillforts or *oppida*, may have been found anywhere in southern England. Nevertheless, despite the lack of certainty in Suetonius' account, archaeologists have assumed that the bulk of Vespasian's British war must have been based around *Vectis* and, given that western Hampshire / Dorset / southern Wiltshire / southern Somerset possesed hillforts (9) that, in the early first century AD, remained both active and battle-ready, that it was here that the fight between Rome and the Britons was at its fiercest. This has now become an Established Fact.

Another Established Fact is that Dorchester, today the market town of Dorset, was originally the civitas or tribal capital of the Durotriges: *Dunovaria Durotrigum*. Unfortunately the tribal suffix *Durotrigum* ('of the Durotriges') which is nearly always given in the modern literature of Roman Britain, is nowhere provided in the ancient primary sources: variant forms *Durnonovaria* and *Durnovaria* appearing in the Antonine Itinerary whilst *Duriarno* is provided by the Ravenna Cosmography. That Dorchester *was* a Roman town is not in doubt (and an important one at that), but that it was the tribal centre of a tribe calling itself the Durotriges must, in the absence of any useful new evidence, such as a tombstone, official inscription or milestone, be noted as 'speculative'. Interestingly the only urban centre where a group identifying itself as Durotrigian, or more strictly 'Durotragian', may be found at Ilchester, the Roman town of *Lindinis* in Somerset.

To make things more confusing, two building stones found within Hadrian's Wall possess the inscriptions:

C DUROTRG ... ENDINESIS

and:

CI DUROTRAG LENDINIESI ...

which may roughly be translated as 'derived from the Civitas of the Durotrages / Durotriges at Lendinesis / Lendiniesis / Lindinis'. Citation of DUROTRAG rather than DUROTRIG suggests that either the modern form 'Durotriges' is wrong (and that Durotrages is the more preferable version) or that the original inscription cutter made a mistake. Whilst it may seem surprising that 'a member of the civitas literate enough to be given the task of cutting the inscription would mistake the spelling of the name of his own people' (Rivet and Smith 1979, 352) it is worth noting that the commonly accepted version of the Roman name for Ilchester, *Lindinis*, is also not provided in either inscription, the name appearing as LENDINIESI ... and ... ENDINESIS. All this may really show is that either the Latinisation of Celtic forms did not follow a set path or that the inscription cutter was used to the spoken, rather than the written, version of the tribe and town and that no one really cared all that much. Today, the names that we give to people and places tend to be rather fixed, but such things were certainly more fluid in the distant past. One has, for example, only to think of the many variant forms of surname provided for that the great Elizabethan poet and playwright

Shakespeare (Shake-speare / Shakspeare / Shakespere / Shakespear / Shackspeare / Shakspere / Shakspear / Shak-speare / Shakespheare / Shaxspere and so on) to realise that rigidity and certainty in spelling is a curiously modern obsession.

We are on no firmer ground when we attempt to explain the derivation of the name Durotriges / Durotrages, an observation not helped by the lack of general agreement on pronounciation (some preferring DUROT-riges whilst others choose Duro-TRIGES). It is possible that the name was originally a combination of *duro*, potentially meaning a fort or defended place, and *riges*, arguably a plural of *rig* / *rigon* / *ricon* meaning 'King'. Hence one could argue that 'Durotrigian' group identity was defined by the existence of multiple defended enclosures (hillforts) each with its own particular leader (king). Many such 'kings' may have been linked by blood or marriage, but few may have neither possessed, nor perhaps desired, ultimate power. Absence of a unified political system or supreme monarchy may further be reflected in the local coinage which, as already noted, was unlike coin series produced by groups to the north and east of Dorset, in that it largely appeared in low denomination bronze and poessessed no great statements, names or titles. A fragmented system of relatively small-scale social groups would presumably have been unable to present a unified response to the arrival of Roman troops in the AD 40s, a general such as Vespasian being able to negotiate or attack various centres in order to achieve ultimate control. The name 'Durotriges' could, therefore, represent an entirely Roman construct: an attempt by the new provincial administration to create order within a dispersed and politically fragmented society. Rome was happier dealing with one tribe and one capital (or perhaps two in the case of Dorchester and Ilchester) than multiple centres and numerous kings.

It is possible that other established tribes appearing in modern maps of Iron Age Britain were, in reality, artificial creations of the Roman state, generated in order to simplify disperate clans or kin-groups that had yet to reach any degree of political unity. The Belgae, for example, whose civitas was established at *Venta Belgarum* (Winchester) possess a name which Caeasr, amongst others, applied to a particular group of tribes which appeared to have been culturally or ethnically distinct from those inhabiting Gaul (and from which we derive the name Belgium). The meaning of the name 'Belgae' itself, as with most other tribal names, is obscure but it may have derived from a term such as *belg*, 'to swell', perhaps implying pride (in the sense of being 'puffed-up') or an ecessively vigorous display of manhood. Establishment of a *Venta Begarum* ('Market of the Belgae') may have been a necessary creation of the Roman government in order that a rather disparate collection of social groups, all of whom shared a common Belgic origin, could be brought together under the control of a single financial and legislative centre. The same can perhaps be said of *Durovernum Cantiacorum* (Canterbury) a town which, rather than serving a single tribe called the 'Cantiaci' was established for the tribes of 'Cantium' (Kent) for Caesar, writing in 54 BC, refers to the 'four kings' of Cantium from which one may deduce that there were at least four discrete tribes.

Of the remaining tribes provided with recognition, identity and status within central and southern Britain following the events of AD 43, the Atrebates are probably the easiest to identify. Their capital was established at *Calleva Atrebatum*, modern day Silchester in Hampshire. The Roman town appears to have been constructed directly over its heavily Romanised Iron Age predeceesor, named in the coins of the British king Eppillus, simply as *Calleva* ('town in the woods' – a name echoing the densely wooded British *oppida* described in Caesar's *Gallic War*). The name Atrebates is itself mirrored by a tribe in Gaul and it is likely that together these represent either two halves of the same ethnic group or the result of a migration to Britain led by the Atrebatic king Commios, a friend and ally of Caesar during the campaigns in Britain of 55 and 54 BC (see below). The tribal name may have derived from a compound of the word *treba*, 'to occupy, settle or inhabit', the Atrebates would in this sense therefore be 'settlers', 'occupiers' or perhaps even 'migrants'. To the north-west of the Atrebates, beyond the Bodunni, lay a group traditionally known as the Cornovii, a name possibly derived from *corn* meaning 'horn', possibly relating to cows, a horned deity or (perhaps) a promontory. Ptolemy refers to them as the Κορναοπιοι (Cornavii), which is perhaps just as likely to represent reality as it is a simple scribal error.

To the south-east of the Atrebatic capital of Calleva, lay the Roman town of Chichester, on the West Sussex coast. Two versions of Ptolemy's *Geography* record the name of the town as Νοιομαγομ (*Noeomagum*) and also as Νοιομαγοσ (*Noeomagus*), the latter noting that it served as a *polis* or capital of the Ρηγνοι (Regni) whilst the *Ravenna Cosmography* names the town as *Noviomagno* and as *Navimagno Regentium*. It is difficult from these sources to gain a definitive version town's Roman identity, although the first element may plausibly have been *Noviomagus* ('new town' or 'new market'). If the town was, as it appears, a civitas, then the second element of the name, *Regentium*, should represent tribal affiliation. Regni, Rigni and Regini, all noted in various readings of Ptolemy's *Geography*, could, like the Atrebates of *Calleva Atrebatum* (Silchester), have been a distinct tribe at the time of the Roman conquest. Depending on the translation preferred, it is possible to suggest that *Noviomagus* was the capital of a people known as the *Regini*, the translation of which could be 'the proud ones'. If true, this would further suggest that Chichester had originally been named *Noviomagus Reginorum*, rather than the more usually suggested *Regnentium* or *Regnensium*.

The problem is that both *Regini* and *Regentium* are sufficiently close to *Regnum*, the Latin word for kingdom, to suggest that the full name of Chichester may have been *Noviomagus Regnensium*: 'the new market town of the Kingdom'. Given the relatively large number of early civilian building projects discovered across eastern Hampshire and Sussex (including the temple sequence upon Hayling Island and the palaces of Fishbourne: see below), it is indeed possible that the 'Regini' were not a distinct *people* but instead a discrete *kingdom*. To whom that kingdom belonged, and how it may have functioned within the province of *Britannia*, is a matter for later chapters.

2
CASSIVELLAUNOS AND CAESAR: THE CIRCUS OF DEATH

Julius Caesar, the first Roman who entered Britain with an army, although he terrified the inhabitants by a successful engagement, and became master of the shore, may be considered rather to have transmitted the discovery than the possession of the country to posterity
(Tacitus *Agricola* 13)

Whichever way you looked at it, the crossing to Britain was an unpleasant experience (*10*). When you consider the swell, the overcrowding on deck, the crashing waves and the overwhelming stench of fear and sickness, then add to that a large 'unwelcoming' party of agitated natives hurling abuse, spears and worse, then the whole thing became totally unbearable. It was late summer in the year 55 BC and Britain was about to burst kicking and screaming onto the pages of history.

The first Roman invasion of Britain is one of the most famous events in the story of Britain (it is certainly the earliest). Thanks to an eyewitness account we have a vivid description of both the disputed landing and the first bout of armed conflict between the indigenous population and the heavily armed psychopaths of the civilised world.

And while our men were hesitating, chiefly on account of the depth of the sea, the eagle-bearer of the tenth legion, after supplicating the gods that the matter might turn out favourably to the legion, exclaimed, "Leap, fellow soldiers, unless you wish to betray your eagle to the enemy. I, for my part, will perform my duty to the commonwealth and my general." When he had said this with a loud voice, he leaped from the ship and proceeded to bear the eagle toward the enemy. Then our men, exhorting one another that so great a disgrace should not be incurred, all leaped from the ship. When those in the nearest vessels saw them, they speedily followed and approached the enemy
(*Gallic Wars* 4, 35)

It's emotive stuff! A tale of heroism and valour; an anonymous foot soldier in the Legions of a Mediterranean superpower struggling onto the shore of an alien land beyond the northernmost limits of the known world. It is also, of course,

10 The sailing to Britain in 55 BC was a major achievement, Caesar and his troops being the first Romans to cross the legendary Ocean and enter the terrifying island of the Britons. *Author*

an unpleasant piece of political spin, adding mythic gloss to an unnecessary war that ultimately cost the lives of thousands of innocent men, women and children. It is propaganda; a piece of self-promotion intended to benefit the political career of a shameless, mass-murdering tyrant.

GAIUS JULIUS CAESAR

Gaius Julius Caesar was a Roman politician, statesman and general who, probably more than anyone else, was instrumental in the death of the Roman Republic. In 59 BC, already one of the most powerful men in Rome, Caesar (*11*) had obtained the governorship of Illyricum, Transalpine Gaul and Cisalpine Gaul. This gave him supreme authority over a block of land covering what is now southern France through northern Italy to the Croatian coast.

Transalpine Gaul – 'Gaul beyond the Alps' (literally the *wrong side* of the mountains) gave Caesar the opportunity for conquest, military glory, power, prestige and wealth. In 58 BC he led his armies across the northern frontier of the Roman world and into *Gallia Comata* ('Hairy Gaul'). Playing on Rome's traditional fear of the barbarian, Caesar managed to legitimise military action as a form of pre-emptive strike against the savage in order to save Rome's allies, territory, lives and investments. The next three years saw Caesar's Legions campaigning across Gaul, reaching the shores of Brittany in 56 BC and crossing the Rhine the following year. When, in 52 BC, the last Gallic revolt against him ended in mass butchery at the hillfort of Alesia, Gaul lay broken: its great towns shattered, its population annihilated.

Julius Caesar is sometimes referred to as 'the most famous of the Romans', a curiously ambiguous description somewhat akin to calling Joseph Stalin the most

11 Julius Caesar. A damaged marble portrait of the man from the sanctuary of Athena, Priene, Turkey. © *Trustees of the British Museum*

famous Georgian or Adolph Hitler the most famous Austrian. Caesar is someone who, even today, divides opinion. Some see him as a remarkable statesman, a general par-excellence, a writer, philosopher and engineer and a politician who almost single-handedly dragged Rome from a small time regional power in the Mediterranean to one of the greatest Empires of the Ancient World. Others view him as nothing more than an opportunistic bully, a callous tyrant and one of the greatest mass murderers in history. It is certainly difficult to view his life and career with a cool and detached calm.

I made this point in an earlier book, *Roman Sussex,* noting that Caesar's systematic slaughter of the Gallic people between 58 and 52 BC was a callous piece of ethnic cleansing conducted purely to advance his own warped political agenda, adding that the crimes that he committed in the name of Rome could easily compare with more recent mass murderers such as Adolph Hitler, Joseph Stalin, Mao Zedong or Pol Pot. This I felt was rather understating the evidence.

A number of classical scholars disagreed. One, who shall remain nameless, commented in a particularly memorable review of *Roman Sussex,* that 'Russell demonstrates his ignorance of the past by crassly comparing the genius of Caesar with the disgusting 'achievements' of Hitler and Pol Pot'. Another, having identified me at a conference, told me, rather politely I thought, that I had destroyed whatever argument I may have felt worth making by denigrating Caesar in such a negative way. To some extent I agree, at least with the spirit of the criticism, for it can be unwise to make comparisons between the ancient and modern world, for the two societies were indeed very different. However it is difficult to remain wholly appreciative of someone like Caesar when, in his own words, he makes statements such as these, relating to the aftermath of his conflict with the Veneti, a Gallic tribe occupying the area of France today called Brittany:

> He [Caesar] resolved to make an example of them in order to teach the natives to be more careful in future about respecting the rights of ambassadors; he had all their councillors executed and the rest of the population sold as slaves
> (Caesar *The Conquest of Gaul* III, 16)

Or following his successful siege of the chief town of the Atuatuci tribe:

> The Atuatuci struggled with the ferocity that was to be expected of brave men fighting a forlorn hope against an enemy who had the advantage of position and could hurl down missiles from an earthwork and towers, and knowing that courage was the one thing that could save them. About four thousand were killed and the rest driven back into the fortress. Next day the gates, now undefended, were smashed open and the soldiers let in; Caesar sold all the inhabitants of the place by auction in one lot. The purchasers reported that the number of persons included in the sale was fifty-three thousand
> (Caesar *The Conquest of Gaul* II, 33)

Or the final moments of the siege of the Gallic town of Cenabum:

> When they [the Gauls] saw the Romans occupying the entire circuit of the wall around them, and not a man coming down to meet them on level ground, they were afraid of being cut off from all chance of escape, and throwing down their arms ran without stopping to the farthest corners of the town. There, some were cut down by our infantry as they jammed the narrow gateways and others by the cavalry after making their way out. None of our soldiers thought about making money by taking prisoners…and spared neither old men nor women nor children. Of the whole population – about forty thousand – a bare eight hundred who rushed out of the town at the first alarm got safely through
> (Caesar *The Conquest of Gaul* VII, 28)

It is the casual, workmanlike way in which the events are described, with no attempt to disguise, excuse or hide the truth, that is truly shocking.

Ultimately, then, despite the passage of two millennia, it is impossible to view Caesar in a totally detached way, much like it is impossible to comment upon the aesthetics of 1930s Nazi architecture without acknowledging the many thousands of innocents who died creating it. Anyone who praises Caesar wholeheartedly whilst turning a blind-eye to the atrocities committed in his name, is in many ways complicit in them as much as the revisionists who, even in the face of damning evidence to the contrary, refuse to acknowledge that anyone died in the ovens of Auschwitz. Caesar can be studied, assessed, reassessed, catalogued, analysed as much as Comrade Stalin or Chairman Mao, but that doesn't make him any easier to like.

As the most 'famous of Romans', it is unsurprising that Gaius Julius Caesar has been portrayed in countless films, plays and other events within popular culture. In film he has been played most memorably by Warren William (*Cleopatra* 1934),

Claude Rains (*Caesar and Cleopatra* 1945), Rex Harrison (Cleopatra 1963), Kenneth Williams (*Carry on Cleo* 1964) and Klaus Maria Brandauer (*Druids /
Vercingetorix* 2001). None of these, however, really seem to get to grips with the
real Caesar, at least as he appears in his own writings. Kenneth William's Caesar
is a tour-de-force comedic performance, whilst Klaus Maria Brandauer presents a
curiously mumbling, insane villain perhaps more at home in the world of James
Bond than that of ancient Rome. Only Warren William in the 1930s *Cleopatra*
conveys some of the brooding intensity of a true megalomaniac, Claude Rains,
although shrewd and statesmanlike, is also witty and brimming with panache.
Rex Harrison, who dominates the first half of the 1963 epic *Cleopatra* (no mean
achievement in a film that runs for a truly bottom-numbing four hours) certainly
bears an uncanny resemblance to the sculptured portraits of Caesar, but he is too
likeable by half, so much so that one is always expecting him to break into song.

BRITAIN

Britain was viewed as a natural target by Caesar for no Roman general had ever
left the known world to explore somewhere so alien and mysterious. He had,
by 55 BC, already conquered much of Gaul and led his armies on a punitive
campaign into Germania, having first thrown a bridge across the River Rhine.
He was, at this stage in his military career, seemingly unstoppable.

   Caesar's attacks upon the island of Britain do not appear to have been intended
to form the basis of a permanent conquest (as had his invasion of Gaul) and,
ultimately, they were not to prove particularly successful (at least from a military
perspective). The important thing about intervening, however temporarily, in British
affairs was that Caesar could demonstrate that he could go anywhere and do
anything. In order to legitimise his actions to the senate back in Rome, he produced
evidence to prove that the Britons had acted against him, discovering that:

> in almost all the wars with the Gauls support had been furnished to our enemy
> from that country
> (*Gallic Wars* 4, 20)

This has often been viewed as a crude piece of self-justification intended to explain
why one of Rome's pre-eminent generals was messing about overseas. There
may, however, be some truth in Caesar's claim for there was much commonality
between tribal groups on either side of the English Channel (certainly Caesar's
translator, Commios, was able to move between the Atrebates of northern Gaul
and similarly named tribe in central-southern England). There may even be the
possibility that British aristocrats really did actively participate in action against
Rome. During the Great Gallic Revolt of 52 BC, for example, Caesar noted that
whilst besieging his enemy Vercingetorix at the hill town of Alesia, a relief army
was sent against him led by:

> Commius the Atrebatian, the Aeduans Viridomarus and Eporedorix, and the
> Arvernian Vercassivellaunus, a cousin of Vercingetorix
> (*Gallic Wars* VII, 76)

Vercassivellaunus? Two years before, in 54 BC, Caesar's chief opponent in the British war was the battle-leader Cassivellaunus ... could this be the same man? The name Cassivellaunos itself may have originally derived from a combination of two elements: Cassi – meaning excelling or surpassing (and possibly, as we have already noted, a tribal group) and Vellaunos meaning good – hence overall we may have a leader bearing the name 'Velluanos of the Cassi', or more simply just 'exceptionally good'. It is worth noting, in this particular respect, that the prefix 'Ver' may originally have meant 'superior' or 'surpassing'; hence Cassivellaunus in Britain (whom, interestingly, Caesar does not allocate a tribe) could conceivably have become Vercassivellaunus (surpassing exceptionally good) of the Arverni in Gaul. Interestingly, in Britain there is also a Cingetorix, perhaps derived from a combination of Cingeto – footsoldier (literally walking warrior) and Rix – king; therefore meaning 'leader of infantry' or 'warrior king'. Using the same logic, Cingetorix could become Ver-cingetorix in Gaul ('superior leader of infantry' or 'great warrior king'). One has to wonder not only how many of these names were duplicated, but also how many were actually titles (rather than personal names) acquired later in life. 'Superior leader of infantry' does seem a curious name with which to saddle an infant.

The first expedition to Britain was not a huge success, something which Caesar seems to disguise when he introduces the campaign noting that:

> the time of year was insufficient for carrying on the war, yet he thought it would
> be of great service if he only entered the island, and saw into the character of the
> people, and got knowledge of their localities, harbours, and landing-places
> (*Gallic Wars* IV, 20)

In other words 'I knew in advance that it was a bit too late in summer to go off on a foreign war but I needed to reconnoitre the island in advance for a more serious invasion in the future, personal experience being far greater than any information I could obtain from torturing Gallic merchants'.

At this point in the narrative Caesar records that his:

> purpose having been discovered, and reported to the Britons by merchants,
> ambassadors come to him from several states of the island, to promise that they will
> give hostages, and submit to the government of the Roman people
> (*Gallic Wars* IV, 21)

Exactly who these ambassadors were and from what 'states' or tribes they were originally sent are things which Caesar fails to record. This is unfortunate for knowledge of which groups felt the desire to surrender wholeheartedly to Rome at such an early stage would be useful, it undoubtedly had a great impact on what was to follow.

Having given the ambassadors an audience, Caesar gave reassurances and sent them home with:

> Commius, whom, upon subduing the Atrebates, he had created king there, a man whose courage and conduct he esteemed, and who he thought would be faithful to him, and whose influence ranked highly in Britain. He instructed Commius to visit as many states as he could, to urge them to embrace the protection of the Roman people, and announce his impending arrival
> (*Gallic Wars* IV, 21)

Commios, a king of the Belgic Atrebates is a man whom Caesar felt he could trust, or at least viewed him as being useful (as well as being ultimately expendable). The 'protection of the Roman people' was a two-edged sword: on the one hand having Caesar as your ally meant that, whilst he was content, others would not dare touch you. Lose his support, or go against him in any way, and that very protection could (in the best mafia way) be used to destroy you utterly.

The landing, when it came, was heavily disputed (*12*). Despite having previously sent scouts to determine a safe harbour, Caesar's troop transports found they

12 A nineteenth-century recreation of the disputed landing of 55 BC. The Britons, a rough lot, clad in animal skins, desperately resist the relentless advance of civilisation. Today, it is sometimes difficult to see which side the Victorians preferred: the invading (alien) army of a great empire or the primitive indigenous (albeit British) tribesmen, courageously fighting back. *Massingheimer Collection*

were unable to ride up and secure themselves into the shallow beach, leaving them wallowing out in deep water. This meant that, in order to get safely ashore, Caesar's men had no option but to jump fully armoured into the sea and wade up towards the enemy, all the time under heavy fire. Typically, Caesar is able to turn the situation to his advantage, at least in the pages of the *Gallic Wars*:

> When Caesar observed this, he ordered the ships of war, the appearance of which was somewhat strange to the barbarians...to be withdrawn a little from the transport vessels, and to be propelled by their oars, and be stationed toward the open flank of the enemy, and the enemy to be beaten off and driven away, with slings, arrows, and engines: which plan was of great service to our men; for the barbarians being startled by the form of our ships and the motions of our oars and the nature of our engines ... stopped, and shortly after retreated a little
> (*Gallic Wars* IV, 25)

Where, exactly, this landing took place is unclear. Once again we are provided with no geographical detail, all Caesar says is that:

> The nature of the place was this: the sea was confined by mountains so close to it that a dart could be thrown from their summit upon the shore
> (*Gallic Wars* IV, 23)

Modern commentators have taken this to refer to the white cliffs of Dover, as there are few 'mountains' in Kent or across the south-east. Alternatively, it is possible that Caesar was referring to the chalk cliffs that form Beachy Head in East Sussex, although this may be too far west for the transport vessels to have strayed in order to find safe haven. Established Fact states that the Roman expedition fleet sailed from Boulogne, from which the cliffs of Dover are visible, but there is no firm archaeological or historical evidence to support this theory, only that it is the 'most sensible' place to have embarked. If the supposition is that Caesar set sail from here, then it may be inferred that he was aiming for the shortest crossing towards Dover. Having observed 'the mountains' Caesar 'advanced about seven miles from that place' whether this is east or west is not mentioned, stationing the fleet 'against an open and level shore' (*Gallic Wars* IV, 23).

That this 'open and level shore' can only be Deal or Walmer beach is something that has now become an Established Fact, although it is worth noting that there is, to date, no evidence for a massed landing here. Coastlines have certainly changed in the past 2,000 years, and it is likely that any beachhead fortification has been lost to erosion, sediment accretion or modern development. Visit Walmer beach today, however, and you will be left in no doubt as to where the standard bearer of Caesar's tenth Legion bravely struggled ashore. Here, a square plinth, supported by a menacingly squat concrete slab embedded within a pathway of uniformly grey paving slabs, informs the world that:

The first Roman invasion of Britain led by Julius Caesar
landed near here LV BC

The white-fenced road beyond is quiet; the architecture, reassuringly British seaside. Seagulls cry somewhere in the distance. A Union Flag, fixed, one must presume in order to prevent anyone forgetting where they are, flutters apologetically in the breeze. A family passes by, parents hungrily devouring ice cream whilst children struggle with a boisterous terrier. Two cyclists, a slow-moving car, a young couple, a red-faced, track-suited man, three children with a large canvas bag: all seem blissfully unaware of both the plinth and its significance. The possibility that two thousand years before, the shingle of Walmer played host to a scene of unmitigated carnage seems wholly incongruous.

It is, of course, possible that neither the beaches of Walmer nor Deal welcomed Rome's first expedition. Although Caesar himself provides no clues as to where his men forced entry to Britain, Dio Cassius, writing over two and a half centuries later, observes that the general

> ... made the passage with the infantry by the most desirable course, but did not select the best landing-place; for the Britons, apprised beforehand of his voyage, had secured all the landings on the coast facing the mainland. Accordingly, he sailed around a certain projecting headland, coasted along on the other side of it, and disembarking there in the shoals, conquered those who joined battle with him and gained a footing on dry land before more numerous assistance could come
> (*Roman History* XXXIX, 51)

This could all be invention, Dio Cassius not being the most objective of historians (sometimes adding extra detail to colour an otherwise uninteresting scene). It has been established, however, that he used a variety of disparate primary sources in order to create his *History* and so he may, in this instance, be providing detail from material now lost to us. If so, the mention 'a certain projecting headland' around which the fleet coasted, is interesting for unless he is refering to an extra prominent chalk outcrop, it could be that Caesar's troops made footfall some significant distance from where the Walmer memorial now stands. Is it conceivable that the fleet, in its desire to outrun the tribal welcoming party on the cliffs, sailed further east (or west?) than anyone has previously thought? Could the 'prominent headland' be elsewhere on the coast – possibly as far as the Isle of Thanet? Given the sources, anything is possible and nothing proven. A landing on the northern coast of Kent could however explain why no evidence of Caesar's expedition has yet been found: everyone has been looking in the wrong place (*13*).

The expedition of 55 BC ended in near disaster for Caesar. Trapped on the beachhead, hemmed in on all sides by the enemy, the general could only watch helplessly as his cavalry reinforcements were scattered in a storm at sea, whilst his own transport vessels were dashed to pieces on the shore. A stalemate ensued,

13 The Kent coast today. Despite the much-repeated certainty that Caesar landed on the beaches of either Deal or Walmer, no evidence to confirm this has ever been recovered archaeologically. *Author*

the Britons being unable to eliminate the Romans or dislodge them from their beachhead, the Romans being unable to break out and attack any fixed British targets. Eventually both sides called for peace. Characteristically, Caesar makes even this sound like a victory:

> Caesar doubled the number of hostages which he had before demanded; and ordered that they should be brought over to the continent, because, since the time of the equinox was near, he did not consider that, with his ships out of repair, the voyage ought to be deferred till winter … For these successes, a thanksgiving of twenty days was decreed by the senate upon receiving Caesar's letter
> (*Gallic Wars* IV, 36-8)

Hostages were traditionally taken as a way of ensuring the loyalty of conquered peoples. If the children of a defeated monarch were retained in the custody of Rome, their parents would be less likely to revolt. Hostage taking also had a more important aspect to it, for the children of native aristocrats could be brought up within the Roman world and introduced to the Roman mindset. If they were ever required to return to their people, they could bring with them a range of new gods, ideas and customs. Having been exposed to a Mediterranean lifestyle, they could help fast track Roman culture within and among their own people.

Within a year of departing the shore of Britain, Caesar was already drawing up plans to invade again. This time he hoped to obtain a more impressive result: ideally to win a pitched battle, take a British town or two, and obtain a greater quantity of slaves and hostages.

CASSIVELLAUNOS

The first Briton that Caesar specifically mentions by name in the *Gallic Wars* is Cassivellaunos, whom he acknowledges to be his main adversary during the campaign of 54 BC (*14*). The significance of Cassivellaunos cannot be overstated: he is the first character to emerge from over half a million years of British prehistory; our first identifiable Briton. Caesar may not have met Cassivellaunos in person during the campaigns of 55 and 54 BC, for he never provides a description of his adversary, but then to be fair he rarely does for any of the secondary characters in his grand narrative.

Cassivellaunos is portrayed as the villain of the piece, intimidating his neighbours by fighting an expansionist war of territorial acquisition across southern England. In the Roman mind, he was a major destabilising influence and therefore target number one; his very existence legitimising Roman military activity. Caesar, ever aware of an opportunity for political gain, could claim that armed intervention in Britain was necessary in order to force regime-change, weeding out dangerous elements (Cassivellaunos) and bringing peace to what was now the northern frontier of the Roman Empire.

The appearance of Cassivellaunos in the *Gallic Wars* is ultimately frustrating for we do not have a face to put to the name, a description or a character that could be derived from a likeness. Caesar does not provide us with a background for Cassivellaunos; we do not even know from which tribe he was supposed to have emerged. All we are told is that the king's territories bordered the northern edge of 'a

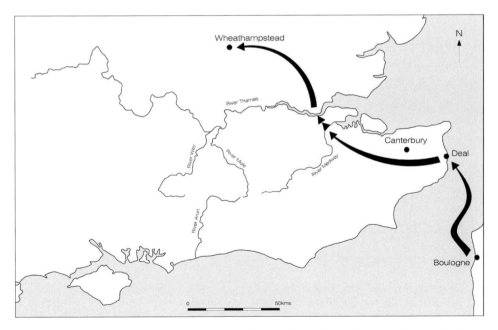

14 The traditional interpretation of Caesar's advance through south eastern Britain in the late summer of 54 BC.

river, which is called the Thames' which neatly separated his lands 'from the maritime states [of Kent] at about eighty miles from the sea' (*Gallic Wars* 5, 11). It seems a fair assumption, therefore, that the 'tribe of Cassivellaunos' and the 'Catuvellauni', later recorded as occupying the area of Hertfordshire, were essentially one and the same and that the king's 'capital', which lay 'not far from' the Trinobantes tribe (located in Essex) was probably in the region of modern-day St Albans.

It is, of course, possible that the name Cassivellaunos itself is in actuality a garbling of a particular tribe, the *Catuvellauni* being prominent players during the later Claudian invasion of AD 43. Alternatively it could be that the Catuvellauni were named *after* this particular, pre-eminent British king and warrior. It is also possible that the king's name was originally misunderstood or garbled by Caesar, whose understanding of the people against whom he fought was limited in the extreme. We know, for example, that in his memoirs he cites a tribe known as the 'Cenimagni', a group unknown from all other sources, which surrendered to him late in the campaign of 54 BC. In all likelihood, 'Cenimagni' is derived from a misunderstanding or mistranslation of 'Eceni Magni', quite literally the 'Great Iceni', a tribal group later identified from Norfolk. Hence 'Cassivellaunus' could be an artificial 'Caesarian' construct created from two separate and distinct names: 'Cassi' (a tribe whom Caesar also recalls surrendering to him following the defection of the Trinobantes led by Mandubracius) and 'Vellaunus'.

Vellaunus, as already indicated, is a name encountered from a number of places from Britain and Gaul including a later religious source at Caerwent, in Gwent. Here an altar was set up in the mid second century 'To the god Mars Lenus, otherwise known as Ocelus Vellaunus' suggesting in turn that the name Vellaunus, possibly meaning something like 'good' or 'excellent', was a perfectly acceptable name. 'Cassivellaunus', as already noted could therefore conceivably be derived from *Cassi*-Vellaunos or 'Vellaunus of the tribe of the Cassi'. If Vellaunus was indeed the name of the British warleader, it would help perhaps explain why the Catuvellauni tribe, although important in AD 43, were not specifically mentioned during Caesar's campaigns. At this time they were simply 'the Cassi' and only after Caesar's departure did they, or a subsect of them, become the Catu-Vellauni, Catu in this instance meaning 'warriors or fighters'. Hence the Catuvellauni were simply 'the warriors of Vellaunus', a rebranding of the group following their successful contribution to the Caesarian war (the Cassi themselves having dishonourably surrendered to Rome).

Cassivellaunos, although largely anonymous as a character, is a barbarian within a very barbarian world. He is also a very dangerous thing, in Caesar's estimation, a savage with intelligence, a man to be feared. He seems to have been feared by his own kind as well, for Caesar tells us that:

> at an earlier period perpetual wars had taken place between him and the other states; but, greatly alarmed by our arrival, the Britons had placed him over the whole war and the conduct of it
> (*Gallic Wars* V, 11)

All differences between rival clan groups were temporarily suspended. Rome was, for the time being, the greater threat and communities, whether coerced or not, now came together to fight the common foe. This was ultimately to prove to be both Cassivellaunos' strength and his greatest weakness. Whilst Caesar looked feeble, his troops unable to find food or safe haven, the British king would succeed. If Caesar was strong, his armies able to gain the upper hand in combat or the taking of field positions, then former inter-tribal enmities could reopen, Cassivellaunos' earlier role as enemy combatant and cattle raider would be remembered; his position as British warleader effectively undermined.

Cassivellaunos' strategy against Rome was one which, had his allies not defected to Rome, would probably have succeeded. He refused to play the Roman game and commit troops to the field. Fighting pitched battles with Caesar, though 'brave' in a conventional sense perhaps, was also futile. Battles were things Rome could win; a guerrilla war, troops being attacked on the march, surprise forays, the ambush of hunting parties, burning of crops and supplies, these were all things that the Roman war-machine found difficult to deal with. Cassivellaunos needed to keep the Britons united by whatever means if he were to defeat the greatest general that Rome could throw at him. His ultimate failure to do so says more about the politics, squabbles and ethnic tensions between tribal groups in southern Britain than anything else.

One other British aristocrat that Caesar had direct contact with during his campaigns was Mandubracius of the Trinobantes (or Trinovantes). Mandubracius is an important figure in British history for he is the first Briton who seems to have embraced 'the protection of Caesar', having previously been ousted from power, or at least threatened, by Cassivellaunos. One version of Caesar's *Gallic Wars* notes that Mandubracius' father, Imanuentius, had earlier been killed by Cassivellaunos, Mandubracius himself only escaping 'by flight'. The tale doesn't occur in all versions (it is something that a later scribe could have inadvertently omitted) but, if true, it provided the young king with sufficient reason to join the Roman cause. Even without a blood feud, it is likely that old ethnic or clan enmities would at some point resurface, certain groups seeing the arrival of Caesar as the perfect opportunity to level old scores and destroy a more ancient foe. Rome, after all some would no doubt have reasoned, would go one day and, if undefeated (possibly also victorious) Cassivellaunos position as great general in Briton would become unquestionable, his grip on power unshakable.

Not everyone seems to have agreed with Mandubracius' actions, for his name, as it appears in the *Gallic Wars*, could be translated as 'the black traitor' (Du brabwr). It seems hard to believe that this was actually what the young prince was called; 'the Black Traitor' being an even more curious name than 'superior leader of infantry' to give a child. An explanation could be found in Caesar himself, possibly garbling or mangling of an original Celtic form. It is possible that the name was derived from a combination of mandu- (pony or small horse) and –brako (trousers, breeches); hence 'pony-trousers' – not a very fierce name it has to be admitted. Perhaps if the prince's father had been Mannuetios (rather than Imanuentius) than he may simply have been Mannuetiagnos (son of Mannuetios). Alternatively, of course, the name which Caesar knew him by may have been derived from a source ultimately hostile to the Essex king ('Who was that man?' 'That, sire, was the black traitor' etc). If so, we can only hope it was not a name that Caesar actually used to his face.

Sometime in the summer of 54 BC, Mandubracius had fled to the headquarters of Julius Caesar in Gaul. Much like the later emperor Gaius (Caligula) would find in AD 41, when the British prince Amminus appeared on the scene with a group of friends, family and retainers, Rome now had an ally: someone who knew the enemy, knew the landscape and, most importantly of all, could provide Roman troops with food, shelter and a relatively warm welcome. With Britons like Mandubracius on his side, Caesar could present himself not as a universal enemy, against whom all Britons could unite, but as a liberator: a friend. It was a continuation of the policy 'Divide and Conquer' that Caesar had used so effectively in Gaul.

Mandubracius himself was in an excellent, and perhaps wholly unexpected situation: he needed Rome (to help restore him to power) as much as Rome now needed him (to provide a secure base, supplies and tactical information). Mandubracius' defection ultimately proved crucial to the Roman cause allowing Caesar to take the war directly to his enemy Cassivellaunos. With the Trinobantes under the protection of Caesar, other tribes, namely the Cenimagni, the Segontiaci, the Ancalites, the Bibroci, and the Cassi, felt that their interests lay in rejecting any perceived authority of Cassivellaunos and joining Rome. The Cenimagni and the Cassi we have mentioned already, probably representing the Eceni Magni (Great Iceni) and a prototype of the Catuvellauni respectively. The Segontiaci, Ancalites and Bibroci, sadly, all remain relatively obscure (see Chapter 1).

Now with a clear idea of where Cassivellaunos' capital was, Caesar marched with all haste where his men simultaneously attacked it from two sides.

> The enemy, having remained only a short time, did not sustain the attack of our soldiers, and hurried away on the other side of the town. A great amount of cattle was found there, and many of the enemy were taken and slain in their flight.
> (*Gallic Wars* V, 21)

Cassivellaunos, attempting to distract Caesar from the task at hand, persuaded four kings of the Cantium district (Kent) to launch a raid upon the beachhead fort, forcing the Roman general to return to the coast. This failed as the British assault was finally beaten off with heavy losses. Finally Cassivellaunos, realising that the game was up, sued for peace.

None of this is detectable on the ground today; there being no trace recovered (to date) that demonstrates either the presence of Caesar's army in Britain, or of any of the geographical landmarks he claims to have encountered. Aside from the beachhead and numerous forts established (we may presume) inland, Caesar mentions only a British stronghold 'admirably fortified by nature and by art' (*Gallic Wars* V, 9), placed some 12 (Roman) miles from the coast, the River *Tamesis* (Thames) and Cassivellaunos stronghold, a rampart and ditch also 'admirably fortified by nature

15 The British stronghold 'admirably fortified by nature and by art' and placed by Caesar at a distance of 12 Roman miles from the sea, is presumed to have been Bigbury hillfort, Harbledown, Kent. Unfortunately, no archaeological evidence has yet been found to confirm this. *Author*

and art' (*Gallic Wars* V, 22). The first British stronghold in Kent has traditionally been presumed to be Bigbury hillfort, Harbledown (*15*), although other sites, depending on where it is presumed that Caesar landed, have been suggested. The exact crossing point of the *Tamesis* or Thames, the only *named* feature in Caesar's account of the war, has proved particularly, although perhaps unsurprisingly, elusive. Despite that, a weathered granite column at Brentford still proudly proclaims that:

BC 54
At this
ancient fortified ford
the British tribesmen
under
Cassivellaunus
bravely opposed
Julius Caesar
on his march to
Verulamium

Perhaps there is a better chance at identifying Cassivellaunos' *oppidum*, for there are only a limited number of candidates north of the Thames where an extensive series of earthworks may be found 'defended by woods and morasses' (*Gallic Wars* V, 21). On occasion the earthwork systems of Camulodunum (Colchester) have been put forward, but these were in the (presumed) territory of Mandubracius and the Trinobantes, the only other possibility being the systems of enclosure at Wheathamstead, Beech Bottom or Prae Wood which cover extensive areas around the later Roman town of *Verulamium* (St Albans) in Hertfordshire.

At the end of the campaign, Caesar was able to leave Britain taking a number of British hostages (to ensure good behaviour in his absence), promises of protection money (euphemistically termed 'tribute') and assurances that Cassivellaunos' tribe would 'not wage war against Mandubracius nor the Trinobantes'. Mandubracius was therefore left as a British ally of the Roman State, someone who could enjoy special trade status and enhanced power and who could, in theory, rely on Caesar's protection in future times of trouble. The concept of allied or client kings and queens was one which Rome found particularly favourable, for they provided the State with a degree of security along unstable frontiers. From a purely economic perspective, client kingdoms also provided Rome with the opportunity to make significant amounts of money through enhanced trading opportunities.

CONSEQUENCES

Caesar's account in the *Gallic Wars* of course represents the 'official version' and, however useful a source, we can never fully get past the obvious bias that permeates it. How Caesar's exploits were viewed in Rome, other than the utterly non-spontaneous scenes of joy enacted by the Senate and the (presumably) more natural excitement of the people, is difficult to gauge. Strabo, writing a few years after Caesar's expeditions, noted:

> The Deified Caesar crossed over to the island twice, although he came back in haste, without accomplishing anything great or proceeding far into the island, not only on account of the quarrels that took place in the land of the Celti, among the barbarians and his own soldiers as well, but also on account of the fact that many of his ships had been lost at the time of the full moon, since the ebb-tides and the flood-tides got their increase at that time. However, he won two or three victories over the Britons, albeit he carried along only two legions of his army; and he brought back hostages, slaves, and quantities of the rest of the booty
> (Strabo *The Geography* IV, 5, 3)

Suetonius, compiling his account a century and a half later, sums up the whole of Caesar's British exploits with a simple, rather sniffy sentence:

> He invaded the Britons too, a people unknown before, vanquished them, and exacted moneys and hostages
> (Suetonius *Julius Caesar* 25, 2)

Another glimpse of the more realistic (some might add cynical) contemporary perspective on Caesar's self-promotion tour of Britain may be seen in the surviving letters of the Roman politician Cicero to his brother Quintus and friend Trebatius both of whom were serving on the second British expedition.

In June 54 BC Cicero wrote to Trebatius:

I hear there's no gold or silver in Britain. If this is so, I advise you to get a war-chariot and hasten back to us as soon as possible
(Cicero *Letters to his Friends* VIII, 7, 1)

Later, in early July he sums up his feelings towards the campaign in a letter to his colleague Atticus:

the outcome of the war in Britain is eagerly awaited; for it is well known that the approaches to the island are set round with walls of wondrous mass. It has also become clear that there isn't an ounce of silver in the island, nor any prospect of booty except slaves. I don't suppose you're expecting any of them to be accomplished in literature or music!
(Cicero *Letters to Atticus* IV, 16, 7)

Towards the end of July Cicero wrote to Atticus again, acknowledging that he had just received correspondence from his brother Quintus, then in Britain. Unfortunately, Quintus' letter does not survive, a shame, for assuming correspondence from the frontline was not subject to close scrutiny or censorship, it would be interesting to hear a more objective account (other than Caesar's) of the campaign. Whatever Quintus said, Cicero was careful to reply in very neutral terms 'I see from your letter that there is nothing for us to fear or rejoice at' (Cicero *Letters to his Brother* IIII, 1, 10), this in marked contrast to the thrills and excitement presented in Caesar's account of the war. Later Cicero remarked candidly to Atticus that:

On the 24th of October I received letters from my brother Quintus and from Caesar which were sent from the nearest point on the shores of Britain on September 25th. The campaign there is complete; hostages have been received; there is no booty; tribute has, however, been imposed and they are bringing back the army from Britain
(*Letters to Atticus* IV, 18, 5)

It is not difficult to picture Quintus, beneath a leaden October sky, overseeing the loading of equipment and men onto ships for the journey back to Gaul. Around him ships roll in the swell, whilst others are dragged through the shingle into the water. Trumpets summon troops to arms, equipment is gathered, expectant horses whinny and impatient centurions curse their weary men back into line. Caesar, in characteristically matter-of-fact tone notes simply that he:

was afraid of being prevented from sailing by the approaching season of the equinox, and so had to pack the men more tightly than usual on the ships he had. The sea becoming very calm, he set sail in the evening and brought all the fleet safely to land at dawn
(*Gallic Wars* V, 23)

For Caesar the British war was over.

3

TASCIOVANUS AND AUGUSTUS: SOMEONE WITH A GRUDGE

In the years following Caesar's departure, the Roman State must to the Britons have seemed a long way off, its armies committed to problems elsewhere. Those British aristocrats hoping to benefit directly from the support of Caesar or his successors may have felt increasing isolated and beleaguered. Individuals like Cassivellaunos, who had fought Caesar and survived, may conversely have found that their political position in the island strengthened with each passing year. Court poets and bards could spin the story of Caesar in Britain to Cassivellaunos' benefit, he had after all single-handedly defied the onslaught. He had, some would undoubtedly have observed, held Caesar at bay before hurling him unceremoniously back into the sea. The Trinobantes had come out of the invasions very well as the allies of Caesar, but it was the people of Cassivellaunos (Vellaunos of the Cassi), the Catu-Vellauni, who would ultimately triumph.

In Britain, the first named 'friend of the Roman People' was Mandubracius, but he would not be the last. Immediately after Caesar's campaigns, a series of powerful dynasties, some possessing close ties to the Roman state, were to emerge across southern Britain. Our evidence for the nature of these clans is fragmentary and incomplete, but it is important none the less for it is derived from a very British type of historic record: the coin.

A BRITISH HISTORY

A crucial element missing from any attempt to categorise, interpret or understand the world that the later Iron Age people of Britain inhabited is a record of their own experiences written from their very own distinct perspective. This period of time is, of course, known as *pre*-history, written perspectives on the Briton not appearing in any quantity until the arrival of Julius Caesar in 55 BC. The absence of any useful indigenous account has meant that, in an attempt to comprehend the lifestyle, belief systems, monuments, landscape and political structure of Iron Age communities in Britain, modern historians have had to rely either upon archaeological sources or on Classical Greek and Roman authors such as Strabo, Caesar and Tacitus, all of whom had the decency to write things down. Such texts, although magnificent works of literature in their own right, unfortunately tell us more about the tastes and (rather

16 A gold ('Gallo-Belgic') stater from Fenny Stratford, Buckinghamshire. Originally copied from the coinage of Philip II of Macedon, this mid second-century BC Celtic issue has a highly stylised, laurel-wreathed head of Apollo on the front and a largely dismembered horse, devolved from the Greek-style two-horse chariot, on the reverse. Coins such as this, which *may* have been minted in Northern France or Belgium, *may* further have crossed the Channel either as payment for goods received, or in the purses of those returning from military service overseas. © *Trustees of the British Museum*

bigoted) world view of a Roman audience than the reality of British prehistoric life. If only the Britons had themselves recorded their experiences in a more meaningful way. If only some form of 'British History' had survived from the Late Iron Age, then a modern audience could more readily comprehend the world that the Britons created, their relationship to nature, the role of monuments and material culture, the experiences they had whilst living in these lands and their perspective on the world of Rome. A clue may be found in the one piece of evidence that the Britons *did* record for themselves, albeit in an unusual, if at times largely incomprehensible, way.

Coins first appear in southern Britain around the mid second century BC, the earliest issues stamped with images influenced by units produced by the Macedonian royal family in the eastern Mediterranean (*16*). This may be because Celtic warriors, largely from the Balkans and northern Italy, had, during the fourth and third centuries BC, been employed as mercenaries by a variety of Mediterranean city states. Any warriors returning home may therefore have carried large numbers of coins with them as payment for services rendered, something which would then have influenced the regional 'barbarian' aristocracy. Most of the first 'Celtic' coins seem to copy popular Macedonian designs, such as the laurel-wreathed head of Apollo appearing on the obverse (front) and a two-horse chariot on the reverse (back). These are often referred to as being of 'Gallo-Belgic' type, for they closely mirror examples found from Northern France and Belgium. They may have crossed the English Channel either as payment for goods received, or with those returning from military service overseas. Some may also have appeared in the purses of those migrating from northern France, Caesar noting that the south-eastern coastal strip was, by 54 BC, under the control of 'those who had passed over from the country of the Belgae for the purpose of plunder and making war' (*Gallic Wars* V, 12).

The exact *function* of these first coins is not easy to resolve for Late Iron Age society was evidently not a monetary economy, at least in the modern sense. The coins being produced were, in any case, not low denomination units of base metal, but discs of more precious gold and silver. They could not be used in simple day-to-day transactions, someone selling you a cow for instance would have been singularly unimpressed had you attempted to pay for it with a gold coin – absence of 'change' rather lessening the use of coins in the market place. Instead of representing disposable cash therefore, coins may more logically have been used by tribal leaders as a way of storing wealth, perhaps to later give a proportion as a gift to the gods, to pay the Roman State for bulk commodities, such as wine or olive oil, or to pay their immediate neighbours for important necessities (horses, grain or a private army). They could also have been used to buy loyalty from another tribe or as a form of political gift, helping to cement alliances and co-operation.

As the concept of coinage spread through Britain, a distinct series of regional variations began to develop. From 70-50 BC a wide range of heavily distorted heads and horses appeared on some coins, whilst others sported lively geometric patterns and stylised (largely indecipherable) images. Towards the end of the first century BC there was a change in imagery combined with a greater desire to use Latin words, names and phrases. The appearance of these later issues is a godsend for archaeologists and historians alike, for they represent the first elements of a British 'history'; the first time that Britons began to write things down. Sometimes the words relate to tribal affiliation, sometimes to the name of a particular deity, leader, town, title or line of descent. Coins now appear to have been used as weapons in British propaganda war; overt statements of wealth and power set upon lumps of precious metal and linked with the names of particularly successful individuals. Although incomplete, and often frustratingly vague, as the first examples of a history written by the British about themselves, coins present an invaluable resource...if only we could make more sense out of them.

Some of the names appearing on the coins may be equated with characters from classical literature, for example the VERICA of coins in found in Hampshire may have been the 'Berikos' (Βερικος) mentioned in the writings of Dio Cassius whilst the AMMINVS of coins in Kent could plausibly be the 'Adminius' appearing in Suetonius' life of Caligula. If such linkages between text and coin can be sustained then specific dates may be established and a rough chronology generated. Unfortunately, only a handful of those named on the coins were ever of sufficient importance to have been noted by the historians of Rome, hence many individuals remain lost in time and space, their true significance, position and status unknown. Unfortunately, as David Braund has observed, few writers of the period today acknowledge that any such uncertainty exists, the coinage of the ancient Britons frequently being used:

17 Silver unit of ALIFF SCAVO, with a wild boar and a horse, an individual (or individuals) whose identity, tribal affiliation, reign, life and full name all remain unknown. *Images of ancient British coins provided by dealer Chris Rudd. Cat. No. 1559*

18 Gold stater of ADDIIDOM / AOOIIDOM / ADDEDOMAROS, an individual minting coin in an area roughly corresponding to modern Essex. As with ALIFF SCAVO, nothing is known of this particular character. *Images of ancient British coins provided by dealer Chris Rudd. Cat. No. 2338*

to construct a chronology of their reigns, complete with historical sketches of their warfare, their relationships and even their thinking. The process has been influential: its principal appeal is its creation of neat and known narrative outline where none otherwise exists

(Braund 1996, 67)

Hence, in reality, we can say little about the dates, reign or full name of EISV, CATTI, INAM or COMVX appearing on coin issues of the English south-western counties, nor AESV, SAENV, ANTED or SCAVO (*17*) of the Norfolk area or even ADDIIDOM / AOOIIDOM / ADDEDOMAROS of Essex (*18*). Even the supposed tribal affiliation of these individuals is unknown, for only the Eceni (Iceni of Norfolk) and possibly the Bodunni (Dobunni of the Cotswolds) were ever specifically cited on coins. The coin-to-tribe distribution maps that appear as Established Fact in many modern accounts of Iron Age and Roman Britain are, in truth, little more than fantasy; a fiction generated from the combination of basic finds distribution maps with the known location of later tribal towns (*civitates*) created by the Roman State (*19*). As noted in Chapter 1, it is highly probable that, in establishing the new *civitas* towns of Britain, Rome recognised only the larger political groupings; less significant social clusters being consigned to cultural oblivion. In some instances, however, the regularity and repetition of coin image design, combined with the use of specific language to denote discrete family relationships, means that some Iron Age dynasties may be reconstructed, at least partially, for the 'interwar' period of Britain between 54 BC and AD 43.

19 A modern coin-to-tribe map, seeking to define areas of Iron Age political control based upon a combination of Celtic coin distribution and the location of later tribal towns (*civitates*) of Roman Britain.

THE DYNASTY OF COMMIOS

At some point in, or shortly after, the mid first century BC, the previously abstract coin series of the Berkshire / northern Hampshire area was subtly altered by the addition of a name, a short sequence of seven letters presented in a neat Latin font: COMMIOS.

A native Gallic king whom Caesar made particular use of as mediator, translator and ally during his British war was an individual whom he called 'Commius of the Atrebates'. Commius, Caesar noted:

> had rendered Caesar loyal and useful service ... and in return Caesar had ordered
> that his tribe should be immune from taxation and have its independence restored
> and had made Commius suzerain over the Morini
> (*Gallic Wars* VII, 76)

Despite such concessions, Commius eventually threw in his lot with Vercingetorix, leader of the French resistance, and joined forces the enemies of Caesar during the Great Gallic revolt of 52 BC. Perhaps he had been coerced, perhaps he was blackmailed or perhaps he simply realised that Caesar and his troops were never going to leave Gaul, remaining forever as an army of occupation. When the uprising was eventually, and perhaps inevitably, crushed at the Gallic *oppidum* of Alesia, Commius found himself in an unenviable situation: should he flee and hope to evade the tentacles of the Roman State or should he submit to the famous mercy of Julius Caesar? Given what he undoubtedly knew of Caesar the man, Commius decided his best interests lay in hasty retreat.

By 51 BC the Atrebates were engaged in peace talks with Rome and Commius, after years of bitter conflict, finally came to terms with the Roman general Marcus Antoninus (Mark Antony).

> Commius ... sent ambassadors to Antoninus, and assured him that he would give hostages as a security that he would go wherever Antoninus should proscribe, and would comply with his orders, and only entreated that this concession should be made to his fears that he should not be obliged to go into the presence of any Roman (*Gallic Wars* VIII, 48)

Antony accepted that Commius had possessed a degree of just cause for his past actions and allowed the king to leave Roman territory unmolested. Commius could not, of course, be returned to his own people, for he represented a figure of defiance, but he may be able to find a place somewhere else, where his kin had already made a home. Commius therefore left for Britain, a rehabilitated, if not entirely forgiven, former friend and ally of Caesar.

Coins bearing the name COMMIOS (20) were soon after issued from around the area of the *Calleva oppidum*, later to become the Roman city of *Calleva Atrebatum* (modern day Silchester in Hampshire). It is tempting to view these as the calling card of the Atrebatic Commius, former colleague of Caesar. Some issues, however, also bear the legend COM COMMIOS, which may plausibly be interpreted as 'Commios son of Commios' indicating a second generation. Whatever the case, the presence of a tribe called the Atrebates in Britain, also the name of the tribe that Commius left when he abandoned Gaul, makes it tempting to link the two areas politically. It is possible that there was a tribe already called the Atrebates in Britain, Commius merely joining them here after his split with Rome, although it is perhaps more likely that Commius and his followers set up a British 'Atrebatic confederacy' along similar lines to the Gallic tribe. This in turn may suggest that the name 'Atrebates' itself had a specific link to Commius / Commios and his family; perhaps as a dynastic, hereditary or family title / name. The iconography on the Commion coin series issued at Calleva demonstrates

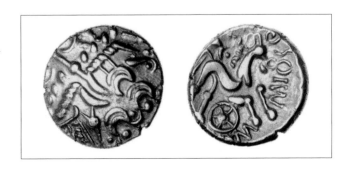

20 Gold stater bearing the name COMMIOS, possibly the same Atrebatic king and ally of Caesar during the invasions of Britain in 55 and 54 BC. *Images of ancient British coins provided by dealer Chris Rudd. Cat. No. 534*

a clear affiliation to Rome, something one would perhaps expect, not from a disgraced enemy of Caesar, but from a rehabilitated ally of the Roman State.

At least three individuals were later to claim direct descent from the Atrebatic COMMIOS (or COM COMMIOS) on their coins, namely TI / TIC / TIN / TINC / TINCO / TINCOM (Tincomarus), EP / EPP / EPPI / EPPIL / EPPILLU / EPPILLUS (Eppillus) and VIR / VIRI / VIRIC / VER / VERI / VERIC / VERCA / VERICA (Verica), all of whom marked their coins with CO F / COM F / COMMI F which may be translated as 'Commi Filius' or 'Son of Commios' (21). If their names are all transcribed (and understood) correctly, they may literally translate into 'Big Fish' (from tanko 'fish' and maro 'big'), 'Horse' (a derivative of epo) and 'Over-King' (from a combination of uer and ric / rigon).

A precise chronology for these three as king is impossible to establish with any certainty, they may have ruled together or reigned over different subsects of the same tribal group. Established Fact tells us that their ruled in sequence from Tincomarus (*c.* 30–10 BC), via Eppillus (*c.* 10 BC–AD 10) to Verica (*c.* AD 10–AD 40), but this is highly speculative. Historically, Verica seems to have fled to the emperor Claudius sometime before AD 43, whilst Tincomarus is cited in the *Res Gestae*, the monumental 'look what I did for you' statement of the emperor Augustus set up before AD 14. Beyond that, all is speculation. Nor is it possible to be 100 per cent sure about the exact relationship of these kings to Commios or, by implication, to each other. If they were all indeed the *sons* of the Atrebatic king, then together as brothers they ruled for some significant time: Commios arriving in Britain at the end of the 50s BC, Verica surviving until the early AD 40s.

If Commios had been in his mid to late 20s when Caesar used him in Britain (not altogether impossible had he shown great ability and promise), then he could still been siring heirs into his 50s, during the mid 20s BC (and we do not of course know precisely when he died). This leaves plenty of chronological scope for sons Tincomarus, Eppillus and Verica, and even the speculative COM COMMIOS (Commios II) to take their place on centre-stage. Alternatively, Tincomarus, Eppilus and Verica could all have been the sons of Commios II, making them the grandsons of Caesar's former ally in Gaul. It is further possible that none of them actually possessed a *direct* link to the great man in terms of blood, 'filius' on the coins perhaps implying an adopted heir or legal successor (with an ideological nod towards their predecessor). Whatever the case, Tincomarus, Eppillus, Verica and the speculative Commios II, all clearly wished to express an unambiguous

21 Gold stater of TIN (Tincomaros / Tincomarus) who styles himself COM F: 'Commi Filius' or 'Son of Commios'. *Images of ancient British coins provided by dealer Chris Rudd. Cat. No. 1090*

link with the Atrebatic Commios. A further dramatic link is provided within the coins of Eppillus and Verica, both of whom styled themselves REX CALLE or 'Rex Calleva' (King of Calleva). *Calleva*, loosely translated as woodland / wooded place, was a large Iron Age *oppidum*, later remodelled by the Roman State and re-branded *Calleva Atrebatum* to serve as the *civitas* of the Atrebates. To claim legitimacy as REX CALLEVA would indeed suggest that both Epillus and Verica were top dog within the Atrebates.

Over time, the imagery that Tincomarus, Eppillus and Verica used on their coins increasingly moved away from the more abstract 'Celtic' designs of Commios. The shift in artistic design seems to have occurred under Tincomarus for, whilst some of his (earlier?) issues made use of the distorted head and chariots derived from Macedonian coins, others possessed images of cavalrymen that appear so accomplished and are combined with lettering that is well proportioned, that it is possible they were taken directly from Roman dies, or at least created by those used to working within the Roman system. Analysis of the metallic content adds an extra twist, for many of these classical-style issues contain a very high proportion of silver (in excess of 95 per cent) which compares favourably with contemporary (early first-century AD) Roman coins. Were these issues of Tincomarus made from imported Roman bullion, coins or ingots, given as a gift by the emperor in order to ensure the long-term loyalty of Commios' descendants?

THE DYNASTY OF TASCIOVANUS

Coins recovered primarily to the north of the river Thames, Hertfordshire to Essex, produce the second example of dynastic succession within the Later Iron Age of central-southern Britain. Here issues produced by TAS / TASC / TASCI / TASCIA / TASCIAV / TASCIO / TASCIOV / TASCIOVAN (Tasciovanus) were stamped with the two mint marks, VER / VIR / VERL / VERO / VERLAMIO and CAM / CAMVL. VER can only really be *Verulamium* or *Verulamio* (of unknown derivation, but note the use of Ver possibly meaning 'superior' or 'surpassing'), an Iron Age *oppidum* remade in the Roman period as the *civitas* of the Catuvellauni (and re-branded again by later Christian communities as St Albans). CAM must be *Camulodunum* (modern day Colchester), the *oppidum* known as 'the fortress of Camulos', a Celtic god of war. To have two centres of coin manufacture may seem excessive, but it is possible that Tasciovanus, either through war or marriage did indeed claim control over both. Established Fact states that these *oppida* were created by two very different tribes, *Verlamio* / *Verulamium* being established by the Catuvellauni and *Camulodunum* by the Trinobantes. Therefore IF Tasciovanus was king of the Catuvellauni first and IF his power was later to extend over *Camulodunum*, an *oppidum* which *may* have been the chief focus of the Trinovantes, then Tasciovanus and the Catuvellauni *may* have finally completed the process of Trinovantian absorption started by

Cassivellaunos (assuming of course that Cassivellaunos *had* been king of the Catuvellauni in the first place). Confused?

Despite the uncertainties noted within that last sentence, the suggestion that both the *oppida* of Verulammium and Camulodunum were controlled by a single king named Tasciovanus, based on the coin evidence available, does at least appear plausible. Either Tasciovanus had begun as a Trinobantian at CAM, later moving to control VERLAMIO or either he began as a ruler of the Catuvellauni at VERLAMIO and swept eastwards to take CAM – these are not things that the coins themselves can usefully resolve. The oft-repeated Established Fact about *Camulodunum*, at least within the archaeological literature, was that it was later to become the *oppidum* of Cunobelinus (22) who, unlike Tasciovanus, has a specific tribal affiliation in that he he is credited as being 'of the Catuvellauni'. He is also, as we shall see, further cited upon his own coins, as the son of Tasciovanus, therefore Tasciovanus himself, so the logic inevitably goes, *must* himself have been a Catuvelaunian monarch. This Fact has been used to suggest that *Camulodunum*, though clearly in Trinobantian territory (modern day Essex), must have been a Catuvellaunian enclave: a colony established deep in enemy territory in order to provide the landlocked Catuvellauni with access to the sea.

Suffice to say that there is no real evidence for any of this. The one reference, from Dio Cassius which demonstrates that Cunobelinus was of Catuvellaunian affiliation actually says:

Ο ουν Πλαυτιος πολλα μεν πραγματα αναζητων σφας εσχεν, επει δε ευρε ποτε (ησαν δε ουκ αυτονομοι αλλ ΄ αλλοι αλλοις Βασιλευσι προστεαγμενοι), πρωτον μεν Καρατακον επειτα Τογοδουμνον, Κυνοβελλινου παιδας, ενικησεν. αυτος γαρ ετεθνηκει. φυγοντων δε εκεινων προσεποιησαυο ομολογια μερος τι των Βοδουννων, ων επηρχον Κατουελλανοι οντες, κανταυθα φρουραν καταλιπων προσω ηει

(*Roman History* LX, 20)

which may be translated as:

Plautius had a good deal of trouble in searching out the sons of Cunobelin, who was now dead, for the Britons were not free people but served under different rulers that they themselves had appointed, but when he did find them he first prevailed

22 Bronze unit of CVNO (Cunobelinus) stamped with the mint mark CAMVLODVNO (Camulodunum – Colchester in Essex) which may mean that the king ruled over the Trinobantes tribe. *Images of ancient British coins provided by dealer Chris Rudd. Cat. No. 2764*

over Caratacus then Togodumnus. Having banished these, he accepted terms of
surrender from that part of the Bodunni having been subject to the Catuvellauni
and, leaving behind a garrison, he followed on until he came to a river

There is, in this translation, no direct connection between Cunobelinus and the
Catuvellauni, nor for that matter between his two sons and the tribe. In fact the
connection is not even *inferred*, Dio Cassius stating simply that Cunobelinus
was dead, that his two sons were called Caratacus and Togodumnus and the
fact that the Bodunni tribe, previously subject to a tribe called the Catuvellauni,
had surrendered to him. That the three named Britons were also part of the
Catuvellauni is not something that Dio Cassius actually says. It may have been
the case that they *were* all Catuvellaunian, and that this fact was more explicitly
stated in whatever earlier source Dio Cassius used to compile his *History*,
but it is not there in his own text and therefore we should not automatically
make the link. *Camulodunum* was in Trinobantian territory and was we may
presume, therefore a Trinobantian centre. Anyone who ruled there, or who was
credited as ruling there, may also have been Trinobantian. If Tasciovanus *and*
later Cunobelinus were credited as ruling both Camulodunum and *Verulamium*,
it might suggest that they were Trinobantian kings spreading their influence
westwards, to Catuvellaunians looking east.

Tasciovanus styled himself as RICON / RICONI, the Celtic for king, on
his coins (23) and not REX, as had Eppillus and Verica. This may have been
because the coins of Tasciovanus were attempting to affirm his British heritage,
rather than by claiming legitimacy through use of a Roman title. It could also
be that the term RICON / RICONI had a specific usage, perhaps meaning
something greater than a REX. Possibly the term implied 'overlordship' of
more than one tribal group (in this instance perhaps both the Trinobantes and
the Catuvellauni)? Was Tasciovanus too unpredictable, or even dangerous, a
character for the Roman State to recognise his authority, therefore denying him
any opportunity to use Latin titles such as REX? This is possible: a destabilising
element in the south-east of Britain would certainly not have been welcomed by

23 Gold stater of TASCIO
(Tasciovanus) who styles himself
RICON, the Celtic for 'king', as
opposed to the Latin term REX.
This may have been because the
coins affirmed a British heritage
(rather than the mere adoption
of a Roman title) or it may be
that RICON possessed a specific
meaning, implying overlordship of
more than one tribal group. *Images
of ancient British coins provided by
dealer Chris Rudd. Cat. No. 2407*

Augustus and his successors. Sadly, this is something that the coins themselves cannot answer.

Certain coins issued with the name of Tasciovanus also possess the words ANDOCO, DIAS, RUES or SEGO. These have caused consternation to archaeologists and classical historians, some of whom have suggested that ANDOCO, DIAS, RUES and SEGO are the abbreviated form of Celtic names; perhaps minor or petty rulers subordinate to Tasciovanus. We have no idea how the Iron Age tribes of southern Britain functioned or whether the hierarchy of power was in any way similar from one social group to the next. It is possible, however, that if one king (Tasciovanus) could rule over two tribes (the Trinobantes and the Catuvellauni) then perhaps it is also possible that any given tribe may have possessed multiple leaders, or was itself subdivided into semi-autonomous clan groups. Such a scenario might explain use of the term RICON / RICONI on the coins of Tasciovanus for he could have been in control of many discrete subsects or smaller territories contained within the area of 'the greater tribe'. Alternatively, ANDOCO, DIAS, RVES and SEGO could all represent more egotistical concerns, a form of boasting or one-upmanship: Ande perhaps meaning 'big', Rues or Ro meaning 'great' and Sego perhaps meaning 'power' or 'force'.

As with COMMIOS to the south-west, Tasciovanus lived long enough, or committed sufficient great acts (including the provision of heirs), to be commemorated upon the British coin series by those claiming direct descent from him. To the east, around *Camulodunum*, CUN / CUNO / CUNOB / CUNOBEL / CUNOBELIN (Cunobelinus) minted coins marked with TASC F and TASCIOVANI F (Tasciovanus Filius) whilst EPA / EPAT / EPATI / EPATICU (Epaticus), primarily based, according to his coins, around *Verulamium* also noted the TASCI F relationship (24). It could be that both men, if indeed the biological sons of Tasciovanus and not simply his political or adopted heirs, divided the two tribal zones based around the *oppida* of *Camulodunum* and *Verulamium* (and consequently the Trinovantes and Catuvellauni) between them; brothers or half-brothers each creating their own distinctive domains following the demise of their father. This theory, though undeniably attractive, fails to explain why Cunobelinus, either the cuno ('hound') of belinos or the bel-cuno (literally 'powerful' hound), also has coins marked with VER and VERV, unless he took control over the *oppidum* of *Verulamio / Verulamium* following the death or exile of Epaticus (a name possibly derived from epo, meaning 'horse'). These are things that, once again, the coins cannot resolve.

24 Silver unit of EPAT (Epaticus) who, like CVNO (Cunobelinus) identifies himself as a son of TASCIOV (Tasciovanus). *Images of ancient British coins provided by dealer Chris Rudd. Cat. No. 1196.*

25 Silver unit of DVBNO (Dubnovellaunos), possibly the same king who, between 30 BC and AD 14, was in Rome, seeking refuge in the court of the emperor Augustus. *Images of ancient British coins provided by dealer Chris Rudd. Cat. No. 282*

Sometime after 30 BC, but before AD 14, Tincomarus, whose coin series had previously extended along the western Thames, northern Hampshire and the southern coast of Sussex, was in Rome, together with one Dubnovellaunos (25), whose coin series had been largely restricted to Essex and Eastern Kent. We know this because the names of both appear on the *Res Gestae*, a monumental statement dedicated by Augustus, grandnephew and principal heir of Julius Caesar. Both British kings are noted as 'seeking refuge', though from what is not recorded. Whatever the cause for their flight, it seems probable that both Tincomarus and Dubnovellaunos were trying to persuade Augustus, the first emperor of Rome, to honour the promises and assurances of protection made by Caesar, his adopted father. Being a friendly, allied or client king was a two-way process they would undoubtedly have reflected, and whoever had threatened their powerbase in Britain should be eliminated with the full military backing of Rome.

GAIUS OCTAVIANUS (AUGUSTUS)

Gaius Octavianus came to supreme power on 1 August 30 BC following the defeat of his rivals Marcus Antoninus (Mark Antony) and Queen Cleopatra VII Philopater at the sea battle of Actium off the coast of western Greece. Actium effectively marked the end of the civil war that had convulsed the Roman world following the assassination of Julius Caesar in 44 BC, and it also emphatically marked the end of the Roman Republic. Octavian, the adopted son of Caesar, spent the following three decades subtly altering the Roman constitution and carefully formalising his position at the very heart of the empire.

In January, 27 BC, less than three years after Actium, Octavian made a public show of surrendering his accumulated powers to the senate. They, perhaps rather wisely, made a very public show in return, refusing his generous offer and handing all his titles back. Critically, Octavian could now claim to hold power 'as a gift' from the senate and not, as Caesar had done before, because he had forced them to do his bidding. Later in the same year he took the name 'Augustus' (26), a name that reflected both his new constitutional powers and his curious, unearthly status as the son (albeit an adopted one) of a god (his deified uncle), Gaius Julius Caesar: it means literally 'revered' or 'sacred one'. His adoption of the name helped confirm that he was 'more than human'.

26 Cameo portrait of Augustus created between AD 14 and 20. Images created for public consumption, of which this does not appear to have been one, emphasised the authority of the First Citizen, without necessarily implying divinity. © *Trustees of the British Museum*

From this point on, Augustus cemented his exceptional position through the gradual accumulation titles and powers. As *princeps*, Octavian was recognised as the 'first citizen' of Rome. In the senate everyone was, theoretically at least, on an equal footing, but Octavian was now *Primus Inter Pares* (First Among Equals) – to paraphrase George Orwell, he was now *more equal* than his colleagues. As *pontifex maximus*, Octavian became chief priest; as *imperator* he took command of the military, outranking all provincial governors in the process. He generously allowed the Senate to maintain control of the long established (and wealthy) provinces of the Roman world whilst he looked after the younger, more troublesome ones (which incidentally just happened to possess the greatest concentration of military reserves). As continually elected consul he had his fingers in the law-making process and as *Pater Patriae* he was formally recognised as being 'Father of the Country'.

Through the stealthy acquisition of power, Augustus persuaded the senate to accept his unusual (and unprecedented) position as head of state. Perhaps mindful of the fate that befell Caesar, being stabbed in the back (sides and front), Augustus was careful to demonstrate that everything he did was for and on behalf of the people. All official inscriptions retained the acronym SPQR – 'Senatus Populusque Romanus': the senate and people of Rome.

As an adopted son and heir to the estate of the divine Julius, what Augustus really needed to show the Senate and People was that he too was successful in the art of war. Wars not only brought prestige they also delivered swift economic cost benefits in terms of slaves (prisoners of war) and the opportunity of taking direct control of conquered resources (rather than having to deal through traders and middlemen). There was not, in the later years of the first century BC, any real concept in the Roman mind of a limit to conquest and the definition of fixed frontiers. The empire was in a state of continual expansion with only the severest constraints of geography or politics holding it back.

Early in Augustus' reign, it seems clear that contact between Rome and a number of prominent British families remained relatively strong, trade and exchange helping to bind the 'barbarians' closely to the State:

> At present, however, some of the chieftains there, after procuring the friendship of Caesar Augustus by sending embassies and by paying court to him, have not only dedicated offerings in the Capitol, but have also managed to make the whole of the island virtually Roman property. Further, they submit so easily to heavy duties, both on the exports from there to Celtica and on the imports from Celtica (these latter are ivory chains and necklaces, and amber-gems and glass vessels and other petty wares of that sort), that there is no need of garrisoning the island; for one legion, at the least, and some cavalry would be required in order to carry off tribute from them, and the expense of the army would offset the tribute-money; in fact, the duties must necessarily be lessened if tribute is imposed, and, at the same time, dangers be encountered, if force is applied
> (Strabo *The Geography* IV, 5, 3)

The calculation of resources required to keep Britain under Roman control seems ludicrously small in Strabo's estimate: one legion 'at the least' with accompanying cavalry. Presumably Strabo is referring only to the area of Britain producing the friendly chieftains, i.e. the south and east, rather than 'the whole of the island' (as he seems to be implying), but then the point is that he is providing the justification to *not* attack Britain. The embassies of unnamed British chieftains, who may have included representatives of both the Trinobantes and Atrebates, as well as the proto-Catuvellauni, the Cenimagni (Eceni) and some of the Cantium aristocracy, were in Rome 'paying court' to Augustus and dedicating offerings in the most holy of Roman sanctuaries. Caesar's campaigns had reaped dividends: those who either wished to avoid antagonising Rome, or who simply wanted to ensure that their neighbours did not gain the upper hand through increased links with the Mediterranean, were actively pursuing Augustus and he was only too happy to advertise the fact. Conquering the Gauls and Germans was one thing; having the Britons emerge from the very edge of the known world in order to pay homage, was quite another.

Gradually, however, attitudes towards Britain began to harden. Possibly the arrival of the two British kings Tincomarus and Dubnovellaunos, as refugees in Rome, around the year 30 BC, provided the catalyst for a planned invasion. Something or someone had disturbed the political *status quo* in Britain, with the result that two pro-Roman monarchs felt it prudent to flee to the relative safety of the imperial court. Tincomarus, who styled himself on coins as the son of Caesar's former ally Commios, may have played on his father's pre-Gallic Revolt loyalty to the Roman State and, perhaps, his rehabilitated status later in life. Augustus was no doubt mindful of the potentially damaging effect that a destabilised northern frontier would have, not just on trade, but also upon the still largely unsettled province of Gaul. He would also have been acutely aware of the glory that had accompanied Caesar's wars in Britain and the potential success that any grand military crossing of the Ocean would bring.

In 34 BC, Dio Cassius tells us that:

> Augustus had set out to lead an expedition into Britain in emulation of his father, and had already advanced into Gaul after the winter which saw the consulships of Antony for the second time and of Lucius Libo, when some newly conquered tribes together with the Dalmatians rose in revolt
> (Dio Cassius *Roman History* XLIX, 38, 2)

Seven years later the political situation appears to have deteriorated further for we hear that Augustus:

> set out with the intention of leading an expedition into Britain, but on his arrival in Gaul he stayed there. For it seemed likely that the Britons would come to terms with him, and affairs in Gaul were still unsettled since the civil wars had broken out immediately after their subjugation
> (Dio Cassius *Roman History* LIII, 22)

The following year, 26 BC, Augustus remained:

> anxious for war against Britain since the peoples there would not come to terms, but he was prevented by a revolt of the Salassi, and the Cantabrians and Asturians had become hostile
> (Dio Cassius *Roman History* LIII, 25)

What are we to make of all these apparently frenzied preparations for war? At face value it would suggest that the 'British Problem' posed a significant threat to the security of the Roman State. Three times in eight years the emperor gathered resources together to force a military solution and instigate regime change within the British political system. It is possible, of course, that Dio Cassius has got his facts wrong: it wouldn't be the first time. As a compiler of material, the third-century historian could have misunderstood his sources, repeating the same event, preparation for war, and creating two or three separate events out of just the one.

The first consideration of war is cited, almost in passing, and as if it were based on nothing more than a whim: an attempt by a vain emperor to obtain a swift military victory 'in emulation of his father' (Julius Caesar). The second set of references, allegedly taken from 27 and 26 BC, suggest a slightly different motive: the unnamed Britons being noted on two separate occasions as 'not coming to terms'. Terms with whom and why, is unfortunately not explained. Was the unrest related to the conditions set by Caesar following the termination of his British war, or were they specific terms of agreement set out by Augustus at a later date?

A clue to Augustus' motives may be provided in one of the few 'policy statements' supplied for the emperor in his relations with the northern barbarians:

Except in a few instances he restored the kingdoms of which he gained possession by the right of conquest to those from whom he had taken them or joined them with other foreign nations. He also united the kings with whom he was in alliance by mutual ties, and was very ready to propose or favour intermarriages or friendships among them. He never failed to treat them all with consideration as integral parts

27 Provincial silver coin minted in Ephesus, Turkey, showing a portrait of Augustus with the legend LIBERTATIS P R VINDEX ('Protector of the Roman People's Freedom') and the female personification of PAX ('peace'). This 'official version' emphasises not only Rome's desire for peace, following a lengthy period of civil war, but also the potentially stabilising influence of the 'First Citizen'. © *Trustees of the British Museum*

of the empire, regularly appointing a guardian for such as were too young to rule or whose minds were affected, until they grew up or recovered; and he brought up the children of many of them and educated them with his own

(Suetonius *Augustus* 48)

This implies that Augustus was interfering in some way with the internal affairs of those tribal aristocracies that bordered his empire (27). This, in itself, was nothing new, Rome had for many centuries attempted to interceed in the affars of state of others, suggesting alliances, overseeing succession or overthrowing an unfriendly government. Regime change through diplomatic means was always preferable to direct military intervention, although, from a Roman perspective, force of arms could always be portrayed more heroically on coins and in statuary. The unilateral imposition of Augustus' will upon British or German tribes through a display of military might would, however, have been extremely costly, both financially and politically (especially if things did not go to plan). As Augustus was to discover, client kingdoms, 'buffer' states at the margins of empire, could be manipulated in far more subtle ways than by mere intimidation.

A key element of Roman society was the institution known as *clientela* (clientage). This ran on the principle that a *cliens* (client) was obligated through a debt of loyalty to repay favours (gifts, financial aid, employment, protection or the granting of their own personal freedom), received from a benefactor or *patronus* (patron). The patron acted, in most instances, as a father-figure to his clients, taking a personal interest in their businesses and financial and legal well being. In return the client could offer financial, political, legal and, during the Republic, sometimes even military support to his patron. The more clients a patron possessed, the greater his support-base and social standing. The system worked tolerably well at a personal level, but at an institutional, when entire families, clans, cities or tribes became *clientes*, the social dynamics could become a little more precarious.

The rulers of states, tribes or kingdoms allied to Rome could perhaps have operated as clients to their patron, Augustus. In such a framework, particular monarchs could be influenced or manoeuvred in many different ways and by many varied means. They could, for instance, be obligated to supply 'gifts' of slaves or metal ore, pay tribute or tax or provide fighting men for the armies of Rome. They may also have been required to surrender their children to the emperor, partially as a way of ensuring their continued loyalty to the Roman state (the young acting as hostages) but also in order that their offspring could receive a 'good education' and mix with the great, the good and the politically influential. Once 'educated', and at a point when the succession of power within a particular kingom was in doubt, the former hostage could be returned to his or her people, fully conversant with the ways and systems of empire (and no doubt speaking Latin). Thus Rome could minimise potentially destablising events within a 'client-kingdom', such as invasion, coup or the unexpectedly sudden death of a pro-Roman monarch, by returning their own preferred candidate to a position of power.

The system, as David Mattingly has already noted, may not always have run smothly, however, for:

> Client kingship was something that had to be agreed by Rome, so anyone seeking to establish their own rule, no matter what their support in Britain, would have to seek recognition from Rome. In succession matters, Rome may often have had a favoured candidate, though that does not mean she always got her way
> (Mattingly 2006, 72)

Such a scenario, with pro and anti Roman factions disputing the nature of succession within a tribe, may explain Augustus' repeated attempts to force his will upon the Britons. The second attempt at military intervention (probably against the Atrebatic or Catuvellaunian / Trinobantian dynasties) in 27 BC, did not materialise, because, so we are told, the Britons came 'to terms', presumably accepting Augustus' demands and agreeing to the succession of a candidate sponsored by (or brought up in) Rome.

Whatever the case, and whether we are discussing three discrete and separate attempts at military action, or one repeated three times, it is important to remember that this would have been no minor foray arbitrarily thrown together by a bored emperor. An expedition to the British Isles would present a significant risk not only to the security of the state, the emperor and large numbers of troops tied up in a distant land, but to the perceived success of Augustus' fledgling monarchy. Catastrophic defeat could prove helpful to those that still hankered after the Roman Republic and craved the permanent removal of the First Citizen.

The 'gung-ho', sabre-rattling mood of the imperial court at this time is captured in the (rather sycophantic) court poems such as those set down by Propertius in around 27 BC: 'Whether on foot the Parthian we pursue or the Briton with our fleet, blind are the perils of sea and land' (*Elegies* II, 27, 5). Horace observed that: 'Augustus shall be a god on earth when once the Britons and the grievous Parthians are added to our empire' (*Odes* III 5, 1). This is all good stuff, but does it really reflect a statement of intent, or is it all spin? In 26 BC Horace asked that 'Fortuna preserve our Caesar soon to go against the Britons, furthest of earth's peoples' (*Odes* I, 21, 13), something that may suggest the imminent launch of a major campaign (rather than being purely wishful thinking). Some time later, possibly in or just before 23 BC, Horace was to comment that 'moved by your prayer Apollo shall take from our people and their leader Caesar tear-inspiring war and plague and wretched famine and inflict them on the Persians and the Britons' (*Odes* I, 21, 13-16). This last statement by Horace sounds particularly aggrieved and may imply that whatever action had been planned by the State in Britain had been thwarted, much to the annoyance of Augustus and those closest to him. Perhaps by calling up a plague of almost Old Testament proportions upon the Britons, Horace is merely reflecting the sense of outrage and impotence that Augustus himself may have been feeling.

4

CUNOBELINUS AND ROME: THE CURRENCY OF PAIN

North Sea storm tides, combining severe weather conditions and a dramatic rise in sea level, can be particularly unforgiving. Ships are sunk, houses and fields are flooded, animals and people die, sometimes in tragically high numbers. The storm that hit the coast of the Netherlands and Germany late in the summer of AD 16 was no exception. It was, so Tacitus tells us, a calamity which transcended all others 'in extent and novelty' (*Annals* II, 24).

> Hail poured from a black mass of clouds, and simultaneously the waves, buffeted by conflicting gales from every quarter, began to blot out the view and impede the steering. The soldiers, struck by alarm and unfamiliar with the sea and its hazards, nullified by their obstruction or mistimed help the services of the professional sailors. Then all heaven, all ocean, passed into the power of the south wind; which, drawing its strength from the sodden lands of Germany, the deep rivers, the endless train of clouds with its grimness enhanced by the rigour of the neighbouring north, caught and scattered the vessels to the open ocean or to islands either beetling with crags or perilous from sunken shoals
> (Tacitus *Annals* II, 23)

The storm hit the Rhine Delta just as Roman ships were returning troops back to their respective bases at the end of a punitive campaign against the Germanic tribes. Many soldiers lost their lives, whilst others were cast ashore in a variety of strange places.

> Some of the ships went down; more were stranded on remote islands; where, in the absence of human life, the troops died of starvation, except for a few who supported themselves on the dead horses washed up on the same beach ... A few had been swept over to Britain, and were sent back by the petty kings. Not a man returned from the distance without his tale of marvels; furious whirlwinds, unheard-of birds, enigmatic shapes half-human and half-bestial; things seen, or things believed in a moment of terror
> (Tacitus *Annals* II, 24)

Southern Britain had been within the orbit of the Mediterranean world for some significant time, and yet to the average Roman, it was still a place that was way beyond the limits of civilisation. It was a place of mythological weirdness, where strange creatures stalked the land menacingly: a classical version of the land *Where the Wild Things Are*. It was not a place where anyone would volunteer to visit.

OPPIDA IN BRITAIN

Archaeology has helped to fill in the blanks in our understanding of life and settlement in late prehistoric Britain. Curiously, none of the 'unheard of birds' or enigmatic half-bestial shapes that Tacitus' hysterical soldiers described in AD 16 have yet been discovered.

The most instantly recognisable type-site of the southern British Iron Age is the hillfort or defended hilltop enclosure (28). Such structures appear to provide confirmation of the warlike nature of Iron Age communities, always feuding, brawling, fighting and stealing from one another. Strong hilltop defences must, so the logic goes, imply a very real fear of neighbouring groups coupled with the desire to protect house and home. Or do they? The terms 'fort' and 'fortress' are emotive, implying imply threats from abroad and the consequent need for defence. They suggest the presence of formidable armies roaming the field and yet it would seem that only a minority of the population lived, worked or worshipped in hillforts. Most Iron Age settlements appear as relatively small-scale, close knit farming communities, trading, interacting and existing within the landscape without the need to massively defend (29).

Warfare between the various Early Iron Age communities may have been endemic, in that there was a semi-permanent state of competition between tribes, clans or farming units, but rarely, if at all, would any group attempt to eradicate another. The total extermination of opposing groups, enemy combatants and civilians is something that may be defined as the modern, 'civilised' concept of war. Conflict between prehistoric societies probably more often took the form of competition. Competition helped foster alliances and enforce allegiances, further increasing the desire amongst the leaders of particular communities for prestige goods and extreme dress items. Ultimately it probably led to more and more forms of visually impressive hilltop enclosure. Hillforts, therefore, could have had less to do with a permanent state of hostilities, and more to do with the definition of a social heart of a specific clan group. Hillforts could be where organised gatherings met at particular times of the year (30). Places where people could come together for the purposes of trade, exchange, taxation, marriage, food distribution or religious ceremonies; places where the leadership of the tribe was reinforced and bonds of allegiance strengthened.

There are many varied and impressive forms of hillfort enclosure in Britain but the main feature common to developed examples is the presence of large internal pits. Such features came in a variety of shapes, including circular, rectangular and triangular, but, when excavated most produced prolific quantities of artefacts suggesting some form of structured deposition. Given the nature of recording

28 Badbury Rings hillfort, Dorset: a prime example of one of the most instantly recognisable, archaeological type-site of the southern British Iron Age. *Author*

29 A recreation of an Iron Age roundhouse at the Cranborne Ancient Technology Centre in Dorset. Despite the prevalence of hillforts in modern literature, the majority of Iron Age settlement types in Southern Britain comprised relatively small-scale farming communities. *Author*

30 Maiden Castle, Dorset. Hillforts probably acted as the social heart of a specific clan group where people came together for the purposes of trade, exchange, taxation, marriage, food distribution, religious ceremonies or to resolve leadership challenges. *Author*

31 Structured deposition within a backfilled 'storage' pit of the Later Iron Age. Bournemouth University Durotriges Big Dig 2009. *Author*

undertaken, it is sometimes difficult to be certain of the exact context of the finds, but it is apparent that a series of special deposits, including weapons, tools, pottery, coins, querns and disarticulated bone (both human and animal) were set down, often following broadly repeatable patterns of deposition (*31*). Whatever was going on at these sites, it does not seem to relate to any 'normal' idea of fortified settlement.

As the hillforts of the Early Iron Age faded from most areas of south-eastern Britain in the later years of the first century BC, a new form of enclosure system developed. These systems are referred to in the archaeological literature as *oppida*. This is something of an unfortunate title, as it is derived from a term that Julius Caesar applied to almost every Iron Age enclosure, settlement or hillfort that he encountered during his campaigns across Britain and Gaul, regardless of location, extent or political affiliation. In fact Caesar never really defines what precisely he believes the term *oppidum* to mean. Given current archaeological considerations, the term probably has more valid application in France, Germany and Switzerland where certain Late Iron Age enclosures possess clear evidence of urban planning in the form of street grids, administrative centres, religious buildings, elite settlement and enclosing masonry walls.

There is nothing remotely comparable to continental *oppida* recorded from Late Iron Age Britain, though the term 'territorial *oppidum*' has at times been applied by archaeologists to a series of discontinuous linear earthworks found in areas where the hillfort appears to have died out. Territorial *oppida* are to be found in relatively low lying areas of southern Britain and they often possess complex systems of banks and ditches that demarcate vast blocks of land. A

Left: 32 Distribution of 'territorial *oppida*' across southern Britain in the Late Iron Age indicating the suggested form of their original names, as indicated on contemporary coinage. The shaded areas identify the 'main zones of hillfort occupation'. *Redrawn from Jones and Mattingly* An Atlas of Roman Britain *(1990, 46)*

Below: 33 The Chichester *oppidum*, West Sussex: a network of ramparts extending for an overall distance of 10km (east–west) by 4.5km (north–south), to the immediate north of the modern town. Although overgrown, the earthworks still present a formidable barrier. *Author*

notable example of the territorial *oppidum* can be found at Colchester in Essex, where an area of just over 32 square kilometres (*c.* 12 square miles) was partially enclosed by a series of ramparts. There have been few extensive surveys of the interior, but it seems clear that only a few areas were in any way intensively inhabited. At Sheepen, to the west of the later Roman town, an area of Iron Age settlement associated with industrial activity, coin manufacture and exotic Roman imports has been located, while at Gosbecks and Lexden, to the south-west, a religious complex and major cemetery have been recorded. Other *oppida* have been identified at St Albans in Hertfordshire, Silchester and Winchester in Hampshire and Chichester in West Sussex (32).

The Chichester *oppidum* comprises a network of ramparts (known as the Chichester Entrenchments or Dykes), which extend for an overall distance of 10km (east-west) by 4.5km (north-south), to the immediate north of the modern town (33). Some 15 separate earthworks have so far been identified, though later agricultural and urban development has almost certainly destroyed significant sections. Situated at the very southern edge of the South Downs, the entrenchments effectively cut off the neck of land between the main north-south river systems of this area from the Arun, via the Lavant and off towards Bosham Stream in the west. The entire coastal plain from Bognor Regis to Bosham, including Selsey Bill and the western limits of Chichester harbour, was therefore separated by these earthworks from the lands to the north.

Dating *oppida* entrenchments has proved difficult. Excavations across the majority of systems have provided only a limited sample of material which confirms only a very general date in the Middle to Late Iron Age. The sheer cost of constructing the entrenchments, at least in terms of labour, must have been immense. Richard Bradley, when examining the Chichester Entrenchments, calculated that the total mass of soil excavated in the course of cutting the ditches and building the ramparts was in the region of 340,000 tons. Labour required to finish such a system would be somewhere in the equivalent to 1,500,000 man hours (or, to put in another way, 410 men working a 10-hour day every day for a year). Even if the entrenchments were created in a series of stages over time, their building must have tied up a considerable part of the population.

Associated with the main *oppida* of south-eastern Britain are a relatively small number of high-status burials. At least some of the graves, which broadly span the period from the late first century BC to the mid first century AD, are presumably of those individuals who proudly defined themselves on coins, sometimes as REX or RICON. In the absence of any firm dates or associations, however, it is perhaps unwise to speculate upon which particular members of tribal aristocracy have been recovered by archaeologists.

At Colchester, the Lexden Tumulus, a 30m diameter round mound excavated in 1924, revealed a large assemblage of artefacts, most of which appear to have been damaged or broken prior to burial, set within a wooden chamber. The individual in question, of whom little was recovered, the body having been cremated then apparently scattered across the western edge the chamber, had been buried with chain mail, set over a leather jerkin, and a variety pots, amphorae, fragments of furniture and imported metal items, including a small portrait of the emperor Augustus. The suggested date range for deposition of artefacts within the chamber has been calculated to the last two decades of the first century BC. At Stanway, to the south-west, a series of burials, some placed within timber chambers, have been dated to between the end of the first century BC and the mid first century AD (possibly as late as AD 59/60). Artefact associations here included weaponry, drinking vessels, amphorae, jewellery, a gaming board (with the pieces set out as if the game were about to start) and a series of medical instruments used in surgery. A burial set within a wooden chamber at Folly Lane, near St Albans, contained a similar range of amphorae, ceramic fine ware and imported metal goods, together with chain mail, hob-nailed boots / sandals and a range of equestrian trappings, all dated to the mid 50s AD.

Unfortunately no one has yet been able to supply a satisfactory answer as to why *oppida* were deemed necessary, how they may have functioned and what, exactly, were they for. It is possible that they were designed to enclose the political heart of the local tribe, clan or community. The sheer quantity of late Republican Roman imports recovered from excavations in and around the entrenchments is suggestive of a trade focus and political control, but few definite structures have yet been found. The sheer size and scale of the *oppida* (*34*) suggest that they were designed to represent the boundaries of important and powerful social groups. Perhaps a single *oppidum* may have represented the political formalisation of tribal authority, a monumental version of the linear ditch systems, or cross ridge dykes, of the Late Bronze and Early Iron Age, which defined more limited spaces. In this context the Dykes could be viewed as the late prehistoric equivalent of the 49th parallel or the demilitarised zone separating North and South Korea. But who in the Later Iron Age community would have had the political will or social need to create such boundaries and what was the perceived threat supposed to be?

34 Chichester, West Sussex. View looking south-east from the top of the Iron Age *oppidum*, towards Chichester cathedral (which lies at the heart of Roman *Noviomagus*). The scale of *oppida* suggests that they were designed to represent and define the boundaries to powerful tribal authorities. *Author*

Perhaps local communities felt afraid of the expansionist tendencies of their immediate neighbours. Historically we know that a number of Late Iron Age kings from southern Britain, including Tincomarus and Dubnovellaunos, were seeking shelter with the emperor Augustus at the beginning of the first century AD, so that theory may not be too wide of the mark. The fact that many of the hillforts of the Early Iron Age were not being refortified at this time however, many apparently going out of use completely, may alternatively suggest that fear of attack (and the subsequent escalation of hostilities) was not a major concern, at least for the bulk of the population.

Only those with a vested interest in maintaining good relations with Rome may have felt the need to define the limits of their power in dramatic new ways. The control of trade with the Mediterranean, and of the profits that ensued, may have led some British leaders to better protect their investments with networks of defensive ramparts backed by displays of intimidation and force. The exploitation of natural resources in return for Mediterranean consumables (such as wine and olive oil) may have provided a route to supreme power for prehistoric entrepreneurs in Britain. Tincomarus, son of Commios based at *Calleva* (Silchester in Hampshire) may have believed he was top dog in matters of trade with the Mediterranean. Other British rulers may have disagreed. Perhaps in reality the Iron Age kings of first-century Britain were little more than mafia dons: their 'tribes' systematically exploiting key resources, controlling access to exotic imports, organising 'protection' and intimidating the local population. The disruption that concerned Augustus, with certain Britons 'not coming to terms' may therefore have been less about territorial acquisition and more to do with a struggle over resources and capital.

FORTS IN BRITAIN

It is generally assumed that the plans for direct military intervention in Britain were eventually shelved by Augustus and, as trade between the Rome and Britain appears to have continued largely uninterrupted, Established Fact tells us that some sort of peace was created through diplomatic channels. Archaeological evidence unearthed from both Essex and Sussex however, suggests that this was most certainly not the case.

Fishbourne is famous for its Roman palace. Visit the site today and you cannot fail to be impressed by the opulence and luxury; the wall plaster, marble and, perhaps more crucially, the fine mosaic pavements. There is another side to the site however, a side that you could be forgiven for overlooking. During the 1960s excavation of the palace, a considerable range of early first-century pottery, together with early first-century coins and pieces of military equipment were uncovered. All seemed to relate in some way with a series of linear gravel roads and post-built timber buildings. The buildings comprised at least two definite structures, one set between two parallel, east-west aligned roads. The footprint of the first structure was formed by six parallel trenches each

35 Recreation of Roman timber buildings at the Cranborne Ancient Technology Centre in Dorset. Structures such as these appear in the early first-century AD military phase at Fishbourne, West Sussex, where they have been interpreted as granaries. *Author*

originally containing upright timbers. The excavator, Barry Cunliffe, interpreted the remains as a granary, the essential food-storage component of every Roman fort (35). The structure had been raised on stilts (in order to permit the regular flow of air underneath) and had possessed a tiled roof. The second building was slightly larger and better defined, its footprint formed by a series freestanding posts originally supporting a raised floor. As with the first, this structure also appears to have functioned as a granary. Phasing for the granaries proved difficult to determine, although the pottery evidence suggested that building 1 dated to before AD 20.

Excavations conducted on the site in the 1980s and 90s added a further twist: a linear, V-shaped ditch which was traced for a distance of over 90 metres. Finds from the primary silts of the ditch included locally produced pottery of the Later Iron Age and a small quantity of early Roman imports. The imported material comprised mainly red slip-ware and included an Arretine cup which can be tied to a specific date, in this case between 10 BC and AD 10. Of the remaining vessels, all of which were unweathered (suggesting fairly rapid deposition after breakage), none were any later than the Augustan period. When the ditch came to an end, it was deliberately backfilled with clay, presumably derived from an abandoned rampart. Pottery comprised a combination of locally produced and imported wares, none of which were any later than *c.* AD 25–30. The profile and form of the ditch were unlike the more irregular, flat-bottomed ditches of the Sussex Iron Age, and strongly suggest a Roman military origin.

The ditch, the granaries and the finds all create something of a conundrum. Dating evidence, of the sort that archaeologists retrieve in order to establish a secure and safe chronology, here caused an interpretational headache for the site cannot be placed within a well-ordered and stable timeline. The Established Facts of the Roman invasion of Britain in AD 43 are that the landings were in Kent (at Richborough) and, only having been safely put ashore and defeated the enemy in a series of decisive battles, did the separate legions spread out, subjugating all native groups they encountered. True, Julius Caesar led two expeditions to

Britain in 55 and 54 BC, but these were also concentrated in Kent. There was no Roman military involvement in Sussex prior to AD 43. Full stop.

The military remains recovered beneath the Fishbourne palace therefore *have to* date to AD 43 or later and they certainly cannot be earlier. Either the dating is skewed (perhaps those who originally built and used the base were using old pottery, carrying old coins and wearing out of date armour) or the evidence has been misread (somehow the ditch fills had been disrupted or the material had been 'kicking around' the site for some significant time before its incorporation in the feature). Whatever the case, the archaeology is clearly wrong: Fishbourne can safely be ignored.

Similar interpretational problems also occur in levels examined beneath the nearby Roman town of Chichester. Here, significant quantities of early imperial Roman military equipment, including projectile weapons, multiple fragments of plate armour, pieces of helmet, belt buckles, shield fittings and at least one sword have been found in association with timber buildings. Archaeological interpretation is, as at Fishbourne, constrained by fixed historical parameters. Because *we know* that the Roman invasion of Britain did not occur until AD 43, the remains recorded 'must' therefore represent a supply base created in order to support troop movements to the west in around AD 44. Needless to say, there is no real evidence to support this hypothesis and the material from Chichester could easily have derived from Pre-Claudian (pre AD 43) military activity (36).

It is worth pointing out that Fishbourne and Chichester are not unique in their suspected chronology. At Colchester, a small, but classic playing-card shaped fort (rectangular ditched enclosure with rounded edges) has been detected through aerial survey at Gosbecks, to the south of the modern town. When first recorded, archaeologists naturally viewed the fort as belonging either to the primary phase of military subjugation in AD 43/4, or to a phase of reconsolidation following the revolt of Queen Boudicca in AD 60/1. Established Fact states that there cannot be any other time that a Roman military presence was considered necessary in this

36 An early first-century AD bronze legionary helmet from Chichester harbour. It is not known whether an artefact such as this derived from the activities of Augustus, Tiberius, Caligula or Claudius in southern Britain or whether it was part of a gift given to (or a trophy obtained by) an important member of the British aristocracy. Author with the kind permission of the Sussex Archaeological Society

part of the world. Unfortunately, the fort at Gosbecks appears, on present evidence, to *predate* a section of the Iron Age defences of Colchester (*Camulodunum*), a stratigraphic impossibility if no troops were in Britain before the accession of the emperor Claudius in AD 41. Such an observation however, with the fort being built at a time *before* the Iron Age earthworks, could suggest that whoever the (presumably) pro Roman king of *Camulodunum* was, they designed their *oppidum* with a Roman fort right from the start, possibly in order to impress, overawe or just plain dominate the southern approach to the complex.

A MILITARY GARRISON?

So how can we interpret the Fishbourne / Chichester and Colchester datasets? Could the assemblages simply represent the product of long distance trade and exchange or do they relate to something else? There is, of course a wealth of archaeological evidence supporting trade contact between Britain and Rome throughout the last century BC and early years AD. Wine and oil storage vessels (amphorae) from the Mediterranean are found across the south and east coast of Britain from Essex through to Dorset and, as we have seen, a number of British dynasts used Latin titles (such as *Rex* for 'king') on their coins. All this implies trade; a process whereby certain Britons bought into a Roman lifestyle whilst Roman traders acquired iron, gold, slaves and hunting dogs at a reduced price. Few have seriously suggested that Roman involvement in Britain may have been more direct than this, but the finds from Fishbourne / Chichester and Gosbecks / Colchester suggest that elements of the Roman army were in Britain at least three decades before Claudius.

How can this be? Why is there no contemporary Roman account of daring military forays into the uncharted, unknown and unfriendly lands of Iron Age Britain? Well, part of the problem lies with our sources. Roman history creates issues all of its own. Something like 'the invasion' of AD 43 is an entirely one-sided, 'Roman' event; there being no eyewitness account to provide the British perspective. To make matters worse, classical historians were not as truthful and objective as, perhaps, we might hope a reporter of today would be. Roman historians wrote for a Roman audience and most of the time they were writing in order to present a particular take on the past, using past events as a warning, morality tale or as propaganda. Most classical historians were also writing about periods that were very distant to them, both chronologically and geographically. These were not freshly drafted reports hot from the frontline and neither were they, in most cases, accounts by people who had actually witnessed events as they unfolded.

Established Fact states that whatever invasion plans the emperor Augustus drew up against Britain, they came to naught and that Britain remained fiercely independent from Rome until the time of the emperor Claudius. The evidence from Fishbourne, Chichester and Colchester may well contradict this. Roman troops appear to have been stationed in Britain in some capacity during the early years of the first century AD. Perhaps they were billeted here in order to protect friendly British kings from outside aggression or to protect Roman trade interests and investments. Possibly, army detachments were here as a sop to British renegade princes such as Tincomarus in order that the northern-most limits of the Roman world remained stable. Perhaps Augustus viewed a low-level provision of troops in Britain as the first stage in a greater plan: the acquisition and eventual conquest of the island. Certainly the provision of military outposts beyond the frontiers of empire was a common enough feature elsewhere in the fledgling years of the Roman superstate; bases having been found in Armenia, Egypt, Judea, Germany, and perhaps even Ethiopia and India.

The thinking behind the placement of Roman troops within territories beyond the frontiers of empire is neatly summed up by Julius Caesar who notes that in Egypt, at that time outside the remit of the Roman State, soldiers were placed in the royal court so that they may:

> support the authority of the king and queen, neither of whom stood well in the affections of their subjects, on account of their attachment to Caesar, nor could be supposed to have given any fixed foundation to their power, in an administration of only a few days' continuance. It was also for the honour and interest of the Republic that if they continued faithful our forces should protect them; but if ungrateful that they should be restrained by the same power
> (Caesar *The Alexandrian Wars*, 33)

Under such circumstances it would perhaps be more difficult to argue why Rome would *not* have been active in Britain: troops protecting British aristocrats; bases to protect Roman trade interests. Given the relative wealth of Britain and the high levels of commerce evident across the south and east, it would be hard to believe that the Senate and People would have left the Britons well alone. Whether the Fishbourne and Gosbecks forts represented *defensive* structures built 'in the style of' a Roman fort, or a military installation constructed by the Roman State so that they could better protect (or watch over) a client king / queen and their families, establishing control over the profitable trade network is, in the absence of detailed information from either the Sussex or Essex sites, unknown. It is interesting to speculate that, as Caesar comments in his *Alexandrian Wars*, that Rome had established bases and billeted troops in at two locations across the south in order to protect investments through a calculated display of intimidation and military force.

CUNOBELINUS

By the mid first century AD, Britain and the Britons were well known to those within the Roman Empire. Rome had been trading with certain Britons on a regular basis and interfering with their internal affairs for some time. A situation of calm stability was good for all parties. In peacetime, the Romans benefited from cheap metals, foodstuffs and slave labour, whilst some Britons grew fat on the proceeds of Roman trade and began to dominate not only their own lands but also those of their immediate neighbours. One such British magnate was Cunobelinus, whom the Roman historian Suetonius refers to as 'King of the Britons' (*Caligula* 44).

Cunobelinus is an important character in the story of the eastern dynasty, for he is mentioned, albeit briefly, by two Roman historians, Suetonius and Dio Cassius. Suetonius, in his *Lives of the Caesars*, observed that, in AD 40, the emperor Gaius (Caligula) whilst engaged in manoeuvres along the north-eastern coast of Gaul received the surrender 'of Adminius, son of Cynobellinus king of the Britons' (*Caligula*, 44) whilst Dio Cassius noted that, during the invasion of AD 43, the Roman general Aulus Plautius 'had many problems in searching out the sons of Cunobelin who was dead' (*Roman History* LX, 20). Both references, whilst noting indirectly that Cunobelinus seems to be one of the premier of British dynasts (Suetonius seems to imply that he is the only one worth speaking of), also record at least three sons. Suetonius mentions Adminius, probably the AMMINVS minting coins in the area of Kent, as a defector to the court of Caligula, whilst Dio Cassius mentions two further sons of the, by then deceased Cunobelin, as being Caratacus (Καρατακον) and Togodumnus (Τογοδουμνον). Togodumnus is apparently unknown from any known coin, unless his name appears in a different form, though Caratacus may plausibly be the CARA appearing on issues made primarily to the south of the Thames.

As with the majority of other Britons appearing in the histories of ancient Rome, we possess no written description of Cunobelinus and there are no (known) works of art purporting to accurately record his image. There are, however, a very large number of coins that were produced under his authority and carrying his name, many of which do carry realistic-looking portraits. Can any of these represent Suetonius' Great King? Possibly. Some of Cunobelinus' portrait issues may indeed have shown the British king dressed and styled as a Roman ruler, clean-shaven in a tunic and with a laurel wreath, although these are clearly modelled upon emperors Augustus and Tiberius (37). The likelihood is, therefore, that such images were intended to be the first citizen of Rome and not a British dynast. One wonders whether, by copying the emperor's face and

37 Bronze unit of CVNOBELIN (Cunobelinus) indicating descent from (or at least some form of direct relationship to) TASCIOVAN (Tasciovanus). This issue may represent an attempt to show Cunobelinus in the style of a Roman emperor, clean-shaven and with a laurel wreath, although it is just as likely that the portrait was modelled upon either Augustus or Tiberius. *Images of ancient British coins provided by dealer Chris Rudd. Cat. No. 2800.*

38 Silver unit of
CVNOBELINVS with
the mint mark of
CAMV (Camulodunum
– Colchester). Note the
similarity in design with the
coin issue of AMMINVS
(see *45*) who is credited
as being his son. *Images
of ancient British coins
provided by dealer Chris
Rudd. Cat. No. 2746*

39 Silver unit of VIRI
(Verica) proudly stating
that he is the son of COM
(Commios), almost certainly
the former ally of Caesar
during his campaigns to
Britain in 55 and 54 BC.
*Images of ancient British
coins provided by dealer
Chris Rudd. Cat. No. 597*

then superimposing his own name around the edge of the portrait, Cunobelinus
was merely creating a facsimile, an imitation designed to flatter his Roman
counterpart, or whether he was indicating the debt of loyalty (or obligation of
service) that he, as a client, owed to his Roman patron.

Cunobelinus (or Cunobelin) was an important figure in the Late Iron Age, and
he is crucial to the way in which the Roman State perceived Britain. He would
appear to have been king of either the Catuvellauni, and therefore (perhaps) a
descendant, in either politics or blood, of Caesar's great opponent Cassivellaunos,
or the Trinobantes, thereby (perhaps) being a descendant of Manubracius.
At some stage in the AD 30s he was minting coins at CAM – *Camulodunum*
(modern day Colchester), apparently the tribal centre of the Trinobantes (*38*) for
whom Caesar had specifically sought protection in 54 BC and VER – *Verulamium*
(modern day St Albans). It is quite possible that Cunobelinus was continuing the
expansionist wars of Cassivellaunos, gradually spreading his influence through
eastern and southern Britain. Cunobelinus was in all probability the Iron Age
equivalent of a Mafia godfather, dangerous, strong, politically powerful and in
control of all economic and financial transactions. Certainly the area around
Camulodunum appears, in the last decade before Roman attack, to have been
the premier importer of Mediterranean and exotic consumables. He was also,
judging by the images appearing on his coins, an ardent supporter of Rome and
may well, like other client kings of the period, have sent his children to Rome to
be educated under the protection of the emperor.

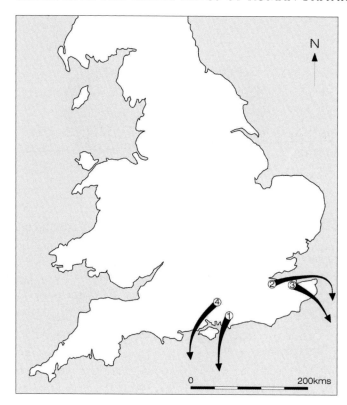

40 Map showing the flight of four British rulers to Rome prior to the invasion of AD 43. 1 = Tincomarus, attested from coins found mainly in Hampshire and West Sussex and from the *Res Gestae* of Augustus, set up before AD 14; 2 = Dubnovellaunos, attested from coins restricted to Essex and Eastern Kent and from the *Res Gestae* of Augustus (before AD 14); 3 = Amminus, attested from coins in Eastern Kent and with Caligula by AD 40; 4 = Verica, attested from coins found mainly in Hampshire and with Claudius by AD 43.

The death of the king, at some time prior to AD 43, may have left a political void that was disputed by at least two of his surviving sons: Caratacus and Togodumnus. The instability following the demise of Cunobelinus and the subsequent interregnum, may have driven Verica, descendant of Commios and king of an area centred upon Hampshire and West Sussex (39), to seek the protection of Rome (Dio Cassius *History of Rome* LX, 19). The flight of both Verica and Amminus (or Adminius) and their followers to the emperor provoked additional unrest, the historian Suetonius observing that Britain was 'in uproar at the time as a result of the Roman refusal to return certain fugitives' (*Claudius* 17). Later, Dio Cassius says that in or around AD 41 'a certain Berikos' was in Rome, bending the ear of the newly installed emperor Claudius. Berikos, who is usually equated with the coin identified VERICA had, we are told 'been driven out of the island as result of an uprising' and was in Rome in order to persuade Claudius 'to send a force there' (Dio Cassius *Claudius* LX, 19, 1). The circumstances that had deprived this descendant of Commios of power in Britain are not set out in any detail. It is interesting to note however, that the greatest concentration of Verica's coins are to be found around Silchester in northern Hampshire as well as along the coastal zone of West Sussex. If the general distribution of these indicates the extent of political power that Verica wielded, then whatever the unrest or 'uprising' entailed, it was presumably played out in this particular part of central-southern Britain (40).

5

AMMINUS AND CALIGULA: THE DIGNITY OF LABOUR

In 40 AD the third emperor of Rome, Gaius Caesar Augustus Germanicus, known to history by his nickname 'Caligula' (little boots: not a name that one would have used to his face), decided that like Augustus and Caesar before him, Britain was the ideal place to pick a fight and, ultimately, to win a triumphal war. Caligula's plans for conquest, such as we understand them today, seem to have closely followed those of Caesar in that not just Britain, but also the area of Germany to the north of the Rhine, were both considered legitimate targets.

Unfortunately the exact nature of events in AD 40 are unclear. History has not been kind to Caligula, and the Roman emperors that followed him were keen to downplay his achievements in politics, social reform, architecture, diplomacy and the field of battle. The minutiae of court life were played out in the pages of later gossip columns and in the salacious detail of the Roman historian Gaius Suetonius Tranquillus. That is not to say that Caligula was a benign ruler whose life has been unfairly vilified, for it is clear that Gaius Caesar Augustus Germanicus was not always a pleasant man to be around.

Born in AD 12 to Vipsania Agrippina, granddaughter of Augustus, and Augustus' adopted grandson, Germanicus Julius Caesar, Gaius became emperor on the death of his great-uncle Tiberius (41) on 16 March AD 37. The citizens marked his accession with great celebration; the austere reign of his predecessor was at an end and the young son of the military hero Germanicus was now in control of Rome. Caligula seems to have maintained the support of the population throughout his short reign. Indeed there was an immense outpouring of anger when his assassination was finally announced to the people. Aristocrats and senators felt differently: Caligula had made no secret of his contempt for them and many viewed his death as the ideal time to reinstate the republican constitution. Caligula was not, as many later writers would like to believe, simply insane, but he was something perhaps rather more sinister: he was morally neutral, lacking in empathy and generally indifferent to the feelings of others (42). He also thought he was a god.

41 Marble portrait of Tiberius created at the time of his formal adoption by Augustus in AD 4. As emperor, Tiberius seems to have no great plans for Britain, adopting a policy of maintaining the *status quo*. © *Trustees of the British Museum*

42 Silver coin of Gaius (Caligula). Minted on Crete around AD 38, it shows the emperor with a sceptre over his left shoulder (implying a god-like status) and, on the reverse, his ancestor, the deified Augustus, sat on a heavenly throne. © *Trustees of the British Museum*

CALIGULA AND BRITAIN

It was his desire to surpass the achievements of his illustrious ancestor Julius Caesar that led Caligula, like Augustus before him, to consider crossing the Rhine and the Channel in order to conquer both Germany and Britain. Our sources for the campaign, undertaken early in AD 40, are overtly hostile, all desperate to establish that Caligula was delusional. 'He had but one experience with military affairs or war' so court gossip Suetonius tells us 'and then on a sudden impulse' (*Caligula* 43) suggesting that the whole idea for the campaign was based upon a whim, a sudden and irrational desire for glory.

> So without delay he assembled legions and auxiliaries from all quarters, holding
> levies everywhere with the utmost strictness, and collecting provisions of every kind
> on an unheard of scale. Then he began his march and made it now so hurriedly

and rapidly, that the praetorian cohorts were forced, contrary to all precedent, to lay their standards on the pack-animals and thus to follow him; again he was so lazy and luxurious that he was carried in a litter by eight bearers, requiring the inhabitants of the towns through which he passed to sweep the roads for him and sprinkle them to lay the dust. On reaching his camp, to show his vigilance and strictness as a commander, he dismissed in disgrace the generals who were late in bringing in the auxiliaries from various places, and in reviewing his troops he deprived many of the chief centurions who were well on in years of their rank, in some cases only a few days before they would have served their time, giving as a reason their age and infirmity; then railing at the rest for their avarice, he reduced the rewards given on completion of full military service to six thousand sesterces (Suetonius *Caligula* 43-4)

This rather surreal chapter in Suetonius' life of Caligula may represent the distorted recollection of a very real event, namely the preparation for significant military action. Reference to the dismissal of officers may indicate action taken against troops following a mutiny (although the punishment for mutiny would

43 Dover, Kent. The *pharos*, or lighthouse, which survives to a height of 19m, the lower 14m of which is entirely Roman. The structure defies precise dating and may have been put up in the first century AD. The only historical reference for a *pharos* in this part of the Roman Empire is that erected by Caligula as a permanent memorial to his 'great victory'. This building is usually thought to have been created in Boulogne, but it could conceivably have been constructed in Kent, assuming that Caligula's troops 'won some slight success' here. *Author*

normally have been harsher than mere dismissal) or the removal of corrupt or incompetent soldiery, rather than being the product of a purely random mind. It is perhaps doubtful, given the catastrophic history of Roman interference in *Germania Magna*, that Caligula, however unhinged, would have considered prolonged military intervention to the lands north of the Rhine, especially if he were also planning a crossing into Britain. Advancing a war on two fronts simultaneously would have been disastrous for Rome, as Caligula's advisers would undoubtedly have told him. *Securing* the Rhine frontier, prior to launching a British invasion would, however, have made perfect sense and it is this particular strategy that the emperor and his entourage may have been pursuing.

Caligula's plan to emulate the deified Caesar ended, so the hostile accounts of Suetonius and Dio Cassius tell us, in fiasco. With his soldiers lined up on the Gallic coast 'in battle order' facing Britain, the emperor apparently ordered his men to 'gather shells and fill their helmets and the folds of their gowns' (Suetonius *Caligula* 46). This 'booty', Caligula claimed, represented 'spoils from Ocean', the mythical and treacherous expanse of water that surrounded the known world. The spoils, once gathered up, were then transported to Rome, as evidence of the emperor's great triumph over the sea. A *pharos* or lighthouse (43) was erected on the shore (possibly at Boulogne, although no one has yet entertained the idea that it may have been set on the British coast) as a permanent memorial to Caligula's great victory, and to each soldier present the sum of a hundred *denarii* was given with the words 'Go your way happy; go your way rich' (*Caligula* 46). Most modern writers have taken the view that Caligula's men had perhaps mutinied, not wishing to cross the English Channel, and the story of the sea shells merely reflects the humiliation that they received at the hands of their emperor. Others, like Suetonius, believe the event was a clear sign of Caligula's developing insanity. Some have even suggested that the shells may have been collected to act as ammunition for Roman catapults.

Our second source for this period, Dio Cassius, is also damning of Caligula's campaigns in the north noting that he had:

> ... set out as if to conduct a campaign against Britain, but turned back from the ocean's edge, showing no little vexation at his lieutenants who won some slight success ...
> (Dio *Roman History* LIX, 21)

Despite Dio's contempt for Caligula, this short and often overlooked paragraph is intriguing for it implies that some officers under the emperor's command were actually involved in a successful military action. Was this a landing, establishment of a defended beachhead, fighting or a combination of all three? Was it in Germany or in Britain? Any potential landing in Britain may have been designed to be small scale, possibly as a precursor to larger invasion. Maybe the speculative action had been designed to aid regime-change or to recover a pro-

Roman monarch in need of allies. Whatever the case, any such success, however 'slight', would certainly have been played down by Caligula's successors.

A further hint of actions forgotten is provided by Dio Cassius when, during his account of the Great Revolt against Rome in AD 60, he has the British Queen Boudicca say:

> it is we who have made ourselves responsible for all these evils, in that we allowed them to set foot on the island in the first place instead of expelling them at once as we did their famous Julius Caesar,— yes, and in that we did not deal with them while they were still far away as we dealt with Augustus and with Gaius Caligula and make even the attempt to sail hither a formidable thing
> (*Roman History* LXII, 4)

Of course these are not the genuine words of a British monarch, but those of a Roman historian relating what he thought Boudicca ought to have said. Even so, they do provide an interesting perspective on events as perceived from the late second century AD. How, exactly, the Britons managed to 'deal with' both Augustus and Caligula, especially as they are both cited as being 'far away', is unfortunately unclear (although this probably relates to the distance between Norfolk and the French coast). Making the 'attempt to sail ... a formidable thing' could refer to either a mutiny or a disputed crossing (or difficult landing). Given the distinctly garbled and overtly negative accounts of Caligula's exploits, from all surviving sources, the truth of the matter is difficult to separate from the fiction, but the possibility of direct Roman military involvement in Britain at this time should not be totally ruled out.

AMMINUS

A major achievement of Caligula's action in Gaul and Britain, in fact the *only* one according to Suetonius, was:

> to receive the surrender of Adminius, son of Cynobellinus king of the Britons, who had been banished by his father and had deserted to the Romans with a small force
> (Caligula 44)

44 Bronze unit of AM (Amminus) and struck at DVNO, possibly the *oppidum* of *Durovernon* or *Dunovernum* (Canterbury). *Images of ancient British coins provided by dealer Chris Rudd. Cat. No. 356*

Adminius is probably a later garbling (or mistranslation) of AM / AMMINVS (44), the name appearing on coins within eastern Kent (*Cantium*) issued by a British king at around the same time Caligula was in power (or at least between the late 30s and early 40s AD). Suetonius is damning of even this defection, claiming that Caligula used the surrender of a petty British princeling to boast that 'the entire island had submitted to him'. As we shall see, Caligula's boast may not have been too far from the truth.

If Amminus had indeed been the son of Cunobelinus, rather than, say, merely his political subordinate, it could be that the distribution of his coins indicates an administrative responsibility over *Cantium*, perhaps given to him by his father (or acquired through marriage or war). It should be remembered that, in this respect, the 'Cantiaci' mentioned in many texts on Roman Britain were not a specific tribe, *Cantium* being a geographical term (possibly meaning 'corner land' – the promontory of Kent) rather than an ethnic name. Caesar mentions four kings of *Cantium* in 54 BC, Cingetorix, Carvilius, Taximagulus and Segovax (*Gallic Wars* V, 22), whom Cassivellaunos, arguably king of a prototype Catuvellauni, seems to have possessed some kind of power over. The possibility that a Catuvellaunian prince or king could move into *Cantium* and take control should not, therefore, be discounted. This is especially pertinent when one considers the case of Dubnovellaunos, whose coin series was restricted to Essex and Eastern Kent, a king whom Augustus records as 'seeking refuge' in Rome on the *Res Gestae Divi Augusti*, a monumental statement set down before AD 14.

One of Amminus' coin series has a neatly drawn Pegasus on the reverse side, atop an abbreviated name or prefix: DVN and DVNO (45). This could, given that many Later Iron Age dynasts had a liking for establishing family credentials, have been intended to represent the lineage of Amminus, DVN / DVNO being the name of father or distant ancestor. Assuming, however, that Suetonius did not get his facts wrong (and further assuming that the Adminius in his text is the same as the AMMINVS on the coins) then the king's father was *Cuno*-belinus NOT *Duno*-belinus. More plausibly, perhaps, given that many of Cunobelinus' own issues possess the mint or ownership marks CAM and VER (for *Camulodunum* and *Verulamium*), DVN / DVNO could indicate where the Amminus coins were being manufactured. The identification of such a potential *oppidum* site in Kent is still hotly debated, although the association with Canterbury, *Durovernum* in later Roman sources, seems reasonable enough, especially if its Latin form is a garbling of an earlier British name, perhaps *Durovernon* or *Dunovernum*.

45 Bronze unit of AMMINUS struck at DVN (probably Canterbury). Note the similarity in the design of the wheat appearing here with that of CVNOBELINVS (see 38). *Images of ancient British coins provided by dealer Chris Rudd. Cat. No. 348*

46 Marble portrait of young man, naked except for a military cloak, riding a horse. The statue, found in the vicinity of Rome in the sixteenth century, is usually credited simply as being of 'a Julio-Claudian prince', although it could represent Caligula in an overtly heroic pose. © *Trustees of the British Museum*

Although the bulk of Amminus' coins, and certainly those bearing the AM / AMM / AMMINVS legend, have been found in Kent, other series, inscribed with an 'A' and somewhat similar in style to the Kentish examples, occur in Sussex. This has led some to suggest that, after falling out with his father Cunobelinus (but prior to seeking refuge with Caligula), Amminus may have fled to a western Atrebatic dynast, possibly Verica (Berikos). In fairness, there is no provable link between the AMMINVS and the Sussex 'A'-series and, even if there were, there are no useful dates on which to hang a possible chronology. There is, however, a second and rather better link between the Kentish king and the lands of Sussex, for in 1823, an altar was found in Chichester which bore the dedication:

GENIO S
LVCVLLVS
AMMINI FIL
D S P

Which is usually translated as meaning:

> Sacred to the Genius (of the place) Lucullus, son of Amminus, set this up from his own resources

Variants of the name Amminus occasionally crop up in Gaul, but there are only two other examples of this occurring anywhere within Britain: from the writings of Suetonius and from the coin series of Kent. The altar, which was set at the heart of Roman Chichester (*Noviomagus*), emphasises the importance and social standing of the donor Lucullus, for only a person of significant wealth and status would have been able (or allowed) to set this up here 'from his own resources'. Intriguingly, the way in which the donor styles himself on the altar, as AMMINI FIL ('son of Amminus'), is not very Roman, though it does mimic the TINCOM COMMI FIL ('Tincomarus son of Commios') style of association occurring on certain Late Iron Age coins. Whoever Lucullus was, he seemed very keen to outline his blood heritage in Sussex.

What ultimately happened to Amminus / Adminius after his flight to Caligula is not recorded, although presumably the emperor would have made much of his catch, the Briton becoming the centrepiece of his return to Rome (46). Amminus' 'surrender', in truth more of a defection, could certainly have masked any potential problems surrounding the abortive nature of Caligula's British campaign. Any triumph or victory parade planned to celebrate the 'conquest' of the Britons and Germans by Caligula seems to have been postponed, not, as some writers have suggested, because the senate did not feel that the emperor deserved it (or because Caligula himself felt that he wasn't appreciated enough), but perhaps because the whole programme of military intervention was merely being *postponed* at this time. Whether Amminus was able to provide tactical information on Britain (possible landing sites, safe havens, friendly tribes, major towns and river crossings) necessary for Caligula's projected 're-invasion', we cannot say. Neither can we be sure whether the British king was himself actively engaged in any covert action, plotting a British coup or counterinsurgency, on behalf of the third emperor.

In hindsight, the court of Caligula was perhaps not the safest place in which to seek refuge, at least if we believe the writings of Suetonius. Of Amminus' fate, we hear nothing, although it is always possible that he ended up like Ptolemy, son of the north African king Juba II, and grandson of Mark Antony, whom Caligula executed 'for no other reason than that when giving a gladiatorial show, he noticed that Ptolemy on entering the theatre attracted general attention by the splendour of his purple cloak' (Suetonius *Caligula* 35). Amminus may never have returned to Britain, although it would be less than three years before Claudius would venture there, but it is possible that his son later made the journey, setting up a dedication in *Noviomagus* (Chichester) in order to fulfil a vow and formally commemorate his lineage.

6

CARATACUS AND CLAUDIUS: THE ONES WHO MAKE A STAND

The third emperor of Rome, Gaius Julius Caesar Augustus Germanicus, better known to history as 'Caligula', lay in a tangled heap upon the floor of a darkened corridor in Rome. It was the afternoon of 24 January AD 41 and the emperor, after ruling almost four years, had, in the words of the Roman historian Dio Cassius just 'learned by actual experience that he was not a god' (*Roman History*, LIX, 30).

The moments immediately following the murder were ones of panic and confusion. In the palace the conspirators turned their attention to the remaining members of the imperial family as well as any senators, slaves and freedmen that they could find. Elsewhere, stray members of Caligula's German bodyguard laid into those they suspected of aiding the murderers, Suetonius noting that they slaughtered 'several of the assassins and a few innocent senators into the bargain' (*Caligula*, 58). At this point, so the story goes, a group of soldiers discovered the dead emperor's uncle Claudius cowering behind a curtain in the palace. Recognising the importance of their find, the troops hustled Claudius from the imperial house, and took him to the praetorian barracks outside of the city. Here the bemused man was proclaimed the rightful successor to Caligula; the fourth emperor of Rome.

Of course we have no way of knowing the truth behind the story: Claudius may well have been complicit in the death of his nephew, only later concocting the tale of a scared innocent, reluctantly accepting a position of power in order to prevent chaos and anarchy spreading out into the streets of Rome. Whatever the case, on the morning of 24 January AD 41, Tiberius Claudius Nero Germanicus found himself as absolute ruler of the Roman State. Now he had to prove his worth. Mindful that he was no great politician and possessed no claim to military prowess, despite hailing from a great and illustrious family, Claudius desperately needed something to capture the hearts and minds of the senate and people. Like politicians of more recent years, Claudius felt that the only way he could achieve this was by starting a war.

ROME AND BRITAIN

Britain was a land of opportunity, as both Augustus and Caligula had no doubt reflected. First and foremost, assuming the propaganda could be correctly spun, it could be shown that the deified Julius Caesar, greatest warrior of Rome, had singularly failed to conquer Britain despite invading on two separate occasions. Whatever he said about the Britons paying tribute and submitting to the government of Rome, it was clear that they had other ideas. If the newly installed emperor Claudius could not only win a victory in Britain but more critically establish a province under direct military control, he could show himself to be greater than Caesar and therefore, by inference, to be greater than a god. Secondly, Claudius' immediate predecessor, the unfortunate Caligula, had already been involved in some form of military intervention in the island, possibly involving the landing of troops. Not only could any such activity be easily downplayed by Claudius' spin-doctors, especially if any possible mutiny, abortive sailing or inconclusive skirmish be turned into clear evidence of Caligula's insanity (collecting sea-shells anyone?).

Whatever the reality of Caligula's activities against Britain, it was clear that not only had a significant player in British politics gone over to the Roman cause with a retinue (Amminus) but also it was likely that all ships, units and provisions remained in place or were at least recoverable. Caligula, and presumably Augustus too, had drawn their plans against the Britons and, together with any logistical information obtained by Caesar (especially relating to harbours and anchor points), battle plans would require only minimal updating and revision. Lastly, as everyone in Rome would be aware, Britain was rich in metal and grain whilst slaves would come in great numbers during a war. Military intervention in Britain would not only therefore make sound political sense, but could also be made economically viable, but only if the emperor could take direct control of all the Island's key resources.

INVASION

Our only reliable source for the Claudian invasion of AD 43 is Dio Cassius, writing in the late second and early third century AD (over 100 years after the events he describes), for the relevant sections in Tacitus *Annals* are missing. Dio Cassius' work is usually treated as a standard discussion of a major military invasion akin to the Normandy landings in France of 1944 or the Norman landings in England during 1066. Established Facts tell us that in AD 43 a Roman general named Aulus Plautius landed in Kent with an immense army which included four Legions (II, IX, XIV and XX), comprising 20,000 soldiers, together with a similar number of second class ('expendable') auxiliary troops. Plautius' intention, it is usually believed, was to drive his army northwards across Kent and over the rivers Medway and Thames, scattering all opposition on the way. The Iron Age capital of *Camulodunum* (modern Colchester in Essex) was the Roman's ultimate objective; their target number one (47). Unfortunately, attractive though this theory undoubtedly is, Dio Cassius actually says nothing of the sort. A careful rereading of his text shows that all Dio Cassius says on the invasion itself is:

> Aulus Plautius, a most respected counsellor, led an expedition to Britain, for a
> certain Berikos, having been driven out of the island by an armed uprising, had

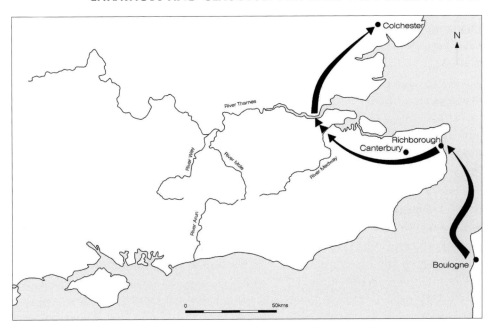

47 The standard, orthodox view of the emperor Claudius' invasion of Britain in AD 43. Here, four Legions plus auxiliaries, numbering some 40,000 men, land at Richborough on the Kent coast, and butcher their way across the River's Medway and Thames. Claudius' chief of staff (and first governor of Britain), Aulus Plautius, effectively clears the way for the emperor himself arrive and take control of the army in the final stages of the advance to Colchester (Camulodunum), where 11 British kings formally surrender. The resistance against Rome is thought to have been led by the brothers Togodumnus and Caratacus, the former dying at the battle of the Thames, the latter taking the fight into South Wales.

persuaded Claudius to send a force there
(Dio Cassius *Roman History* LX, 19)

Nowhere does Dio state that Plautius was leading a full scale invasion and the assumption that four legions were involved is actually modern speculation. The four legion fiction is based on the observation that in AD 60 the II, IX, XIV and XX Legions were all present in Britain and must therefore have been so earlier. If one looks carefully at what Dio Cassius actually *does* say, then there is evidence for only one Legion being directly involved in the initial landings and their aftermath: the II. We know this because the then general of the II Legion, Titus Flavius Vespasianus (later emperor), is specifically noted as taking part in at least one of the subsequent disputed river crossings. One Legion (assuming it was complete and not operating as a small detachment) gives us a maximum accountable figure of 5,500 men for the preliminary stages of the AD 43 Channel crossing.

With regard to the landing itself, Dio Cassius observes that the troops:

were carried across to the other side, having been divided into three sections in order not to hinder one another and to disembark section by section ... They put

into the island, no one opposing them
(Dio Cassius *Roman History* LX, 19)

But where did these troops land? Dio Cassius' description of the landings, in 'three sections' do not supply any specific geographical detail, nor (again) is any mention made of the exact numbers of Roman soldiers involved. Unfortunately an unknown number of soldiers divided by three remains an unknown number.

An obvious choice for the landing, if one was siding with Verica or any of the other banished British kings in Rome, was to create a villain or villains and focus the attack somewhere close to their home territory. Clear candidates for villainy may have been the surviving sons of Cunobelinus, Caratacus and Togodumnus, both of whom were the first Britons to be specifically sought out during the initial stages of the invasion. This, in turn, may have made the *oppidum* of *Camulodunum* (Colchester) a key objective: target number one. If *Camulodunum* was the main target, then it could be hit straight away, perhaps by an army landing on the Essex coast close to the site. Such a landing, however, could result in strong and effective resistance to Rome, and general carnage on both sides. What Claudius really needed was the opportunity to get his troops ashore, obtain a secure series of bases, make friends (ideally by restoring Verica and his pals to their kingdoms), wear down the enemy and the perhaps prevent the dynasts of *Camulodunum* from presenting a united front against him by securing peace with tribes in the south-east, exactly as Caesar had done in 54 BC. Only then, if *Camulodunum* refused to surrender, would his army need to approach Essex under arms.

A detailed examination of Dio Cassius' text indicates that the 'British intervention' of AD 43 was almost certainly not a full blown invasion, at least in its initial stages, but rather an attempt to curtail and control civil unrest. Such unrest had presumably exploded following the death of King Cunobelinus, the pro-Roman dynast who ruled the much of what is now south-eastern England from his capital at *Camulodunum* (Colchester). Britain, as a stable entity, was not only a valuable trading resource for Rome but was also important as a peaceful buffer, protecting the northern shores of Rome's empire in Gaul. The political upheaval that followed Cunobelinus' death may have threatened that stability. It was the responsibility of Rome to resolve any difficult or disputed succession within a client or allied kingdom, and the need for regime change may well have proved the motive for military involvement in Britain.

Given the logistical and military problems that faced Caesar in his attacks in 55 and 54 BC, and the political issues that presented themselves to Claudius, the Kent coast may not have been the landing site of choice for his expeditionary force. And yet if we look today at any modern study of Roman Britain, the Kent coast, specifically the area around Richborough, is cited as *the* primary landing site of Claudius's invading army. This has become the most entrenched Established Fact in the history of the province. The identification of Richborough as the key beachhead is based on the discovery of early Roman timber buildings, and of a series of linear ditches. Unfortunately, we also get similar evidence from other sites on the south coast, particularly around

48 The view into Portsmouth harbour, Hampshire, with the Historic Naval Dockyard and the Isle of Wight in the distance, as seen from the later Roman fortress of Portchester. Given that there are a number of great natural harbours on this stretch of the coast, between Chichester to the Solent, and that this was within the area belonging to the pro-Roman king Verica, a landing here during the initial phases of the AD 43 'invasion' would have made more strategic sense than along the more exposed (and unfriendly) coast of Kent. *Author*

Chichester, Portsmouth and Southampton. Ultimately, given the paucity of literary and archaeological sources, the landing could legitimately have been anywhere from the Hampshire/Sussex coast to the fringes of the Thames estuary. Established Fact states that the invasion *must* have been in Kent, but there is no compelling evidence to say that this was so. Given that the Sussex/Hampshire coast provided not only a series of great natural harbours, from Chichester to the Solent (*48*), but was also close to where Verica, and his predecessor Tincomarus claimed kingship, a landing here could potentially receive a friendlier welcome than, say, a landing in Kent or Essex. Here the Romans could, if they played their cards right, be seen as liberators, restoring a series of rightful kings to their disputed thrones.

What is particularly interesting is that any suggestion that the Roman invasion of AD 43 may have been anywhere *other* than Richborough in Kent has provoked strong rebuttals in the pages of archaeological magazines and the national press. At a number of recent conferences, prominent Romanists have argued and fought (sometimes physically) over something that, to most people, appears largely irrelevant. We know Rome invaded and we know that there is good evidence that this invasion hit the south coast first. The absence of any strong evidence one way or another to pinpoint where exactly it happened, shouldn't really affect our understanding of Roman Britain at all – should it? Sadly, the strength of feeling displayed against the 'heretical' view that Claudius' troops may have gained first foothold in Britain elsewhere (and not Richborough), serves only to demonstrate the entrenched close-mindedness of some traditional Romanists. Richborough was in all probability a very early Roman base, but the weight of archaeological and historical evidence used to support the idea that it was the *primary* base simply does not add up:

> *Richborough was the primary landing site because that's what everyone has said since the early twentieth century. They can't all be wrong.*

First, not *everyone* has said it was Richborough and, secondly, just because large numbers of people say (or believe) in the same thing, doesn't make it right. Before Richborough became the preferred landing site, academics had suggested a number of alternative potential beachheads, from Southend in Essex to Southampton in Hampshire. It wasn't really until the Society of Antiquaries of London commenced an archaeological examination of Richborough, under the direction of J. P. Bushe-Fox in the 1920s and 30s, that Kent became the favoured choice. Admittedly the evidence recovered from Richborough, in the form of granaries, ditches, roads and military hardware, all looked good, but since the 1980s similar evidence, especially granaries, ditches, roads and military hardware, have been found elsewhere.

> *Kent has to have been the primary landing site because it is the only area where one could safely and efficiently disembark 40,000 heavily armed troops with all their equipment, Sussex or Hampshire being too far away.*

But, as already mentioned, the number of 40,000 is a modern fiction. We have no idea how many soldiers were involved in the first wave led by Aulus Plautius, although the fact that Cassius Dio calls it simply 'a force' then later describes the arrival of the emperor in Britain with 'an army and much equipment' implies that the first wave did not comprise a major 'mass-invasion' fleet. The bulk of the armed forces, complete with elephants, probably *did* arrive as *reinforcements* with Claudius at Richborough, this being the shortest crossing against the tides, landing in an area which by then had been secured by Plautius.

> *Richborough preserves the remains of a large triumphal monument, set up by the emperor Domitian, to commemorate the landing of Claudius. If the landing was not here, why is the monument?*

Opposite below: 50 AD 43: The 'Hind Alternative', first set out by John Hind in 1989 (The Invasion of Britain in AD 43 – an Alternative Strategy for Aulus Plautius: *Britannia* volume 20). Here, the primary landing site for the massed legions of Rome (*c.* 40,000 men) is within the 'Great Harbour' at Portsmouth and / or Chichester, with a 'flying column' sent to help the Bodunni / Dobunni (Cirencester). Having established a degree of order within the kingdom of Verica (Hampshire / West Sussex), the Roman advance is halted first at a crossing of the River Arun, and later at the Thames, near Staines. Having destroyed the Britons and killed Togodumnus, word is sent to Claudius, who arrives a few weeks later, probably on the Kent coast.

1 Octavian: Gold issue of 28 BC minted to celebrate the victory of Octavian (Augustus) over Marcus Antoninus (Mark Antony) and Queen Cleopatra VII of Egypt and the 'Restoration of laws and rights to the people of Rome'. Such coins disguised the political reality of Octavian's position as monarch. © *Trustees of the British Museum*

2 Silver unit of TINCOMARVS, from Hampshire, credited on other coins as the son of COMMIOS, the ally of Julius Caesar during his British campaigns of 55 and 54 BC. By AD 14, Tincomarus was in Rome 'seeking refuge' at the court of Augustus. © *Trustees of the British Museum*

3 Detail of the Battersea Shield, a highly decorated bronze sheet with red glass inlay. A masterpiece of Late Iron Age 'Celtic' art, the shield was recovered from the River Thames where it may have formed a part of a ritual deposit. © *Trustees of the British Museum*

4 Detail showing the terminal ends of the 'Great Torc' from Snettisham, Norfolk, land of the Eceni, a gold neck-ring covered in stylised designs typical of 'Celtic' art. © *Trustees of the British Museum*

5 Reconstruction of a Late Iron Age burial assemblage recovered in 1965 from Welwyn, Hertfordshire. The group contains five wine amphorae, a Roman silver wine cup and a variety of high status imported pottery forms. © *Trustees of the British Museum*

6 A variety of imported Roman table ware, recovered from the King Harry Lane cemetery site at St Albans, Hertfordshire, and dated to between 20 BC and AD 50. © *Trustees of the British Museum*

7 The *pharos*, a Roman lighthouse, now within the walls of Dover Castle, Kent, possibly dating to the first century AD. *Author*

8 A cast section from Trajan's Column in Rome, showing a Roman invasion fleet (in this case crossing the Danube). *Author with the kind permission of the Sussex Archaeological Society*

9 A section of the re-excavated 'Claudian' ditch at Richborough, Kent, as it appears today. *Author*

10 Bronze shield boss belonging to Junius Dubitatus of the *VIII Augusta* Legion, a unit rarely credited to Britain, found in the river Tyne, Newcastle, in 1867. © *Trustees of the British Museum*

11 Gold coin issued to commemorate Claudius' victory against the Britons and the building of the great Arch in Rome during AD 51. The arch, now lost, is shown on the reverse with the accompanying text: DE BRITANN ('over the Britons'). © *Trustees of the British Museum*

12 A rare surviving fragment from the Arch of Claudius in Rome, now in the Louvre Museum, Paris. The piece shows four soldiers and a standard-bearer, standing in rather stiff, formal poses. If, as some have suggested, the soldiers are Praetorians, then they represent elements of the emperor's personal bodyguard during his two-week stay in Britain. *Massingheimer Collection*

13 Statue of 'Boadicea' (Boudicca), on the Thames Embankment by Westminister Bridge in London, surrounded by the paraphernalia of modern life. *Author*

14 The southern wall of Caistor St Edmund (*Venta Ecenorum*), Norfolk, a market town created by the Roman State for the Eceni following the suppression of the Boudiccan revolt. *Author*

15 Fragment of a life-sized portrait, probably of the young Nero, aged 14, at the time of his adoption by the emperor Claudius in AD 51, found in the foundations of Fishbourne palace, West Sussex. The piece presumably formed part of a more formal group contained within the earlier 'proto-palace'. *Author with the kind permission of the Sussex Archaeological Society*

16 Gold coin of the young Nero, aged 14, at the time of his formal adoption by the emperor Claudius in AD 51. © *Trustees of the British Museum*

17 Gold ring belonging to TI CLAVDI CATVARI ('Tiberius Claudius Catuarus'), recovered from near to the palace at Fishbourne, West Sussex. © *Sussex Archaeological Society18*

18 A monumental portrait of an emperor, possibly Nero, found at Bosham, near Chichester in West Sussex. © *Sussex Archaeological Society*

19 View from the Roman frontier in the early AD 50s: Old Burrow, north Devon, looking out across the Bristol Channel and the South Welsh coast. *Author*

20 View from the Roman frontier in the late AD 70s: Tomen-y-Mur, Gwynedd, looking out at the landscape of Snowdonia National Park. *Author*

21 View from the Roman frontier in the early AD 120s: Maryport, Cumbria, looking out across the Solway Firth to Dumfries and Galloway on the southern Scottish coast. *Author*

22 View to the Roman frontier in the mid AD 120s: looking up at the battlements of Hadrian's Wall, recreated at Vindolanda, Northumberland. *Author*

23 Housesteads, Northumberland: The northern frontier of *Britannia*, designed by Hadrian in the early AD 120s in order to 'separate the Romans and the barbarians'. *Author*

24 Cawfields, Northumberland: the gateways of milecastle 42, originally designed to control access through the northern frontier of Hadrian's Wall. *Author*

Above: 49 The immense foundations for the triumphal, four-way arch commissioned by
the emperor Domitian at Richborough in Kent. The structure, constructed around AD 85, is
sometimes thought to commemorate the initial landing of Roman troops in AD 43, although it
actually celebrates the official *conquest* of Britain, as achieved by the Roman governor Agricola.
The site was undoubtedly chosen as home for the monument because Richborough had, by the
80s AD, become the primary port of entry to *Britannia*, and it may well have been here that the
deified Claudius arrived with substantial reinforcements during the second wave of AD 43. *Author*

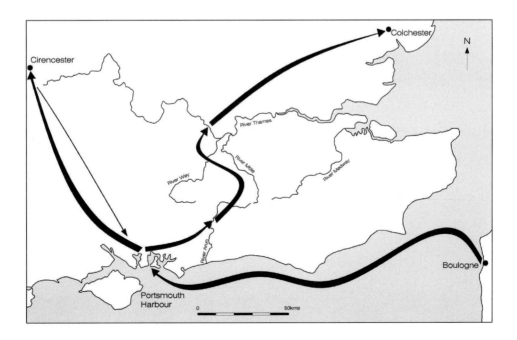

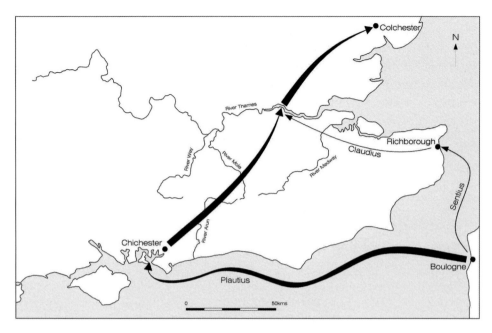

51 AD 43: The 'Black Alternative', first set out by Ernest Black in 2000 (Sentius Saturninus and the Roman Invasion of Britain: *Britannia* volume 31). Here, the primary landing site for the invasion, comprising three legions plus auxiliaries (*c.* 30,000 men) is Chichester harbour. Having resolved the political situation within the Atrebates (under Verica) and the Bodunni / Dobunni (at Cirencester), Aulus Plautius' advance towards Colchester stalls at the River Thames. In this interpretation, the 'two disputed river crossings', become one, Black suggesting that our only written source for the event, Dio Cassius, cited the *same* river battle twice by mistake (the error perhaps arising from Dio's use of two very different primary sources). Following the Thames battle, in which Togodumnus is killed, Claudius arrives with reinforcements led by Sentius Saturninus, a senator later credited with major involvement in the campaign, at Richborough, before advancing to meet Plautius at the Thames.

The point here is that the monument at Richborough (49) seems to commemorate the *conquest* of Britain, finally achieved by the Roman governor Agricola in the early 80s AD and not the initial *landing* of Roman troops in AD 43. Richborough was probably chosen for two reasons: first, because it became the primary, prestige port of entry to the province, and where better to erect a triumphal monument to both welcome visitors and also direct them to the official start of the road network, and second because this was probably where Claudius, fourth emperor of Rome, symbolically landed with reinforcements during the second wave of AD 43.

> *Richborough makes more sense as the primary landing site as it is closer to Colchester, Claudius' stated objective, than any site in Sussex or Hampshire.*

But we don't know what Claudius' stated objective was. If he only meant to attack Colchester, in Essex, why did his army land in Kent? Given Julius Caesar's lengthy description of constant running battles on the way to the Thames, why did Claudius think that Kent was a good idea? Why did he not send his army somewhere else, preferably where they might receive a friendlier welcome? Why, given that the primary wave was probably no more than an expeditionary force with a peace-keeping (or at least succession-resolving) remit, why didn't they aim for the kingdom of Verica (Berikos) in Sussex / Hampshire (50, 51)? Verica was, according to Dio Cassius, after all the man who persuaded Claudius to invade in the first place.

Richborough makes more sense as the primary landing site because any advance north from here will cross the River Medway, undoubtedly where Aulus Plautius fought his first major battle with British forces, whereas a landing in Sussex or Hampshire will only bring you up against Rivers such as the Arun, which are little more than drainage ditches.

Unfortunately, other than the Thames, site of Aulus Plautius' second major conflict, Dio Cassius provides no geographical information to help place the actions of the first expeditionary wave. The 'Medway Battle' has become an Established Fact, firmly embedded in the history of Roman Britain, but that doesn't make it true. The Arun is just as formidable an obstacle as the Medway and it is also one of the few rivers in Britain to have been specifically identified by the Roman geographer Ptolemy, who calls it *Trisantonis Fluvii* (Τρισαντονισ Φλυϖιι), the 'great wayfarer'.

CONSOLIDATION

Wherever they landed, events following the initial phase of the expedition seem to have gone well; Dio Cassius stating that:

the Britons, not learning of their arrival, had not assembled beforehand. Not even then did they come to hand but, seeking refuge, fled to the swamps and woods, expecting without reason to be rid of them, even as once before, the very same thing had happened with Julius Caesar, since it would be fruitless of them to repeat this. However Plautius had a good deal of trouble in searching out the sons of Cunobelin, who was now dead, for the Britons were not free people but served under different rulers that they themselves had appointed, but when he did find them he first prevailed over Caratacus then Togodumnus
(*Roman History* LX, 20)

This is usually thought to mean that the Britons were ill-prepared, having not mustered their forces to combat the Roman landings as they had done against Caesar in 55 BC. Eventually, having located the armies of Togodumnus and Caratacus, Plautius manages to defeat them in battle. Once again, this is not what Dio Cassius says. Louis Francis, in a new reanalysis of the *Roman History*, has noted that there:

... is an obvious interlude implied after the landing, while Plautius pursues his enquiries, presumably into the cause of the armed insurrection and those responsible. Also implied is the fact that he had travelled from the landing point and had great difficulty, having learned that the sons of the late Cunobelin were responsible, in locating them. When he does so, first Caratacus then Togodumnus, there is no mention of an armed conflict with them, only that he [Plautius] got the better of them in some way. However the verb that he uses has many shades of meaning in Greek, from the battlefield to the law courts and the fact that, unlike other incidents to be mentioned, there are no details of any fighting, we are justifiably left with the possibility of an alternative meaning. If the mission of Plautius were that of peacekeeping, then talking would surely have preceded fighting (Francis 1991, 3)

In other words, the Established Fact that fighting between Romans and Britons commenced once Plautius had discovered the hiding places of Togodumnus and Caratacus, and that the Roman general prevailed (in a military sense), is flawed. There may have been fighting, Togodumnus and Caratacus may have led the resistance and been defeated, but they may, just as plausibly, simply have been engaged in *negotiation* with the Romans. If we are looking at the aftermath of a disputed succession, both Togodumnus and Caratacus arguing over who was the rightful heir to Cunobelinus' kingdom, then Plautius' role, as the representative of Claudius, was to resolve the issue peaceably. Eventually Plautius *prevailed* over both parties, and, at the end of the negotiations, urged them to accept the decision and comply with the wishes of Rome. It was at this point, however, that things started to unravel.

FIGHTING AT THE RIVERS

Having 'banished' the two British kings back to their respective territories, Aulus Plautius 'accepted terms of surrender from that part of the Bodunni having been ruled by the Catuvellauni' (Dio Cassius *Roman History* LX, 20). As has already been argued, the 'Bodunni' are almost certainly the tribe usually referred to in modern literature as the Dobunni (although Dio Cassius' original form *Bodunni* is more likely to have been their real name), a group credited with occupying an area centred upon modern day Cirencester. Had Plautius indeed landed in Kent, the surrender of a tribe in the Cotswolds may appear curious, although a landing in Sussex or Hampshire may make slightly more geographical sense.

As Plautius oversaw the safe return of all parties involved in the disputed succession, he arrived at a major river. Here it became apparent that the mission was no longer peaceful, for a barbarian army awaited his arrival on the opposing bank. Francis has noted that from this point we seldom hear reference to 'Britons' (Βρεττανοι) in the account of Dio Cassius, but 'Barbarians' (Βαρβαροι): 'it cannot be a slip of the pen because it happens again. The inhabitants are always Britons while the insurrectionists, presumably they, are always Barbarians' (1991, 4). Perhaps, as Francis notes, the distinction was being made between allied, friendly Britons, those who had perhaps accepted the decision of Plautius made at the negotiation table, and those who blatantly had not.

All attempts by the Roman troops to cross the unnamed river were thwarted by the barbarian faction. At this point Plautius 'sent over a detachment of Celts who were accustomed to swim easily through rough water in armour' (*Roman History* LX, 20). The 'Celts' are usually assumed, in modern literature, to have been auxiliary troops in the pay of Rome, but there is nothing in the *Roman History* to suggest this was the actually case. In fact, given what Dio Cassius says later, it seems more likely these 'Celts' were allied British troops, native friendlies distinguished from the enemy faction who are, from this point on, merely 'Barbarians'. In other words we are seeing a series of events (such as occurred between Cleopatra VII and her brother Ptolemy XIII in Egypt during the late first century BC) where one native faction has allied itself to Rome whereas another has been identified as the aggressor.

The location of the disputed river crossing has never been firmly identified, and probably never will. Most modern commentators place the events at the River Medway, assuming that Plautius had landed at Richborough (and after he had

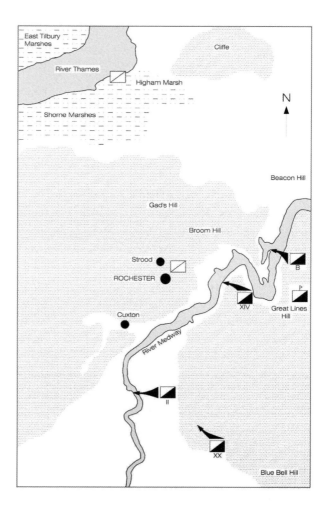

52 The 'Medway Battle' phase 1: an interpretation based upon Dio Cassius' description of the first disputed river crossing, redrawn from John Peddie's book *Invasion: the Roman Conquest of Britain* (1987, 81). Here, the battle occurs to the east and south of modern Rochester, high ground is shaded, unshaded areas represent 'low-lying, marshy land'. On Great Lines Hill, the Roman commander, Aulus Plautius, directs the XIV Legion towards the Medway, whilst the II Legion, under Vespasian, prepares to cross the river from the south. To the north-east, the Batavian auxiliaries easily cross the Medway under arms and in full view of the opposing British army.

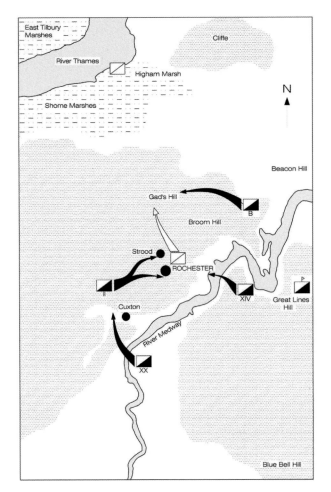

53 The 'Medway Battle' phase 2: an interpretation based upon Dio Cassius' description of the first disputed river crossing, redrawn from John Peddie's book *Invasion: the Roman Conquest of Britain* (1987, 83). Here, British combatants, distracted by the actions of the Batavians, are caught out by the sudden appearance of Vespasian and the II Legion. Fighting lasts until nightfall, with neither side gaining the upper hand. With the arrival of the XX and later the XIV Legions, the Britons to retreat to the Thames.

evidently visited the Cotswolds to say hello to the Bodunni) (52, 53). A landing in Hampshire or Sussex presents alternatives, the most plausible, perhaps, being the River Arun in West Sussex. The uncertainty hasn't stopped people making big, definitive and utterly unprovable statements, however, as a visit to Burham in Kent today will amply demonstrate. Here, about a mile from the medieval church of St Mary the Virgin, stands a small, but undeniably impressive memorial stone and information board. The stone, erected by the Kent Archaeological Society and Maidstone Museum in 1998, bears the inscription:

This stone commemorates
the battle of the Medway
in AD 43
when a Roman army
crossed the river
and defeated the British tribes
under Caratacus

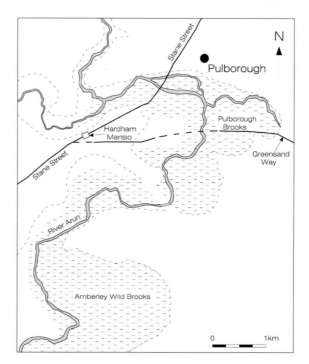

54 The River Arun to the south of Pulborough in West Sussex, in the first and second centuries AD, with 'Stane Street', the Roman road linking Chichester and London, the 'Greensand Way', an offshoot road into the Weald, and all low-lying marshy areas marked.

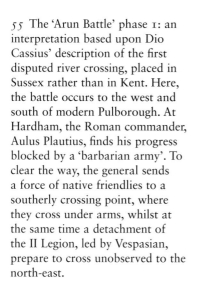

55 The 'Arun Battle' phase 1: an interpretation based upon Dio Cassius' description of the first disputed river crossing, placed in Sussex rather than in Kent. Here, the battle occurs to the west and south of modern Pulborough. At Hardham, the Roman commander, Aulus Plautius, finds his progress blocked by a 'barbarian army'. To clear the way, the general sends a force of native friendlies to a southerly crossing point, where they cross under arms, whilst at the same time a detachment of the II Legion, led by Vespasian, prepare to cross unobserved to the north-east.

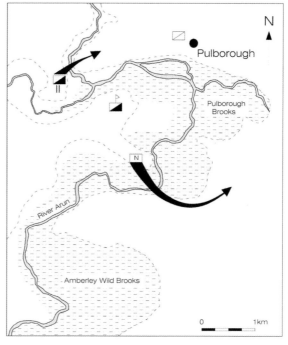

For the sake of consistency, if nothing else, a second stone, commemorating 'the battle of the Arun' and confirming the crossing of the Roman army to defeat 'the British tribes under Caratacus', ought to be set up at Pulborough (54, 55), for this is just as likely to be the site of the conflict as is that currently proposed at Burham.

TOGODUMNUS AND THE KELTOI

Dio Cassius' description of the battle, its aftermath and immediate consequences, is probably the most important thing that he ever says about Rome in Britain and yet it is also a section that is frequently overlooked, its significance widely ignored or simplified. The relevant text (Dio Cassius *Roman History* LX, 20, 5 – 21, 1) reads:

αναχωρησανυων δε εντευθεν των Βρεττανων επι τον Ταμεσαν ποταμον, καθ ΄ δ εσ τε τον ωκεανον εκβαλλει πλημμυροντος τε αυτου λιμναζει, και παδιως αυτον διαβαντων αυε και τα στεριφα τα τε ευπορα του χωριου ακριβως ειδοτων, οι Πωμαιοι επακολουθησαντες σφισι ταυτη μεν εσφαλησαν διανηξαμενων δ ΄ αυθις των Κελτων, και τινων ετερων δια γεφυρας ολιγον ανω διελθοντων, πολαχοθεν τε αμα αυτοις προσεμιξαν και πολλοθς αυτων κατεκοψαν, τους τε λοιπους απερισκεπτως επιδιωκοντες ες τε ελη δυσδιεξοδα εσεπεσον και συχνους απεβαλον. δια τε ουν τουτο, και οτι και του Τογοδουμνου φθαρεντος οι Βρεττανοι ουχ οσον ενεδοσαν αλλα και μαλλον προς την τιμωριαν αυτου επισυνεστησαν, φοβηθεις ο Πλαυυιος ουκετι περαιυερω προσεχωρησεν, αλλ ΄ αυτος τε τα παροντα δια φυλακης εποιησατο και τον Κλαυδιον μευεπεμψατο.

Which is usually translated as:

Thence the Britons retired to the river Thames at a point near where it empties into the ocean and at flood-tide forms a lake. This they easily crossed because they knew where the firm ground and the easy passages in this region were to be found; but the Romans in attempting to follow them were not so successful. However, the Germans swam across again and some others got over by a bridge a little way up-stream, after which they assailed the barbarians from several sides at once and cut down many of them. In pursuing the remainder incautiously, they got into swamps from which it was difficult to make their way out, and so lost a number of men. Shortly afterwards Togodumnus perished, but the Britons, so far from yielding, united all the more firmly to avenge his death. Because of this fact and because of the difficulties he had encountered at the Thames, Plautius became afraid, and instead of advancing any farther, proceeded to guard what he had already won, and sent for Claudius.

In this particular, much quoted version, Dio Cassius seems once more to be indicating the difficulties experienced by *Roman* troops (presumably the II Legion commanded by Vespasian) in crossing a prominent river. Once again it is the timely aid provided by their *Celtic* allies which saves the day. The 'Celts' or German (Batavian) auxiliaries swam across, pursuing the enemy faction and chasing them into swamps before being ambushed and annihilated. Established Fact states that at this point, Cunobelinus' son Togodumnus, who, we are told, was co-ordinating the resistance *against* Rome, perished and all those Britons in the immediate area were roused to avenge his loss. This is all well and good and has the plausible ring of truth about it, but unfortunately it is not what Dio Cassius said.

First, it is worth reiterating that the 'Germans' or Batavians cited today represent a modern fabrication, an interpretative fiction woven from the original term Κελτους as used by Dio Cassius. They are Keltoi / Celts; nothing more. They are just as likely to have been native friendlies operating under the command of their own leaders of behalf of Aulus Plautius than fully trained auxiliaries in the pay of Rome. The suggestion that Dio Cassius may originally have been referring to Roman auxiliaries, specifically Batavians, a Germanic people from the area of the Rhine delta, was first put forward by Mark Hassall in an influential article published in the journal *Britannia* for 1970. In this, Hassall noted that Batavian cohorts were certainly in Britain by AD 67 and that, given their 'proud boast and peculiar skill' was to 'swim rivers fully armed' (Hassall 1970, 131), the possibility existed that they may have been present even earlier, as the 'Celtic' troops that Dio Cassius described in AD 43. The article is well researched and persuasive, but as Hassall himself freely admits, the evidence is circumstantial.

Unfortunately, since 1970, the circumstantial nature of the Batavian theory has tended to be forgotten, at least by those compiling books on Roman Britain. In her novel of 1978, *The Eagle and the Raven*, author Pauline Gedge could write:

> They rolled forward quickly, the chiefs running behind, spears raised and swords drawn, their clamour a constant, terrifying din, but when they reached the bank they stopped incredulously. There were soldiers in full armour in the river, swimming strongly, and behind them troops splashed into the shallows and struck out, hundreds of them…Caradoc felt his heart sink. The men who were now almost halfway across were not Roman. They were auxiliaries, Batavians or Thracians or both, tribes renowned for their water skills
> (1978, 148)

In a similar vein, although this time in a work of non-fiction, Graham Webster's *The Roman Invasion of Britain* could also confidently assert that:

> while the Britons watched all this with fascinated anticipation, the Batavians were quietly entering the water and swimming across virtually unnoticed
> (1980, 99)

Secondly, the 'death' of Togodumnus, falling in defence of his homeland was actually nothing of the sort. As long ago as 1991, Louis Francis observed that within Dio Cassius' original Greek text:

> the use of φθαπεντος the Aorist Passive Participle of the verb φθειρω, to describe the death [of Togodumnus] itself is a strange choice because the strict translation of this verb in the Passive is not so much 'to kill' as 'to destroy.' Something is done to the individual that causes his death, unlike the usual αποκυεινω which means 'to kill', pure and simple, in the Active as well as the Passive
> (Francis 1991, 4, iii, h)

BLOODLINE: THE CELTIC KINGS OF ROMAN BRITAIN

Francis assumes, quite understandably, that the death of Togodumnus must therefore have been in some way abnormal. Perhaps the Roman army, having captured the king, tortured or maimed him before decapitating him in order to destroy the man completely. Such a death, Francis considers, may have been of sufficient horror to rouse 'normally placid Britons to fight in his name'. Whilst plausible, it is worth noting that this particular theory is still working within the well-Established Fact that Togodumnus was killed during the course of the second river battle. If one takes the paragraph as a whole, however, it becomes apparent that Dio Cassius is not actually describing the bloody, violent demise of an anti Roman king on the battlefield, but something altogether more intriguing. For that reason it is worth analysing the English translation of this critical segment of text again, this time using Francis' new translation and taking in the new inflexions and emphases:

> However the Celts straight away swam across while others got across by a bridge a little way upstream, engaged with them from many sides and cut many of them down. But in the headlong pursuit of the remainder, chased them into swamps with no way out and many of themselves perished. However, because of this action and also, at the same time, the destruction of Togodumnus, those Britons not greatly involved, but of a gentle and mild disposition, deemed it worthy to stand together at his side, against them (*Roman History* LX, 20)

The paragraph remains confusing precisely because Dio Cassius is trying to convey what was a complicated event, one that he may not actually have fully understood himself when compiling the narrative from whatever original source material was available to him. Let us read it again, this time with some clarification:

> However the *Celts* straight away swam across while others [more Celts] got across by a bridge a little way upstream, engaged with them [the Barbarians] from many sides and cut many of them [the Barbarians] down. But in the headlong pursuit of the remainder, chased them [the Barbarians] into swamps with no way out and many of themselves [the Celts] perished. However, because of this action and also, at the same time, the *destruction* of Togodumnus [Celtic army], those Britons not greatly involved, but of a gentle and mild disposition, deemed it worthy to *stand together at his* [Togodumnus'] *side, against them* [the Barbarians] (*Roman History* LX, 20)

In other words it is Togodumnus' army that is being *destroyed* in the swamps by the enemy (barbarian) faction led (presumably) by his own brother Caratacus. It is not the *man* being 'killed', but the Κελτους (Keltoi). It is precisely this particular 'destruction' by ambush which prompts certain 'Britons not greatly involved' in the struggle (i.e. those neutral groups previously not taking sides within the area of Sussex / Kent / Hertfordshire) 'to stand together at *his* (Togodumnus') side against *them*' (Caratacus' army). The crucial thing about this rereading is that not only was Togodumnus and his army of Keltoi operating *with* Plautius, on the Roman side, but, more importantly it is clear that he evidently survived the ambush for the next thing the text states is that the Britons previously unaffected, now stood 'together *at his side*'. This implies a people joining the still living king in order to fight the barbarian foe, rather than, as usually thought, native warriors joining the Barbarians in order to fight Rome and avenge his death.

At this point Plautius, 'becoming alarmed' at the obvious deterioration of events, sent word back to Rome for reinforcements. What seems to have begun as little more than a peace keeping mission to resolve a disputed succession had now degenerated into open civil war. Interestingly, though Dio Cassius tells us little about the nature of these 'reinforcements' other than they included 'extensive equipment, including elephants' which 'had already been got together for the expedition', he does later refer to 'Legions'. Claudius had, it would seem, been fully prepared to take the credit for bringing peace to Britain through diplomatic means, but had also collected sufficient military reserves in case he needed to resort to force. At this point we can legitimately talk of an 'invasion', reinforcements that Claudius was later to lead into Colchester comprising many of the military units that were later to garrison Britain. These reinforcements would presumably have taken the more direct route to Britain from Gaul, landing somewhere in Kent, the early military presence at Richborough being a prime candidate for the arrival of the emperor, his men, horses and elephants.

Quite how many troops (legionaries and auxiliaries), horses, elephants, friends, colleagues and general hangers-on Claudius took with him to Britain is unknown, but it seems clear from the writings of Dio Cassius that the second wave represented the main invasion force so it was likely to be impressive; a reflection of the status of the emperor himself. It is possible that the 'Legions' that Dio Cassius mentioned included those not taking part in Aulus Plautius' initial task force: the ninth (IX), fourteenth (XIV) and twentieth (XX). It is also possible that, if the preliminary force had only contained components of the second, under the ultimate command of Vespasian, the remainder of that legion was only now involved in Claudius' great maritime adventure (56).

Ultimately, of course, unless the lost section of Tactitus' *Annals* covering the 'invasion' ever appear, we are unlikely to ever know the exact numbers and composition of either wave. Thanks to a variety of disparate tombstones, honorific inscriptions and other dedications recovered from around the empire, we do have some idea of the high officials present within the entourage of the emperor in AD 43, one of which was Lucius Coiedius Candidus, a *quaestor* (junior magistrate). It is worth pausing to consider the career of Candidus for a moment as some have suggested that he received decorations for the 'British War' whilst acting as a tribune in the *VIII Augusta*, a legion which Established Fact tells us was not part of the invasion. In fact the *VIII* is generally overlooked in any debate concerning the events of AD 43 on the grounds that *we know* it wasn't part of the invasion force. Unfortunately, of course, we *do not know* this at all. Considering that we actually possess no clear idea what units *were* actually involved in the initial phases of the invasion, except perhaps the *II Augusta*

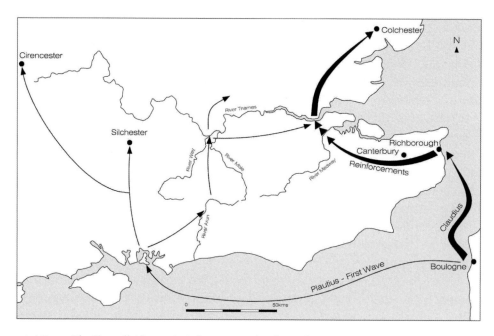

56 AD 43: The 'Russell Alternative', first set out by the author in 2006 (*Roman Sussex*). Here, the primary-wave 'force' (numbering between 2,000 and 5,000 men) are sent to Britain under the command of Aulus Plautius, in order to resolve a hotly disputed succession following the death of king Cunobelinus. Landing somewhere within the Portsmouth / Chichester harbour area, Plautius restores order within the kingdoms of the Atrebates (based at Silchester) and Bodunni / Dobunni (Cirencester) and negotiates between the two main Catuvellaunian / Trinobantian candidates, Togodumnus and Caratacus. Having decided in favour of Togodumnus, Plautius finds himself at the centre of an escalating civil war. Caratacus' 'Barbarian' army attempts to block Plautius at the Arun and later the Thames, being thwarted in both cases by the timely intervention of Togodumnus' Keltoi (Celts). At the Thames, Togodumnus' force is, however, cut to pieces in an ambush, an action which serves to make many wavering tribes join the Roman cause (as they fear the aggressive nature of Caratacus). Realising that the situation is now beyond his control, Plautius sends word to Claudius, who arrives at the head of a substantial army of reinforcements at Richborough, in Kent. Claudius' army of conquest, which has now replaced the peace-keeping primary wave, heads towards the centre of British resistance, the Trinobantian capital of Colchester (*Camulodunum*).

under Vespasian, then there is no automatic reason to exclude the *VIII* at all. In fact when we do look at the evidence for Legionary units designated to the island province, there is a surprising amount of evidence to suggest that the *VIII* was indeed a major player in the invasion of Britain and its immediate aftermath.

TOGIDUBNUS

It is at this point in the narrative of Dio Cassius, Togodumnus disappears, even though it is now clear that there is no evidence to support the theory that he died on the banks of the Thames fighting Rome. Soon afterwards, however, we start to hear about a 'Tiberius Claudius Togidubnus'. Can the two be the same? If we temporarily discard the 'Tiberius Claudius' aspect of the latter, it is clear that Togodumnus and Togidubnus are essentially the same name (both meaning something like 'deep axe'). Given the general level of uncertainty already noted over the correct form of British names when transcribed (or mangled) into Latin, I have no doubt that both names and, indeed, both men were in reality one and the same.

Our first source for Togidubnus comes from the quill of the Roman historian Publius Cornelius Tacitus, writing at the very end of the first century AD, who comments rather sneeringly that:

> Certain states were handed over to King Cogidumnus – he in fact remained totally loyal down to our times – in accordance with the Roman people's old and long-standing policy of making even kings their agents in enslaving people (Tacitus, *Agricola* 14)

Stepping aside from matters of spelling for a moment (as most now recognise that *Cogi*-dumnus has far less validity in Celtic than *Togi*-dubnus), the man appears in one other historical document, a monumental inscription found in the town of Noviomagus, Chichester in West Sussex. The inscription was found (and damaged) during the excavation of a cellar close to the centre of town in 1723. How many pieces the inscription was originally in, is unknown, but it does appear to have suffered considerably at the hands of its discoverers. Enough survives, however, to be able to name a certain '...IDUBNI', giving him his full name and title.

NEPTVNO ET MINERVAE
TEMPLVM
PRO SALVTE DOMVS DIVINAE
EX AVCTOITATE TIBERI CLAVDI
...IDVBNI REG MAGN BRIT
COLLEGIVM FABRORVM ET QVI IN EO
SVNT DE SVO DEDERVNT DONANTE AREAM
PVDENTE PVDENTINI FILIO

This may be translated as:

> To Neptune and Minerva, for the welfare of the Divine House by the authority of Tiberius Claudius Togidubnus, Great King in Britain, the guild of smiths and those therein gave this temple from their own resources, Pudens son of Pudentinus, donated the site

The inscription formed the centrepiece of a temple dedicated to two key Roman deities, Neptune god of the sea and Minerva goddess who together with Jupiter and Juno formed one of the key deities of the so-called Capitoline Triad. Unfortunately the piece remains undated (and ultimately undatable), as no emperor is specifically cited by name or title as benefactor. Mention of the 'Divine House' would relate either the Julio-Claudian dynasty (Julius Caesar, Octavian / Augustus and Claudius all being deified by the Roman senate) or to the Flavians (the same thing occurring later to Vespasian and his son Titus, respectively father and brother to Domitian). This means that the piece must have been set up in the reigns of those immediately succeeding divine emperors, either Claudius (AD 41-54), Nero (AD 54-68), Titus (AD 79-81) or Domitian (AD 81-96). Given the form of the text and lettering, it has been suggested that the piece is more plausibly to have been made during the either the reign of Claudius or Nero.

Addition of the names Tiberius (TIBERI) and Claudius (CLAVDI) to …IDVBNI's own tells us that not only was he a full Roman citizen, but more significantly that his sponsor for citizenship was one of the members of the Julio-Claudian House, in all likelihood the emperor himself, but which one? The issue is not helped by the observation that three emperors at some stage bore the three names Tiberius Claudius Nero, these being the second emperor, Tiberius, the fourth, Claudius and fifth, Nero. Tiberius himself can be discounted, as he showed no real interest in Britain (and we have no record of any ethnic Britons coming to his court seeking refuge as we do under Augustus), whilst anyone made a citizen by him tended to adopt the names 'Tiberius Julius'. Adoption of the names Tiberius Claudius' to the Celtic …IDVBNI (Togidubnus) therefore suggests enfranchisement under Claudius or Nero. Established Fact tells us that the grant of citizenship occurred under Claudius (AD 41-54) but in truth we cannot really be that precise. Official recognition of …IDVBNI's status extends further than his grant of citizenship however, for the Chichester inscription acknowledges his title 'Great King in Britain' (REG MAGN BRIT).

The big problem with Tiberius Claudius Togidubnus 'the Great' is that, although he appears as an important figure in the years immediately after the conquest of southern Britain, his background before remains stubbornly obscure. Unfortunately, other than the brief comment provided by Tacitus, we possess no clear idea about who exactly who he was: there is no biography, no family tree, no *curriculum vitae*. Therefore, although he is mentioned today by modern authors who describe him as either an enlightened promoter of Roman civilisation or a dirty quisling who betrayed his people, what we 'know' about his career, life and achievements is nothing more than speculation. Established Fact claims that he was probably the descendant of a British King, such as Dubnobellaunus, Tincomarus or Verica, who had fled the British Isles to the protection of the Roman People. Alternatively, perhaps, he was a relatively insignificant local aristocrat, elevated by the emperor as a puppet king to serve Rome. Unlike other British kings in the first half of the first century AD, Togidubnus does not seem to have minted coins and does not feature in any historical text relating to the initial stages of the Roman invasion. He seems to have quite literally sprung out of nowhere. If Togodumnus and Togidubnus are the same man, however, the problems surrounding his background and significance simply evaporate. He was there all the time, we just couldn't see him.

Togodumnus / Togidubnus, leader of the Keltoi or 'Celts' was presumably the man whom Plautius, acting on behalf of the emperor, had chosen to succeed

57 'Certain States were handed over to king Togidubnus': here a series of tribal areas, some existing before AD 43 and some created by the Roman State, are given to the 'Great King', freeing up Roman troops and allowing them to advance westwards into Wales. Togidubnus and the Catuvellauni, as chief allies of Rome during the disputed succession of AD 43, are provided with a high status *municipium*, close to the former tribal centre at St Albans. The Belgae, a conflation of Belgic communities and associated groups, are provided with a new prestige centre at Winchester, whilst high-status construction

work commences at Bath. At Silchester, Romanised development continues within the former *oppidum* of *Calleva*, whilst the 'Kingdom' (Regnum), an artificial, non-tribal creation, is established upon land around Chichester on the East Hampshire / West Sussex coast.

Cunobelinus. His brother, Caratacus, leader of the 'Barbarians' was the loser in every sense, for, having rejected the decision of Plautius concerning the disputed succession, Caratacus made himself Rome's enemy. With Togidubnus firmly on Plautius' side, at a time when Rome was desperately trying to save its trade investment in Britain, the whole situation remained salvageable. Togidubnus would have been vital to the Roman cause and would almost certainly have been well rewarded afterwards. Identification of Togodumnus with Tiberius Claudius Togidubnus may also help to explain how and why he was given the title of 'Great King in Britain', for this is akin to the recognition given by the Roman State to his father Cunobelinus, at least according to Suetonius.

As a king of the Catuvellauni, Togidubnus' power would almost certainly not have originally centred around Chichester and Western Sussex. As joint heir to his father Cunobelinus' estate together with his brother Caratacus, the two brothers should theoretically have been based either at the Trinobantian capital of *Camulodunum* (Colchester in Essex) or the Catuvellaunian one at *Verulamium* (St Albans in Hertfordshire), the two *oppida* which Cunobelinus had claimed lordship over (57). As *Camulodunum* became the chief target of Claudius' army, later having a legionary fortress implanted directly across it, whilst *Verulamium* became a *municipium* (a favoured town whose population was granted Roman citizenship) we can only assume that it was in Hertfordshire that Togidubnus first reigned. Chichester and the lands that surrounded it could, in such a scenario, have been one of the cantons or states given to Togidubnus to repay his loyalty to Rome. Whatever the case, it would appear that Chichester soon became a favoured place amongst the Iron Age elite, the quantity and quality of palatial buildings established on land surrounding the town surpassing all other areas of Britain.

CARATACUS

Claudius' arrival at the head of major reinforcements brought the troubles in Britain to an end, the emperor receiving the submission of 11 (unnamed) British kings 'defeated without any reverse'. Claudius could now celebrate his triumph over Britannia, something that he continued to do throughout the remainder of his reign. Southern Britain, or at least that part previously belonging to the Trinobantes, Catuvellauni, Eceni, the Atrebates and the various tribes of Cantium, was now formally part of the empire, having been 'liberated' from a potentially messy civil war. It was clear, however, that the larger conflict was not over, however much the emperor's PR machine said otherwise, for Caratacus, now leader of the British resistance movement, was still at large.

Unlike Togidubnus, Caratacus (meaning something like 'the ram') seems to have minted his own coins prior to AD 43, a small series marked with the legend CARA being found in northern Hampshire and southern Oxfordshire (58). The coins, featuring a relatively well executed bust and a suspiciously Roman looking eagle, are almost identical to issues previously minted with the name EPATI (Epaticus), and are all derived from the same general area. Assuming that Dio Cassius was right, and Caratacus WAS the son of Cunobelinus (along with Togodumnus / Togidubnus and Adminius / Amminus), then Epaticus should have been his uncle; for both Epaticus and Cunobelinus are identified on their coins as TASCI F, 'son of Tasciovanus'. That the CARA coins so closely emulate those of EPATI, may however indicate that Caratacus was actually the son of Epaticus (and therefore the nephew of Cunobelinus and cousin to Togodumnus / Togidubnus), Dio Cassius getting the family relationship wrong. Alternatively, Caratacus may have been deliberately copying the style of his uncle's coins, having acquired Epaticus' kingdom following the latter's (childless?) demise. Whatever the case, the coins themselves

58 Silver unit of CARA (Caratacus), typically found in northern Hampshire and southern Oxfordshire. Note the suspiciously Roman looking eagle. *Images of ancient British coins provided by dealer Chris Rudd. Cat. No. 1223*

59 The earthwork remains of a Roman fortlet at Old Burrow, on the north Devon coast, built in the early 50s AD to oversee the Bristol Channel and the South Welsh coast during the campaigns against Caratacus and the Silures. *Author*

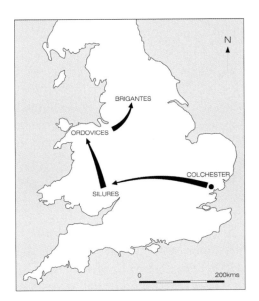

Above left: 60 Map showing, in general terms, the fighting retreat of Caratacus from Trinobantian territory around Colchester, to the lands of the Silures, Ordovices and Brigantes, AD 43 to 51.

Above right: 61 'Claudius defeating *Britannia*': a stone relief from a temple dedicated to the imperial cult of the Julio-Claudian emperors at Aphrodisias, Turkey. Claudius is depicted as an 'heroic nude', savagely grasping the hair of the pleading *Britannia*, a semi-naked amazonian, with his left hand whilst (presumably) about to deal the death blow with a sword or spear in his right. *Massingheimer Collection* are very Roman in design and one wonders, if the disputed succession had gone in Caratacus' favour, whether Togodumnus / Togidubnus would have become leader of a resistance movement and target number one of the Roman military.

After the events of AD 43, Caratacus disappears, finally remerging in AD 47, stirring the Silures tribe of south-western Wales and co-ordinating their fight against the advancing Roman army (59). How he obtained such as position, we do not know, Tacitus noting only that his 'successes, partial or complete, had raised him to a pinnacle above the other British leaders' (*Annals* XII, 33). Perhaps, like Cassivellaunos before him, he was simply the best man for the job: a seasoned warrior with extensive combat experience. Certainly his presence in Wales seems to have livened things up for the new governor of Britain, Publius Ostorius Scapula, who's job it now was to capture the Briton 'dead or alive' in order that Claudius' final triumph could at last be celebrated. Caratacus then shifted the theatre of war to the Ordovices in north Wales, but, after a disastrous battle in which his unnamed wife and 'brothers' were captured, he fled to the Brigantes in what is now northern England (60). The Brigantian queen, Cartimandua, realising perhaps that where Caratacus went the Roman army was soon to follow, arrested the fugitive king and immediately handed him over to Scapula. The year was AD 51. After nearly 9 years of living life on the run, Caratacus was in the custody of his greatest foe.

Claudius used every means to glorify the conquest of Britain (61), staging a variety of 'events' in Rome for the benefit of his people. On his return to Rome in AD 43, following his brief visit to Colchester, the senate granted Claudius a triumph and a title: Britannicus, a name he later gave to his only son. An annual festival of thanksgiving was added to the calendar, whilst two triumphal arches were constructed, one in Boulogne where his army of reinforcement had disembarked, and one in Rome itself. Unfortunately neither arch is in existence today, though fragments of the monumental frieze, showing the emperor's bodyguard, and random sketches of at least one of the battle scenes (made centuries after) set originally upon the arch in Rome, do thankfully survive. Celebratory coins with the legend DE BRITANNIS above the arch in Rome, were also minted. Just in case people missed the point, Claudius also staged a mock-up of *Camulodunum* on the *Campus Martius* (Field of Mars) in Rome, so that that its siege and capture could be re-enacted. Later on a (no doubt highly theatrical) version of the 'Surrender of the British Kings' was staged, with Claudius doubling as himself.

In AD 44 Claudius celebrated a grand triumph, climaxing in his ascent of the Capitol on his knees, followed by the presentation of rewards, gifts, titles and ornaments to those who had accompanied him on his British campaign. In AD 47, when the first governor of Britain Aulus Plautius returned to Rome, having completed his tour of duty, Claudius went out in person to greet him and awarded him an ovation. Poems and verses proliferated; monumental statues were sent out to the provinces. The capture of Caratacus in AD 51 now provided Claudius with another chance to capitalise on his military prowess.

Tacitus relates the arrival of the British king in Rome, and Claudius' attempts to milk the situation for all it was worth, in glorious detail:

The populace were invited as if to some spectacle of note; the praetorian cohorts stood under arms upon the level ground in front of their camp. Then, while the king's humble vassals filed past, ornaments and neck-rings and prizes won in his foreign wars were borne in parade; next his brothers, wife, and daughter were placed on view; finally, he himself. The rest stooped to unworthy entreaties dictated by fear; but on the part of Caratacus not a downcast look nor a word requested pity. Arrived at the tribunal, he spoke as follows: 'Had my lineage and my rank been matched by my moderation in success, I should have entered this city rather as a friend than as a captive; nor would you have scorned to admit to a peaceful alliance one spring from famous ancestors and holding sway over many peoples. My present lot, if to me a degradation, is to you a glory. I had horses and men, arms and riches: what wonder then if I regret their loss? If you wish to rule the world, does it follow that everyone welcomes servitude? If I were dragged before you after surrendering without a blow, there would have been little heard either of my fall or of your triumph: punishment of me will be followed by oblivion. If on the other hand you spare my life, I shall be an everlasting memorial of your clemency.' In response to this Caesar [Claudius] pardoned Caratacus and his wife and brothers (*Annals* XII, 36-7)

Claudius' stage-managed pardon of Caratacus is in direct contrast to the actions of Julius Caesar, who, following the celebration of his victory against the Gauls in 46 BC, had the leader of the Gallic resistance, Vercingetorix, paraded through the streets before being strangled. Claudius had not only surpassed Caesar in achieving the conquest of Britain (against Caesar's rather pitiful expeditions), he surpassed him in humanity, forgiving his enemy rather than condemning him to death.

Caratacus' speech may have been written for him, although given that he was, in his early reign, essentially a pro-Roman client (who may in his youth have even lived in Rome as a hostage), he was clearly no tourist, hopelessly lost in an alien environment; he could no doubt understand Latin and knew exactly how to speak to an emperor. Much of his address, however, chimes with what we know about Tacitus' own mindset and attitude, so it could easily be the Roman author's own words coming through the mouth of the captive king. One aspect of the speech, however, certainly rings true, Caratacus' comment that if he had been 'dragged before you after surrendering without a blow, there would have been little heard either of my fall or of your triumph'. Was this a sly dig at Togodumnus / Togidubnus who had wholeheartedly gone over to the Roman cause? Certainly the relationship of the brothers and their respective attitudes to Roman imperialism may go some way to explain Tacitus' later caustic statement that the loyalty of king Togidubnus was in accordance with Rome's policy of 'making even kings their agents in enslaving people'. Tacitus wrote in praising terms about Caratacus, who spoke defiantly and with 'not a downcast look' nor appeal for mercy. His brother Togidubnus, however, lived on in grand and luxurious splendour in Britain, not because he had bravely defied the Romans, but because he had voluntarily surrendered to them, an act that would not have appealed to Tacitus' view of the noble and honourable savage.

7

BOUDICCA AND THE CATUVELLAUNI: BLIND REVENGE ON A BLAMELESS VICTIM

Business parks are curiously uninspiring places, and the Fison Way estate, one of a number of similarly-themed constructions set at the northern limits of Thetford in Norfolk, is no exception. Built in the later half of the twentieth century, it, like most other industrial estates in the UK, boasts a 'dedicated business infrastructure' in a 'tightly demarcated zone' away from the 'main residential area' of the town, something which 'reduces social and environmental impact' whilst still being close enough to road and rail to provide 'excellent transportation access'. Today, multi-unit brick-built offices, slate-grey warehouses and plate-glass fronted showrooms loom menacingly at the roadside, a world of concrete and steel enclosed behind a multitude of barbed wire fences.

The concept of 'activity-specific zoning' is, however, nothing new to Thetford. Today it is the fear of environmental pollution (light, air and water) that keeps business and light industry away from the main residential area of the town. In the Late Iron Age, the fear of pollution for those in the settlement zone may have had more to do with the sacred and spiritual. Had you visited the area of Fison Way in the first century AD, you would have found no glorified industrial park, but a ceremonial estate set aside for a range of non-domestic, ritualised activities. Instead of lost motorists, business executives and lorry drivers eating their lunch by the roadside, the place would, 2000 years ago, have probably have been the haunt of the religious and political elite.

In its final form, the 'Fison Way site', uncovered in the early 1980s, comprised two rectangular ditched enclosures, the smaller set within the larger, the 34m wide space between the two being filled by eight concentric palisade, wooden fence or tree bedding trenches. The smaller ditch surrounded an area measuring just over 220 by 170m and contained, at its westernmost end, at least five round, post-built structures. The excavators of the site have argued that the well-organised system of internal planning, 'excessive' numbers of enclosure system and lack of any clear defensive nature, especially around the entrance, when combined with the near total absence of any 'normal' domestic debris, make the sanctuary interpretation by far the most plausible. Perhaps this was the spiritual hub of the local clan-group, the Iceni / Eceni; a tribal centre, meeting point or place of assembly. Perhaps, as some claim, it was here that the Boudiccan Revolt, the single bloodiest act of mass butchery ever recorded on British soil, began.

NERO CLAUDIUS CAESAR DRUSUS GERMANICUS

Our view of the emperor Nero Claudius Drusus Germanicus is a decidedly unflattering one, the biographer and historian Suetonius noting that:

> He was about average height, his body marked with spots and malodorous. His features were regular rather than attractive. His eyes were blue and somewhat weak. His neck was over thick, his belly prominent, and his legs very slender ... He was utterly shameless in the care of his person and in his dress, always having his hair arranged in tiers of curls.
> (Suetonius *Nero*, 51)

Throughout history, Nero (62) has been vilified and condemned as a monster, wife-beater, mother-killer and torturer. The golden age of the Hollywood epic has added an extra layer of gloss to the myth, with screen greats such as Peter Ustinov (*Quo Vadis*) and Charles Laughton (*Sign of the Cross*) playing him as a spoilt and petulant child with psychopathic tendencies.

Roman biographers and historians, such as Suetonius, undoubtedly exaggerated the more unpleasant aspects of Nero's character, as one would expect for an emperor who, after death, was declared an enemy of the state. Nero's accession in AD 54, however, had been met with great celebration, the 17-year-old emperor and adopted son of Claudius being acclaimed as an athletic hero, in marked contrast to his aged and rather austere predecessor. Nero was a Julio-Claudian through and through, a direct descendant of the emperor Augustus (his great, great grandfather) via his mother Julia Agrippina (sister of Caligula), daughter

62 A modern copy of an original portrait of the emperor Nero from early in his reign, before the Boudiccan Revolt (AD 56-58). © *Trustees of the British Museum*

of war hero Germanicus and Vipsania Agrippina, herself daughter of Marcus Agrippa and Julia, daughter of Augustus. This was in contrast to Claudius, who descended from Augustus' sister Octavia, via Antonia the younger, daughter of Octavia and Mark Antony. The glorious accession of Nero, then a young *princeps*, is something that is often overlooked today, in much the same way that the popular view of the Tudor king Henry VIII is that of a bloated, bearded and debauched monarch, not the muscular warrior prince of his early reign.

The later portraits of Nero (as with those of Henry VIII) certainly all show the marked effects of a thoroughly decadent lifestyle, the emperor becoming heavy in the face, possessing prominent multiple chins and a thick neck. It is difficult to know how to judge these images today, for whereas modern dictators prefer to project a youthful and athletic image (even if the reality is very different), the ancients equated obesity with wealth, luxury and success. An over-fleshy image of Nero, such as those made in the mid 60s AD, when he was in his late 20s, would therefore have communicated his god-like status to the Roman people. Nero's earliest official portrait type, however, is quite unlike those made in his final years. The Nero we see in sculptures produced at the time of his official adoption by the emperor Claudius in AD 51, are slender and boyish with a delicate, centrally-parted coiffure and lengthy sideburns which curl decoratively in front of slightly protruding ears. The face is smooth and regular with a rounded chin, crisply defined lips and enlarged, almond-shaped eyes. This was Nero aged 14, at the time of his first wearing of the *Toga virilis*, an official dress marker of his progression into manhood.

The reign of the new emperor began well, Nero delivering a speech to the senate reassuring them that he would return to the principles of the deified Augustus. Furthermore, he told them that the senate itself would be permitted greater autonomy and a more defined role in the governance of empire and freedom of speech would once more be tolerated. It was exactly the sort of 'back to basics' speech that the aristocracy of Rome loved. The official imagery of coins convey the sense of 'a golden age': a youthful portrait of the emperor combined with symbols of prosperity and wealth. The only sign of things to come perhaps was the sudden and unexpected death of Britannicus, Claudius' natural son, who had, for some reason, not inherited his father's position as first citizen. On 11 February AD 55, less than four months after the death of Claudius, the unfortunate Britannicus collapsed at the dinner table in front of Nero. No one ever resolved the cause of death, but many suspected foul play. Nero claimed it was probably a seizure of some kind, and swiftly disposed of the body.

Policy-wise Nero broadly continued the strategic decisions of his predecessor. Unlike Claudius or Caligula, however, Nero does not seem to have desired glory in the form of mass territorial acquisition. In Britain, although the policy of expansion westwards seems to have prevailed, there may have been a general lack of direction, stemming from a failure to understand the British problem. During the final years of Claudius' reign things had not been going too well in the province, despite the imperial PR machines' attempt to assure the Senate and People that 'all of Britain lay conquered'. The war had not ended following the capture of the Caratacus; in fact the loss of the insurgency leader did not diminish the resolve of the western tribes to strenuously resist the advancing might of Rome. Legionary detachments within the territory of the Silures in what is now South Wales, were ambushed, serious casualties being inflicted. Shortly afterwards a Roman foraging party was attacked, the reinforcements sent to help being routed. 'Frequent engagements followed' Tacitus says, 'generally of the irregular type, in woods and fens; decided by individual luck or bravery' (*Annals* XII, 39). Guerrilla warfare was a form of combat that Roman troops were neither trained nor equipped to deal with. In AD 52, the second governor of Britannia, Publius Ostorius Scapula died in office, 'broken by the weary load of anxiety' (*Annals* XII, 39). His replacement, Aulus Didius Gallus, arrived to find that the Silures had defeated a legion (presumably the *II Augusta*). To make matters worse, the northern frontier of the province was becoming increasingly unstable with the Brigantes, nominally led by their Queen Cartimandua, descending into civil war. Events were spiralling out of control.

Following the death of Claudius in AD 54, Nero may have seriously considered the possibility of withdrawing from Britain. True, significant amounts of time, money and (specifically military) resources had been tied up there for over a decade, but the invasion and conquest of the island had been little more than Claudius' pet project. Now that he was dead, was there really any need to continue in Britain? Suetonius, in his *Lives* of the Caesars suggests that any such thoughts of abandoning the province were swiftly dropped by Nero, presumably after listening (for once) to his immediate circle of advisors, 'because he was ashamed to seem to belittle the glory of his father' (*Nero*, 18).

Whilst official frontier policy was being discussed, in Britain the strategy adopted was simply one of maintaining the *status quo*. In the south and east towns developed, fledgling Romano-British elites encouraged, roads built, mines expanded and forts constructed. In the north, a shaky alliance with the Brigantes secured the frontier, whilst in the west the policy seems to have been one of containment. Overall, there may have been little or no consensus as to what could realistically be achieved. Tacitus, in his epic work the *Agricola*, bemoans what he perceived to have been a general lack of activity in the province, observing that the governor Didius Gallus merely 'preserved the acquisitions of his predecessors, and added a very few fortified posts in the remoter parts, for the reputation of enlarging his province' (*Agricola*, 14).

By the winter of AD 57 / 58 a decision had finally been made: Britain was not to be abandoned after all. In fact the forward policy of Claudius was to be accelerated and a brand new governor with experience in dealing with unruly mountain tribes, Quintus Veranius Nepos, was appointed to the task. Nepos, however, 'after harrying the Silurians in a few raids of no great significance' (*Annals* XIV, 29), died in office. He was soon replaced with Gaius Suetonius Paulinus, first Roman general to cross the Atlas Mountains of North Africa. At last the final subjugation of the Britons seemed assured.

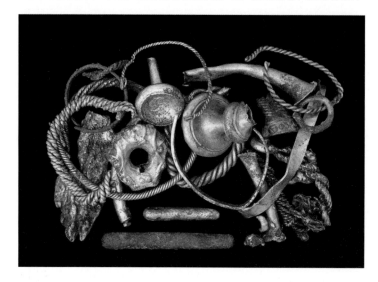

63 One of a number of hoards found at Snettisham, Norfolk, containing torcs (neck rings), bracelets, finger rings, ingots and coins belonging to the Eceni. © *Trustees of the British Museum*

PRASTOTAGUS

As the army moved westwards into Wales, the long-term stability of territory acquired by Rome to the south and east appears to have been guaranteed by the continued acknowledgement of client states, kingdoms that maintained a semi-autonomous existence under the watchful eye of Rome. Togidubnus and the Catuvellauni we have already noted, but the Eceni / Iceni of Norfolk / Suffolk represent another group which seem to have been left largely to their own devices. The material culture of this region suggests that some of the Eceni benefited from Roman contact, many of the torcs (neck rings) and other decorative dress items recovered from hoards of the period suggest that the raw material necessary to manufacture such items was derived from Roman bullion (63). They also appear to have been allowed to continue minting coins.

In 1960, a hoard of Late Iron Age coins was recovered from a site at Joist Fen in Suffolk. Contained within the hoard were a number of silver issues bearing a clean-shaven Romanised head, a well-executed depiction of horse on the reverse and an unusual sequence of letters, later interpreted as reading SUBIDASTO and ESICO (64). Further discoveries of the same basic issue lead coin experts to conclude that a full reading of the original text was likely to have been SVBRIIPRASTO or SVB RI PRASTO around the head with ESICO FECIT on the back. This, if taken at face value, seemed to demonstrate a combination of both Latin and Celtic word-forms, SVB RI PRASTO (sub ricon Prasto) meaning 'under King Prasto', with the phrase continuing on the reverse with ESCIO FECIT or 'Escio made me / made this'. The conclusion was that Escio was probably the coin manufacturer whilst 'King Prasto' was King Prasutagus who, according to Tacitus, was ruler of the Eceni in the mid first century AD.

That the coins were of an historically attested king whose wife, Boudicca, later led the great revolt against Rome, became an Established Fact, at least until a

64 Silver unit of ESV PRASTO (Prasutagus / Prastotagus), presumably the pro-Roman husband of Boudicca. *Images of ancient British coins provided by dealer Chris Rudd.* Cat. No. *1565*

new series of discoveries cast doubt over the interpretation. In the late 1990s, three new PRASTO-related coins were recovered by metal-detectorists. Two of the coins bore the legend SUB ESVPRASTO and not SVB RI PRASTO. Prasto was not a RICON or 'King'; neither was he a 'Prasutagus', reports circulating at the time stating that the Ecenian king cited by Tacitus and the man on the coins were undoubtedly two different people, an Established Fact that some hold to this day:

> There was another king, called Esuprastus, who was issuing coins in what is today East Anglia in the middle of the first century AD, using a Roman style. The idea that the Iceni may have had multiple kings recalls the complexity of Late Iron Age tribal organisation in Britain. Perhaps there were effectively several kings in this area and Prasutagus was the one who had the closest relationship with Rome
> (Hingley and Unwin 2006, 38)

That the text on the new coins clearly reads SVB ESVPRASTO is not in debate, but what exactly does ESVPRASTO mean? The name could conceivably be broken into two halves, the prefix Esu or Esus deriving from 'master' or 'lord', prasto / brasto perhaps deriving from Celtic forms for 'big' or 'large'. Hence in Esu-Prasto we could have a compound name meaning something akin to 'Big Lord' or 'Great Master'. The enlarged form Prasutagus / Prastotagus contains the element tago, which on itself can mean 'chief', hence the rather garbled-sounding, but no less impressive, 'Lord Big-chief'. It could even be possible that the ESV prefix was more of a descriptive term (as with Eceni *Magni*), hence we return to the possibility that Prasto / Prastotagus was the name of the individual in question who, on later issues, decided to qualify his standing (perhaps under direct Roman patronage) as 'Lord' Prastotagus, a point that Amanda Chadburn noted in an article published in the March/April edition of *British Archaeology* in 2006:

> In other words we have two friendly kings, at the same time, in the same place, with very similar names, the one known from archaeological evidence and the other from historical evidence. The current academic fashion is to be extremely cautious when relating classical texts to archaeological evidence. But it would seem perverse not to consider that there is a strong possibility that Esvprasto is indeed the king Prasutagus of history.

Exactly. The chances are that PRASTO, whatever its full original form, was garbled by either by Tacitus or other contemporary authors or officials, the transformation of Celtic names into Latin causing, as we have already seen, considerable mangling, or during the textual transcription of Tacitus' works in the Middle Ages. Either way, the creation of two individuals on the basis of a single PRASTO name-form would appear unnecessarily complex. The full translation of the coin legend SVB ESVPRASTO ESCIO FECIT would therefore read 'under Lord Prasto, Escio made this'.

The facial image depicted on the PRASTO coins is an interesting one, a realistic portrait of a clean-shaven male youth with a very distinctive coiffure of long comma shaped locks and curling sideburns. It has been suggested that this might be the face of Prastotagus himself, depicted as the model Roman citizen wearing the latest fashions. This could be, and it would be very interesting if, in these latest coin issues, we possess a genuine image of a British king, modelled on contemporary portraits of the Julio-Claudian house. Unfortunately, the image could just as easily depict the then emperor, the youthful Nero, his face being placed so prominently on the coins as a way of confirming loyalty to the State.

BOUDICCA

Boudicca ('victorious one'), wife of Prasutagus / Prastotagus and member of the Ecenian royal family (65), is the only Briton appearing in this book for whom we have a description:

> In stature she was very tall, in appearance most terrifying, in the glance of her eye most fierce, and her voice was harsh; a great mass of the tawniest hair fell to

65 The monumental statue to 'Boadicea', by Westminster Bridge in London, designed by Thomas Thorncroft and officially unveiled in 1902. *Author*

her hips; around her neck was a large golden necklace; and she wore a tunic of divers colours over which a thick mantle was fastened with a brooch. This was her invariable attire

(Dio Cassius *Roman History* LXII, 2)

It is important to bear in mind that the author of this piece, Dio Cassius, was writing over a century and a half after Boudicca's death so it is possible that he is relaying only an impression of how he *thinks* a British warrior queen *ought* to have looked. Certainly Tacitus, our only other source for the period, never provided a description of Boudicca, despite possessing a direct link to the events of the time, his father-in-law Gnaeus Julius Agricola having served as a junior officer in Britain during the Great Revolt. It is possible, of course, that Dio Cassius had access to sources of information unavailable to Tacitus (that certainly is true at other times), although in the absence of any corraoborating information we can never be sure.

Boudicca exists only in the written word of her bitterest enemies, there being no independent verification of her in the coins of the period. This may not be surprising, for the coins of ESVPRASTO recovered from East Anglia and assumed to have been her husband, appear to have been among the last Celtic issues minted in Britain. After the death of Prasutagus / Prastotagus, there was no desire amogst the Eceni to slavishly emulate the ethnic markers of Rome and they may well now have returned to their indigenous culture patterns. Some modern writers have even gone as far to suggest that Boudicca herself may have been a myth, a fictional, assertive female character, created by historians like Tacitus in order to contrast with the weak and ineffectual Roman emperor, Nero. This is an interesting theory but given that we possess as much evidence for Boudicca as we have, say, for Cassivellaunos or Caratacus, we should acknowledge that she was in all probability very real.

None of the surviving sources actually refer to Boudicca as queen. Tacitus describes her simply as the *wife* of the king; Dio Cassius as a 'woman of the royal family'. Only Boudicca herself, in a pre-battle speech provided for her by Dio Cassius, calls herself 'queen', and the audience are left unsure as to whether she was genuinelly entitled to assume such a title. It is possible, given how little we understand society in Later Iron Age Britain, that Boudicca was not the recognised heir to Prastotagus, or perhaps that there was another wife, of whom we hear nothing, who held a better claim than she. More likely, perhaps, the absence of a specific title, may be due to the rather skewed world-view of Roman writers, all of whom were male and all of whom were derived from a very patriarchal Mediterranean society. For Tacitus and Dio Cassius, that a woman could rule just as effectively (if not more so) than a man was unthinkable, and we can see some of this bias when Dio Cassius comments that Boudicca was 'possessed of greater intelligence than often belongs to women' (*Roman History* LXII, 2). Perhaps, given the events of the Great Uprising against Rome, and the atrocities committed within it, neither Roman source wished to provide

Boudicca's cause with legitimacy. In their view, she was not formally a queen and therefore, having taken the title, had assumed a degree of status which had not been hers by right.

The death of Prasutagus / Prastotagus created immediate problems for the Eceni. Tacitus says that he had named Nero his heir, together with his two (unamed) daughters, 'an act of deference which he thought would place his kingdom and household beyond the risk of injury' (Tacitus *Annals* XIV, 31). This perhaps highlights the vague nature of client states within the developing province as well as the uncertain status of the clients themselves, something that a king like Prasutagus would only have been too aware. He had made his peace, we can presume, with Nero's predecessor Claudius – did the treaty still stand, with exactly the same terms, now that Claudius was dead? So far he and his family had steered the Eceni through difficult times with their status and position intact. It had not been easy, in fact some could argue that aspects of the relationship, such as the foreceable disarmament of the tribes, had been deeply humiliating, but the Eceni had survived and thrived. Roman gold and silver bullion had flooded into Norfolk, much of it being melted down and reformed into the kind of Celtic power statements that the native Briton preferred: torcs (neck rings), brooches, coins and equestrian equipment.

The finer details of the king's last will and testament ultimately mattered not one jot, Tacitus noting that:

> ... his kingdom was pillaged by centurions, his household by slaves; as though they had been prizes of war. As a beginning, his wife Boudicca was subjected to the lash and his daughters violated: all the chief men of the Icenians were stripped of their family estates, and the relatives of the king were treated as slaves
> (Tacitus *Annals* XIV, 31)

Dio Cassius provides a more prosaic, but no less plausible reason for the sunbsequent unrest:

> An excuse for the war was found in the confiscation of the sums of money that Claudius had given to the foremost Britons; for these sums, as Decianus Catus, the procurator of the island, maintained, were to be paid back. This was one reason for the uprising; another was found in the fact that Seneca, in the hope of receiving a good rate of interest, had lent to the islanders 40,000,000 sesterces that they did not want, and had afterwards called in this loan all at once and had resorted to severe measures in exacting it
> (Dio Cassius *Roman History* LXII, 2)

An unexpected recall of all loans, which certain members of the British aristocracy may have perceived as gifts, would have suddenly crippled the ruling, pro Roman classes within the Eceni. All accounts were now frozen, all royal assets seized by the emperor's debt collectors, co-ordinated through the procurator Decianus

Catus. Today in the UK, debt collection agencies are licensed and regulated and (in theory at least) operate within clearly defined legal boundaries. The majority of such agencies operate on behalf of creditors, those who originally provided the loan, either for a fixed fee or for a percentage of the amount owed. They are not permitted to misuse or misrepresent their powers, harass, detain or injure debtors in the process of reclaiming of goods or material assets. As far as we can tell, the agents of the Roman procurator were not constrained by such legal niceties. The Ecenian ruling and religious classes now found themselves at the mercy of the Roman State and, where money was concerned, the State had no qualms about getting what it wanted.

Dio Cassius echoes these sentiments in a speech that he gives to Boudicca, his leading lady in the story of the British revolt:

> You have learned by actual experience how different freedom is from slavery. Hence, although some among you may previously, through ignorance of which was better, have been deceived by the alluring promises of the Romans, yet now that you have tried both, you have learned how great a mistake you made in preferring an imported despotism to your ancestral mode of life, and you have come to realize how much better is poverty with no master than wealth with slavery. For what treatment is there of the most shameful or grievous sort that we have not suffered ever since these men made their appearance in Britain? Have we not been robbed entirely of most of our possessions, and those the greatest, while for those that remain we pay taxes? Besides pasturing and tilling for them all our other possessions, do we not pay a yearly tribute for our very bodies? How much better it would be to have been sold to masters once for all than, possessing empty titles of freedom, to have to ransom ourselves every year! How much better to have been slain and to have perished than to go about with a tax on our heads!
> (*Roman History* LXII, 4)

Although these are the words of a Briton as filtered through the cultural perspective of a Roman, they are worth noting, if only to provide an alternative perspective to life in a client kingdom.

The overtly harsh treatment of the Eceni, a tribe allied to the Roman cause, may appear strange, an action not particularly designed to win the hearts and minds of the native elite. Unfortunately it *does* reflect the way in which some Roman officials viewed an overseas posting: multiple opportunities to get rich quick. In the absence of war, involving the indescriminate plunder of towns and the rounding up of prisoners for the slave market, opportunities to make money were relatively few and far between. A Roman financial administrator, especially one on the take, would have seen the uncertainty surrounding succession and status within the Eceni as the perfect chance to make a huge amount of cash. Hence, in the short term, tax revenue could be supplemented by extreme examples of rampant profiteering. Ultimately, such activities were to prove hugely detrimental to the new province.

66 ... are they? More than any other aspect of Later Iron Age culture, it is the druids that capture the public imagination. *Author*

DRUIDS

It is worth taking a brief diversion at this point to highlight one of the more significant of Established Facts to permeate the literature of Roman Britain: the existence of Druidism. That the Druids were not only enmeshed within all aspects of Later Iron Age life, but that they were the motivating force behind the Boudiccan Revolt of AD 60, today seems something of a certainty (*66*). In 2006, for example, David Mattingly, in his book *An Imperial Possession*, could confidently assert that the Druids:

> Were a particular threat to Rome in that they were both the teachers and the practitioners of native religion and were the most likely focus for cultural resistance to Rome. In common with more recent empires, the Romans encountered strong revitalization movements after periods of apparent pacification. The druids were a focus for such resistance precisely because of their overlapping religious and political prestige
> (Mattingly 2006, 105)

Later adding that the attack on Anglesey by the Roman governor Suetonius Paulinus in AD 59/60 was the spark that ignited revolt within the Eceni for 'it is probable that in their hour of need the Druids did their best to stir up trouble elsewhere in Britain' (Mattingly 2006, 106). Mattingly is of course only the last in a long line of writers to make the link between Boudicca and the Druids. It is, however, a sobering reminder of the limitations of historical and archaeological fact that at no stage can such a link ever be proven. It is, in short, a fantasy; a plausible-sounding if ultimately unfounded fiction. In fact, if you want to be particularly pedantic, it is stretching the evidence to even suggest that the Druids contributed anything to Iron Age political or religious life beyond the confines of Anglesey. If they were a firm part of Later Iron Age culture in Britain, as most modern writers stress, then they left no mark in either the literature or in the material culture of the period. They may have been there, but proving it is nigh on impossible.

That the Druids existed, at least in one part of Gaul during the mid to late first century AD, is not disputed. Julius Caesar, in his *Gallic Wars*, breaks off his account of the events of 53 BC to explicitly refer to them in the following terms:

The Druids are engaged in things sacred. They conduct the public and the private sacrifices, and interpret all matters of religion. Large numbers of young men go to them for instruction, and they are greatly honoured by the people. In almost all disputes, between communities or individuals, the Druids act as judges; and if any crime has been perpetrated, if murder has been committed, if there be any dispute about an inheritance, if any about boundaries, these same persons decide it; they decree rewards and punishments. If anyone, either in a private or public capacity, has not submitted to their decision, they ban him from the sacrifices. This is regarded amongst the Gauls as the most severe punishment. Those who are banned in this way are esteemed to be sacrilegious criminals: all shun them, and avoid their society and conversation, lest they receive some evil from their contact; nor is justice administered to them when seeking it, nor is any dignity bestowed on them. There is one Druid above all the rest, with supreme authority over them. Upon his death, he is succeeded by whichever of the others is most distinguished. If there are many equal, the election is made by vote, though sometimes they even fight to decide who will be their leader. These assemble at a fixed period of the year in a consecrated place in the territory of the Carnutes, which is reckoned the central region of the whole of Gaul. People who have disputes to settle assemble from every part, and submit to their decrees and determinations. This doctrine is supposed to have been devised in Britain, and to have been brought from there into Gaul; even today those who want to study the doctrine in greater detail usually go to Britain to learn there. The Druids are exempt from military service and do not pay taxes with the rest. Induced by such great advantages, many embrace this profession of their own accord, while others are sent by their parents and relatives. They are said there to learn by heart a great number of verses; accordingly some remain in training for twenty years. They do not think it right to commit their teachings to writing, though in almost all other matters, in their public and private transactions, they use Greek characters. That practice they seem to me to have adopted for two reasons; because they neither desire their doctrines to be divulged among the masses, and they did not want their pupils to rely on the written word and so neglect to train their memories. For it does usually happen that if people depend on writing, they relax their diligence in learning thoroughly, and their memories become less efficient. The Druids attach particular importance to the belief that the soul does not become extinct, but passes after death from one body to another, and they think that this belief is the most effective way to encourage valour, the fear of death being disregarded. They hold long discussions about the stars and their motion, about the extent of the world and the earth, about the nature of things, and about the power and the majesty of the immortal gods, subjects in which they also give instruction to their pupils ... The Gallic people as a whole are deeply superstitious; and on that account those suffering from severe diseases, and they who engaged in battle, either sacrifice men as victims, or vow that they will sacrifice them, and employ the Druids as the performers of those sacrifices; because they think that unless the life of a man be offered for the life of a man, the mind of the immortal gods can not be appeased. Some have figures of vast size, the limbs of which formed of wickerwork they fill with living men, which being set on fire, the men perish enveloped in the flames. They consider that the sacrifice of those caught in the act of theft, or in armed robbery, or any other offence, is more acceptable to the immortal gods; but when a supply of that class is wanting, they have recourse to the sacrifice of even the innocent

(Caesar *Gallic Wars*, VI, 13-16)

I felt that it was important to quote the section by Caesar in full, for this is the only ancient source to document the activities, belief systems and organisational structure of the Druids. Everything that you have ever heard or read about the Druids and their position in Iron Age society is based upon this single piece of text. This is it – full stop. Other Roman and Greek writers, such as Pliny the elder, certainly do mention the Druids, albeit as a shorthand for priest or 'religious leader', but none go into the detail of Caesar's writing. Bearing in mind that Caesar is our only source and that, as noted before, he is by no means an objective historian or social anthropologist, writing to entertain not educate his audience, we must be very careful of taking everything (or indeed *anything*) that he says as the literal truth. He demonised his foe and, in the case of the Germans and Britons, made them every bit the savage barbarian. He was, furthermore, only describing the religions and religious practices of those tribes in *Gaul* with which he was familiar. He did not say that things were comparable in Britain. He may further have misunderstood the significance or nature of religion in Iron Age society. He may have made it all up.

Pliny the elder, writing in the early 70s AD, but making use of Caesar as a primary source, notes that:

The Gallic provinces too, were pervaded by the magic art, and that even down to a period within memory; for it was the emperor Tiberius that put down their Druids, and all that tribe of wizards and physicians. But why make further mention of these prohibitions, with reference to an art which has now crossed the very Ocean even, and has penetrated to the void recesses of Nature? At the present day, struck with

fascination, Britannia still cultivates this art, and that, with ceremonials so august, that she might almost seem to have been the first to communicate them ... Such being the fact, then, we cannot too highly appreciate the obligation that is due to the Roman people, for having put an end to those monstrous rites, in accordance with which, to murder a man was to do an act of the greatest devoutness, and to eat his flesh was to secure the highest blessings of health
(Pliny the elder *Natural History* XXX, 4)

The most interesting section in Caesar's description of the Druids, other than their apparent delight in human sacrifice, is his almost throwaway comments that the doctrine of Druidism had been 'devised in Britain' and that in his day (50s BC) people can go to Britain to learn more. Pliny is equally vague, noting that in his day (*c.* AD 75) Britain 'still cultivates this art'. These represent the only time that a specific link is made between the religious classes that Caesar observed in central Gaul, with communities in Britain. The references are vague, but may indicate that Druidism was progressively on the wane, perhaps any Druidic groups left in Britain acting more in an advisory capacity than the more developed system of justice and conflict resolution described in first-century Gaul. It is also worth noting that, according to Pliny, Tiberius 'put down' the Druids: a rare act of religious suppression within the otherwise generally tolerant Roman world. This act was, it must be remembered, excused by the apparently 'monstrous rites' of cannibalism and human sacrifice, not because the Druids were perceived to be turbulent priests or religious fanatics stirring up political dissent. Ironic perhaps that the Roman State frowned upon the Druids for sacrificing people in religious ceremonies, but was more than happy to endorse mass execution for the sake of entertainment in the amphitheatre.

67 The Menai Strait (*Afon Menai*) seperating Anglesey from mainland Wales. *Author*

The evidence for the nature, importance and general existence of the Druids in Britain can therefore be seen to derive from two discrete, not to say brief, asides. One third and final source appears, at face value, to place the Druids at the very epicentre of the Great Revolt. Written by Tacitus, in the early years of the second century and relating to the Roman attack, led by Suetonius Paullinus, upon Anglesey in AD 59 or 60 (67), it has been used to generate all manner of theories concerning the nature of Druidic power in Britain:

> He prepared accordingly to attack the island of *Mona*, which had a considerable population of its own, having served as a haven for refugees; and, in view of the shallow and variable channel, constructed a flotilla of boats with flat bottoms. By this method the infantry crossed; the cavalry, who followed, did so by fording or, in deeper water, by swimming at the side of their horses. On the beach stood the adverse array, a serried mass of arms and men, with women flitting between the ranks. In the style of Furies, in robes of deathly black and with dishevelled hair, they brandished their torches; while a circle of Druids, lifting their hands to heaven and showering imprecations, struck the troops with such an awe at the extraordinary spectacle that, as though their limbs were paralysed, they exposed their bodies to wounds without an attempt at movement. Then, reassured by their general, and inciting each other never to flinch before a band of females and fanatics, they charged behind the standards, cut down all who met them, and enveloped the enemy in his own flames. The next step was to install a garrison among the conquered population, and to demolish the groves consecrated to their savage cults: for they considered it a duty to consult their deities by means of human entrails (*Annals* XIV)

This is another undeniably dramatic scene from the quill of the Roman historian, but its purpose in the *Annals* is to serve only as a prelude to the Boudiccan war. Hence Tacitus' audience, hearing that the last haven of resistance, harbouring all manner of dangerous fugitives, has been taken, its barbaric rites abruptly curtailed, would reel in shock at the sentence concluding chapter 30: 'While he was thus occupied, the sudden revolt of the province was announced to Suetonius'. This is the perfect Tacitean cliff-hanger, a surprise ending leaving the audience wanting to know what happens next. The expected climax to the war has not materialised; something far worse than mere war has erupted behind the lines; insurrection in an area considered to be safe, secure and undeniably Roman.

It is hard, in this light, to be sure whether the attack on Anglesey and the revolt of the Eceni are in any sense connected, other than in a literary way, the one adding a dramatic prelude to the other. Was Anglesey merely the focus of the Druidic faith, the spiritual home of Druidism to which all British, Gallic or Germanic devotees naturally migrated, or were there Druids in mainland Britain acting in defence of their besieged colleagues by attempting to open a second front in East Anglia? In the absence of hard evidence, especially from Tacitus or Dio Cassius who would undoubtedly have told us if there been the merest whiff of a religious fifth column, the Druid-connection, although tantalisingly plausible, cannot be sustained. As far as we know, Anglesey was the be all and end all to the Druid faith; certainly Druidism is not mentioned elsewhere in Britannia. Worse, Tacitus may just have been using artistic licence, grabbing a term which a Roman audience was already familiar; a word already resonant with fear, loathing and suspicion; a barbarian word mired deep within the filth of human sacrifice. Certainly the description of a sacred island populated by fire-brand wielding, dishevelled furies, fresh from the altars of blood and wicker men, screaming curses and abuse at their Menai-Strait crossing foe, is a potent one. Who says Tacitus didn't spice it up somewhat?

Tacitus' invasion story is so intoxicating a tale, the stark truth, that in the whole of Britain, Druids (and then only 'a circle of Druids') are only ever placed once, on Anglesey, is frequently lost; the 'truth' of the Druidic-inspired resistance movement having become firmly embedded within all historical literature. Sometimes the desire to find Druids everywhere has reached bizarre proportions. In the book *The Life and Death of a Druid Prince* by Anne Ross and Don Robins, the expert analysis of Lindow Man, the famous Iron Age 'body in the bog', takes an unexpected twist:

> ... on the one hand he had the appearance of an unblemished sacrificial victim and on the other the physique of a powerful man of action who was not a warrior. Unlike a Celtic warrior he had a full beard rather than the sweeping, tusk-like moustaches so evident in Roman descriptions of Celtic warriors ... If we went back to the earlier premise that there were no idle aristocrats in Celtic times, and we were convinced that Lindow Man was not a warrior, there were two possible careers or occupations that would have been open to him: bard or priest ... there was little likelihood that a bard would be killed or sacrificed, because of his great power within the tribe, and the havoc his colleagues would wreak on the reputations of any who dared to strike such a blow. And Lindow Man did not look like a bard. His surviving hand and fingernails provided no evidence for any practice in harping: there were no calluses, no chipping or roughening of the beautiful nails. We are left, then, with but one choice: he was a pagan priest. Since he was a Celt, that meant only one thing. He was a druid
> (Ross and Robins 1989, 50)

That the hypothesising does not end here, however, is unfortunate, the authors doing little to aid their cause by further suggesting that they believe the name of the man recovered from Lindow to have been 'Lovernios' (primarily because he wore a fox fur armband and may himself have had red hair – Lovernios being one Celtic variant for 'fox') and was originally from Ireland. Having arrived too late to help his colleagues fight Rome, the authors suggest that Lovernios, 'having witnessed the destruction of the British Druids, could not simply return to a now vulnerable Ireland' and so was sacrificed by his entourage. Although a profoundly colourful and exuberantly written book, *The Life and Death of a Druid Prince* is a prime example of how interpretation can far exceed the limits of archaeological inference. All we can really say about Lindow Man is how he died, when he died, how old he was at death, how he may have appeared in life and what his last meal comprised, together with some informed statements concerning his perceived ethnicity and cultural background. All else is fiction.

COLCHESTER AND LONDON: CITIES OF OPPRESSION

The Eceni were joined in their new found 'liberty' by other disenfranchised groups, most notably the Trinobantes, a client state since the time of Mandubracius in the mid 50s BC. The case of the Trinobantes highlights another element in the failure to successfully transmit *Romanitas* to the British. The Trinobantes were evidently the losers of AD 43 and its aftermath, for they had been singled out as the enemies of Rome. Their aristocracy broken and their liberty restricted, the Trinobantes had also lost their capital, the *oppidum* of *Camulodunum*. *Camulodunum*, appears to have been the main focus of the Roman advance under the emperor Claudius following the destabilisation of the south-east during the AD 40s. Having served as the centrepiece for Claudius' victory in Britain, the *oppidum* was first heavily garrisoned, by the *XX Valeria* Legion, before being rebuilt, not as a *civitas* or tribal town, but as a *colonia*. *Coloniae*, or 'colony-towns' were founded in freshly conquered enemy territory. Their purpose was to act as a model town (to help Romanise the natives) but also to perform as a military reserve, premium space within the *Colonia* being allocated to soldiers approaching retirement age. *Camulodunum* was now re-branded, its old tribal name being rejected in favour of *Colonia Claudia Victricensis* 'the city of Claudius' victory'.

Colonia Claudia Victricensis seems to have been provided with all the luxuries expected for a classical city, including an organised street grid, established directly over the earlier internal road network of the legionary fortress, a forum (the prestige market centre), basilica (the focal point of local government authority), a theatre, shops and baths. It also had a temple complex, a large religious building dedicated to deified emperor Claudius. Nothing of the temple superstructure survives, though the foundations suggest a substantial building set within a large sacred precinct. It was, according to Tacitus, a 'citadel of an eternal tyranny' whose priests, chosen by the State from amongst the native aristocracy 'were bound under the pretext of religion to pour out their fortunes like water' (*Annals* XIV, 31). Whether the main residents of the town, the retired soldiery, appreciated their new surroundings is unclear. Most of them may have lived in the fort whilst still on active service. Now they were being 'rewarded' by the state with property built within incompletely demolished military buildings. Worse, they were being encouraged to live in peace with the very people whom, only a few months or years before, they were killing, imprisoning and generally conquering. 'The veterans,' so Tacitus tells us, 'were acting as though they had received a free gift of the entire country, driving the natives from their homes, ejecting them from their lands' (*Annals* XIV, 31). It is clear, in retrospect, that experimental 'model-town' of *Colonia Claudia Victriensis* was on the verge of catastrophic failure.

It would seem that the inhabitants of the town were aware that 'something was up'. Presumably the signs of discontent within the surrounding Trinobantian population were clear enough; perhaps a whispering campaign was starting to unnerve the citizens. Tacitus, in a piece of pure theatre, outlined a range of supernatural occurances that foretold the city's imminent demise:

> ... for no apparent reason, the statue of Victory at Camulodunum fell, with its back turned as if in retreat from the enemy. Women, converted into maniacs by excitement, cried that destruction was at hand and that alien cries had been heard in the senate-house: the theatre had rung with shrieks, and in the estuary of the Thames had been seen a vision of the ruined colony. The Ocean had appeared blood-red and the ebbing tide had left behind it what looked to be human corpses, these indications were read by the Britons with hope and by the veterans with corresponding alarm
> (*Annals* XIV, 32)

This is one of the rare occaisions that accounts of a single event, recorded by both Tacitus *and* Dio Cassius, may be compared, a luxury we do not possess for the narrative of the AD 43 invasion. Here, when also outlining the premonitions of disaster, Dio evidently paraphrases Tacitus:

> ... at night there was heard to issue from the senate-house foreign jargon mingled with laughter, and from the theatre outcries and lamentations, though no mortal man had uttered the words or the groans; houses were seen under the water in the river Thames, and the ocean between the island and Gaul once grew blood-red at flood tide
> (*Roman History* LXII, 1)

Colonia Claudia Victriensis lay undefended; the rampart surrounding the old legionary fort had been levelled, the ditch filled in to make way for housing. Apart from the retired soldiers, some of whom may have (illegally) retained armour or swords, there was, according to Tacitus, only a 'small body of troops' in the town. An appeal to the *procurator* (the provincial finance administrator) Catus Decianus in *Londinium* resulted in the arrival of less than 200 men 'without proper weapons'. There was no preparation made within the town, bemoans Tacitus, no creation of defensible positions, no mass evacuation of women and children. When Boudicca's army descended upon the city, those with any sense fled to the temple of Claudius, where they held out for two days. No quarter was given; no prisoners taken.

Archaeological evidence for the destruction is not hard to find. Although it is often difficult, not to say downright dangerous, to conflate archaeological discoveries with an historic event, the thick deposit of charcoal, baked clay and burnt earth that lies guiltily beneath the city of Colchester like a soiled mattress, cannot really be associated with anything else. The deposit masks burnt, high status pottery, molten lumps of metal and glass, food remains, furniture and collapsed wall plaster. To the west of the city, one of the cemeteries also seems to have been desecrated, tombstones thrown over and vandalised (68, 69). The city

Above left: 68 The tombstone of Marcus Favonius Facilis, centurion of the *XX Valeria* Legion from Colchester, Essex, and now in Colchester Castle Museum. Damage to the face may have been sustained during the sack of *Colonia Claudia Victriensis* in AD 60. *Otto Fein Archive*

Above right: 69 Tombstone of Longinus, a Thracian auxilliary trooper from Colchester, Essex, and now in Colchester Castle Museum. Damage to the face of Longinus may also have been sustained during the sack of *Colonia Claudia Victriensis* in AD 60. *Otto Fein Collection*

Left: 70 Bronze head from the River Alde, near Saxmundham, Suffolk, now in the British Museum. The piece, which has been removed from the main body with an axe, is usually thought to be that of the emperor Claudius, possibly part of a group associated with the temple to the deified Claudius in *Colonia Claudia Victriensis* (Colchester), sacked by Boudicca in AD 60. Alternatively, the portrait could represent the emperor Nero, at, or shortly after, his accession in AD 54. As the adopted son and heir of Claudius, the piece could still have been in Colchester and therefore looted during the Great Revolt, but it could also represent the product of *Damnatio memoriae*, the eradication of memory which followed Nero's suicide in AD 68. *Otto Fein Collection*

was recovered and rebuilt after the revolt was over, but the stain runs deep; the horror cannot easily be wiped away. Further afield, evidence of burning detected at a number of early villa sites in Essex and Cambridgeshire, may indicate the murder of landowners and the destruction of their rural estates, but the dating and associations are less secure than that recovered from Colchester.

One of the more famous finds, apparently associated with the sack of Colchester, is a head of bronze, recovered from the River Alde near Saxmundham, Suffolk in 1907. Established Fact tells us that the head, now on display in the British Museum, is that of the emperor Claudius, its deposition in the river Alde being due to its looting from the temple precinct during the sack of *Colonia Claudia Victriensis* in AD 60. Certainly the head has been forced from its original context (*70*), the axe blow to the back of the neck and subsequent jagged tear around the throat are evidence enough for that, but its identification as Claudius, fourth emperor of Rome, may be misplaced. The portrait, which seems to possess none of the features associated with Claudius, such as the high forehead, receding hairline, double chin and fleshy mouth, does, however, possess characteristics of the young Nero, especially evident in the hairstyle, mouth, eyes and ever-so-slightly lopsided ears. As Nero, the piece is still likely to represent a trophy, violently removed from Colchester before being deposited in the river, but it could conceivably also relate to the period after Nero's suicide in AD 68 when, as an enemy of the state, all images of the then reviled emperor were overthrown.

As *Colonia Claudia Victriensis* was being attacked, the closest Legion to the area, the *IX Hispana*, alerted by some unknown intelligence, raced south to relieve the city. Unfortunately, the Legion's commanding officer, Quintus Petilius Cerialis, later to become governor of the province, fell straight into an ambush, the Britons 'slaughtering the infantry to a man' (Tacitus *Annals* XIV, 32). Cerialis managed to extricate himself with some difficulty and fled to safety, with the remnants of his cavalry. One city, one quarter of the garrison of Briton and an unknown number of civilians were dead. 'At no other time in truth was Britain more agitated or in a state of greater uncertainty' Tacitus was to later comment, 'our veterans slaughtered, our colonies burnt, our armies cut off, we were then contending for safety' (Tacitus *Agricola* 5). Sensing that ultimate victory was in their grasp, Boudicca's army descended upon *Londinium*.

Londinium or London was the first-century equivalent of a Wild West shanty town, and probably just as lawless. It was not, at this stage in its history, the priemier city of Britain, nor even a major town in its own right, but business was booming; *Londinium* was a commercial success. Here were the riverside wharves, the warehouses and store rooms of provincial commerce, the shops and markets, the banks and offices of the tax collector, *procurator* Decianus Catus. At this point in the Tacitus narrative, the governor, Suetonius Pauulinus, arrived in London, having heard news of the uprising whilst overturning the native altars on Anglesey. Swiftly appraising himself of the situation, he realised he could do nothing to save the city and, if he stayed, was likely to become a victim himself. Taking with him those 'capable of accompanying the march', Suetonius left Londinium to its fate.

The end came quickly, Tacitus recording that:

> ... the enemy neither took captive nor sold into captivity; there was none of the other commerce of war; he was hasty with slaughter and the gibbet, with arson and the cross (*Annals* XIV, 33)

Dio Cassius again paraphrases Tacitus, but adds detail of his own, either culled from an alternative primary source, or derived from his own fertile imagination in order to titillate or horrify his audience:

> Those who were taken captive by the Britons were subjected to every known form of outrage. The worst and most bestial atrocity committed by their captors was the following. They hung up naked the noblest and most distinguished women and then cut off their breasts and sewed them to their mouths, in order to make the victims appear to be eating them; afterwards they impaled the women on sharp skewers run lengthwise through the entire body. All this they did to the accompaniment of sacrifices, banquets, and wanton behaviour, not only in all their other sacred places, but particularly in the grove of Andate. This was their name for Victory, and they regarded her with most exceptional reverence
> (*Roman History* LXII, 7)

VERULAMIUM: VICTIM OF 'ETHNIC CLEANSING'?

What happened to *Camulodunum*, *oppidum* of the Trinobantes under the Roman provincial government, namely conquest, garrison and total re-branding, is in marked contrast to the Catuvellaunian *oppidum* at *Verulamium* which, following the removal of Roman armed units in the south and east, was modified into a regional town. *Verulamium* was furthermore accorded the status of a *municipium*, a self-governing community of Roman citizens. The disparity between the treatment between the two tribes presumably had its origins in the way in which their respective leaders, Togidubnus / Togodumnus and Caratacus, greeted the arrival of Rome. Caratacus actively campaigned against the Roman army, and was later hunted down in the mountains of North Wales. Togidubnus, however, sided with Rome and was well rewarded by both Claudius and Nero. It is probable that the followers of the pro Roman Togidubnus were accorded high status in the *municipium* of *Verulamium*, whilst their more anti Roman neighbours within the Trinobantes became a conquered people possessing no official status within the new political system. When the revolt kicked-off, *Verulamium* was an obvious target.

The enmity that existed between Catuvellauni and Trinobantes and Eceni had, if we believe the writings of Julius Caesar, been simmering for well over a century. When Caesar invaded Britain in 54 BC he found that the (unnamed) tribe of the British warlord Cassivellaunos was the major destabilising force in central south-eastern Britain. The tribe, which as argued earlier were almost certainly the forerunners of the

Catuvellauni, had fought 'perpetual wars' against all the 'other states' of the region (*Gallic Wars* V, 11) presumably during the course of major territorial acquisition. All infighting between the disparate tribal groups was temporarily suspended by the arrival of Caesar, Rome, for the time being at least, representing the greater threat. Whether the tribes *elected* Cassivellaunos as 'over-king', (literally Ver-Cassivellaunos), for his experience in war or whether he took ultimate control for himself, we have no way of knowing. What is clear, however, is that when Cassivellaunos' unity government started to unravel, it was the Trinobantes, followed immediately by the Cenimagni (Great Eceni) who were among the first to defect. Their desire to see the British warlord overthrown was to prove greater than their wish to hurl Caesar and his army back into the sea. The events of 54 BC had conspired to create the perfect opportunity to neutralise Cassivellaunos once and for all.

Following the conclusion of Caesar's British expedition, the Roman general 'strictly forbade Cassivellaunos to harm Mandubracius or the Trinobantes', a clause in the armistice that must have enraged the warlord. We do not know how long the agreement on the cessation of hostilities between the tribes of Cassivellaunos and Mandubracius lasted, but coin evidence, together with the later presence of pro-Roman kings in Rome, has usually been taken to indicate that Cassivellaunos' people, by this stage the Catu-Vellauni, were replaying the old game and terrorising their neighbours. It may appear unlikely that tribal grievances could survive and fester for over a century, from 54 BC to AD 60, but sadly modern experience in areas as different as Northern Ireland, Iraq, Bosnia Herzegovina, Georgia and Afghanistan demonstrate, almost on a daily basis, that events occurring generations before, can still impact upon the present in very real and terrifying ways. As Stuart Laycock has convincingly demonstrated in his 2008 book, *Britannia: the Failed State*, tribal loyalties and clan memories can last for centuries; each new generation being taught the concept of hate.

Verulamium may well have been deliberately targeted because of deep-seated tribal tensions between the Catuvellauni and their neighbours; Ecenian and Trinobantian pay-back for decades of hurt. The fact that it was an obvious centre of Romanitas, proudly displaying its new-found status, was another good reason to eradicate it. Tacitus chides the British rebels for 'their relish for plunder and wish to avoid hard work' which ensured that they 'steered clear of the forts and military garrisons and made for places rich in spoil but unprotected by any defending force' (*Annals* XIV, 33), but this strategy made sound sense. Those facing the might of Rome in open battle ended up dead; those who employed guerrilla tactics, ambushing troops, burning crops and attacking soft targets, avoiding well-defended military installations in the process, could wear down the Roman resolve. Given that Nero had already considered pulling out of Britain, such a strategy could reap dividends.

Aside from the more obvious ethnic / tribal motivation for attacking *Verulamium*, other considerations may have driven the rebels. The reasons for the uprising, as already noted, were essentially two-fold: the mistreatment of the Ecenian aristocracy following the death of Prastotagus and Trinobantian hatred for the colonists at *Colonia Claudia Victriensis*. By the time *Londinium* had been sacked and the offices of the *procurator* destroyed, the revolt may have taken on a life of its own, with many people, each with their own discrete agenda, now joining the call to arms. The uprising was in danger of losing its primary aim, revenge against Rome and the rejection of Roman authority, and descending into a free-for-all in which any target was fair game. The sack of *Verulamium* could therefore have had as much to do with indiscriminate looting and sating of blood-lust, than the organised destruction of identifiable Roman targets. To be fair, Boudicca is not mentioned by either Tacitus or Dio Cassius with respect to the burning of *Colonia Claudia Victriensis, Londinium* or *Verulamium*, she is only the initial fomenter of discord and the rallying speech-maker around whom the Britons converge in a final battle against Suetonius Paulinus. Boudicca's main objective may therefore not have been the total annihilation of Rome and her allies, but only the forced removal of Roman tax-collectors from Ecenian territory. The insurgency, having started, however, was prey to other groups, each with their own private grievance, and could easily be hijacked.

Both Tacitus and Dio Cassius present a relatively clear view of the rebellion, its causes and impact. Tacitus describes the destruction of three cities, Dio Cassius mentions only two. Neither indicate that the insurgency spread further than the basic East Anglia / Midlands zone implied in their respective narratives. That the concept of open revolt may have infected areas beyond, has rarely been considered, at least in mainstream literature, although many modern historians have suggested that the reason why the *II Augusta* Legion failed to join Suetonius Paulinius in his efforts to destroy Boudicca, was that they were tied down in the west country (Devon / Somerset / Dorset) putting down minor uprisings there. Archaeology has also presented evidence that may question the standard Colchester / London / St Albans / final battle sequence of events, most notably at excavations conducted in the Roman towns of Winchester and Silchester (71). At Winchester, examination of Roman levels during the 1960s found evidence that was broadly consistent with that recorded from London and Colchester, suggesting that *Venta Belgarum* (or at least bits of it) may have been hit by a catastrophic fire around the middle of the first century AD. As Established Fact tells us that Winchester was not destroyed by Boudicca, the 'Boudiccan-period' fires in the town can't have anything to do with her – a wonderfully circular and eternally self perpetuating argument. Similarly at Silchester, fieldwork conducted in 2008 found widespread evidence of fire, dated to between AD 50 and 75, accompanied by the blocking of wells and demolition of buildings. The director of excavations, Michael Fulford has further made the observation that, following the fire, the town street grid was re-laid on a completely different orientation. As the town was designed to serve the Atrebates, a key pro-Roman power in the region, one has to wonder, as with the destruction of *Verulamium*, whether such targeting was opportunistic or ethnically inspired.

Tacitus is ultimately largely quiet about the fate that befell the citizens of *Verulamium*, noting only that their numbers contributed to the 'seventy thousand Roman citizens and allies' who died during the destruction of the British cities (*Annals* XIV, 33). The pattern of evidence recovered from excavations conducted in the city, combined with that from Winchester and Silchester, although not as dramatic as that recorded from Colchester and London, seems to tell the same story of multiple fires and the destruction (or at least semi-demolition) of all buildings.

Suetonius finally managed to face the British insurgents at a place, today unfortunately unknown, where his troops could not easily be ambushed: 'a narrow defile … secured in the rear by a wood' (Tacitus *Annals* XIV, 34). He had with him the *XIV Gemina* Legion and elements of the *XX Valeria*, together will any auxilliary units that he had been able to muster on his march south from Anglesey. The *IX Hispana* and *II Augusta* Legions, comprsing half the elite garrison of Britain, would not be joining him; the IX had already been heavily mauled outside of Colchester whilst the II may have been otherwise engaged in conflict in the south-west. In all he had around 10,000 men. Before him the army of insurgents numbered between 80,000 (the final death toll provided by Tacitus) and 230,000 (Dio Cassius). The sheer size of Boudicca's army proved its downfall, for, after failing to break through the Roman shield wall in one frenzied charge, the Britons were hemmed in, those trying to retreat finding themselves unable to do so, whilst the restricted nature of the landscape ensured they could not easily surround the enemy. Driven back upon the large number of camp followers and spectators, the Britons were butchered, Tacitus calmly recording that 'the troops gave no quarter even to the women: the baggage animals themselves had been speared and added to the pile of bodies' (*Annals* XIV, 37). Paulinus and his troops won a victory so complete, that, according to our Roman sources, the revolt collapsed overnight. Boudicca, we are told, 'ended her days by poison'.

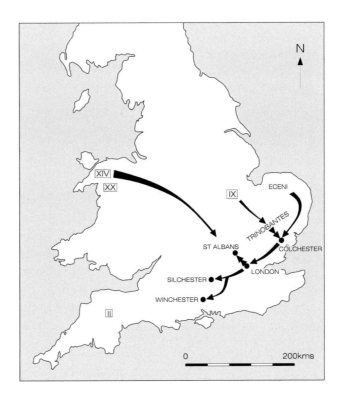

71 Map showing the major events in the Boudiccan Revolt of AD 60/61. The Eceni and Trinobantes destroy Colchester and ambush a relief army, the *IX Hispana* Legion. The Governor, Suetonius Paulinus, races from Anglesey to London, but decides he cannot defend the city. The Eceni and Trinobantes sack London and St Albans, then turn their attention to Silchester and Winchester. Togidubnus and the pro-Roman tribes to the south fight to protect their interests whilst Paulinus, together with the *XIV Gemina* and *XX Valeria* Legions, defeat Boudicca and the rebellion is crushed.

8

TOGIDUBNUS AND NERO: THE PATH OF LEAST RESISTANCE

What first made the emperor Nero unpopular amongst his people was not the rumour that he had started the Great Fire of Rome, that came much later, but that he had profited from it. The year was AD 64 and the fire, which Tacitus later described as being 'more terrible than any other that has struck Rome in terms of the violence of the flames' (Tacitus, *Annals* XV, 38) had burned for well over a week, devastating a large area of the eternal city. Of Rome's 14 districts, three were completely destroyed whilst a further seven were badly damaged. Nero, who had been out of the city when the fire had started, returned to find part of his new imperial residence, the *Domus Transitoria*, ablaze. Taking shelter with his retinue, the emperor allegedly 'dressed up in theatrical clothes' and proceeded to sing 'of the destruction of Troy' (Suetonius, *Nero* 38), an act which perhaps understandably did not endear him much to his immediate entourage. When the flames finally abated, the emperor helped to coordinate the relief effort but then, in what later turned out to public relations catastrophe, started to clear an area of around 80 hectares within the old city centre. It was here that he now planned to build his new home.

The *Domus Aurea*, or 'Golden House', is the name given to the complex of buildings designed by architects Severus and Celer for the emperor Nero following the Great Fire. It was the sheer extravagance of the building project that was truly shocking, for in the *Domus Aurea* Severus and Celer created an artificial rural idyll in the very heart of the city. The scheme that the emperor commissioned comprised, not a single great house or palace, but an impressive collection of luxurious villas and bathing establishments set across both the Esquiline and Caelian hills and the valley between them. The whole was aesthetically and tastefully created within an artificial parkscape, a humanly constructed area of forests, 'sacred groves', colonnades and an ornamental lake. The former heart of Rome was cut out in order to develop a rustic folly; the reality of town life replaced by a garish fantasy. Like all aristocratic families in Rome, the emperor now had his town house and rural retreat, but Nero's grand design surpassed all others in the sheer scale of its ambition.

Unfortunately, little of the ground plan survives, later emperors choosing to ignore, and then finally demolish the houses of Rome's foremost megalomaniac. One section, known as the Esquiline Wing (or the 'Pavilion of the Oppian Hill') has survived, but only because its rooms were filled with rubble so that the ground level could be raised in order to build the great Flavian Amphitheatre, known today as the Colosseum. When the buried remains of the Esquiline Wing were revealed in the fifteenth century the vibrancy of the images caused a stir. Among frequent visitors to the site were the Renaissance artists Perugino, Ghirlandaio, Pinturicchio, Filippino Lippi and Raphael, all of whom were inspired by the freshness of the paintwork, the dramatic use of colour and texture and the breathtaking beauty of the design.

The rich internal schemes of the *Domus Aurea* were further supplemented by a range of Hellenistic sculptures, generated through Nero's pillaging of artistic sites in Greece. Amongst the statues looted were pieces taken from a monument dedicated to Attalus I from the Acropolis in Pergamun. These sculptures are of particular interest, for they were part of a victory group designed to commemorate the defeat of the Galatians, a vigorous Celtic people, by king Attalus around 230 BC. The Galatians, depicted at the very moment of their defeat, are all committing suicide rather than endure capture and slavery. Two of the more famous pieces from the group show a Celtic noblemen, plunging a sword deep into his heart having just slit the throat of his wife. A second, universally referred to as 'the Dying Gaul', depicts a mortally wounded warrior, naked but for his gold torc, sprawling onto his shield. The significance of these sculptured pieces is that Nero, less than three years on from the humiliating events of the Boudiccan Revolt in Britain, chose to decorate the dining room of his new house with the dramatic scenes of a Celtic people in defeat.

The uprising of AD 60/1 had resulted in the near total destruction of levelled at least three cities and the deaths of many thousands of citizens, soldiers, provincials and natives. The whole of Rome's investment in Britain had been at stake and, had it not been for the swift action of the governor, Suetonius Paulinus, then the loss of the province would have been inevitable. If the revolt had succeeded, then the political fallout for Nero and his advisors would have been severe, especially as the key grievance of the rebels had been the rapaciousness of both emperor and his delegated officials. At the end of the revolt, many of the British leaders, including (apparently) Queen Boudicca herself, had taken their lives rather than risk capture, something that mirrored the final actions of the defeated Galatians in the sculptures from Pergamun. Did Nero particularly relish the installation of these stone figures in the *Domus Aurea*? Did their setting, in the Octagon Suite, the main banqueting hall of the Esquiline Wing, represent an eternal monument to his victory over the forces of barbarism? We shall never know for sure but it is certainly a very tantalising possibility.

TOGIDUBNUS THE GREAT

Tacitus' comment in the *Agricola*, that king Togidubnus remained loyal 'down to our times' could be taken as indicating that the Great British King survived into very old age (Tacitus was writing after the reign of Domitian at some point in the late 90s or early 100s AD), or it could be a generalisation to suggest within 'living memory'. Whichever is the case it is probable, given the high level of early civilian architecture recorded from around Chichester in the late first century AD, that Togidubnus or his descendants successfully weathered the storm of the Boudiccan revolt. The revolt, which seriously weakened Roman control over the province, very nearly extinguishing it forever, would have been an ideal time for Togidubnus, his friends, family and followers to distinguish themselves by proving fidelity to their emperor. That Togidubnus was revered into the last decade of the first century AD, would strongly suggest that he had remained stubbornly loyal to the Roman cause throughout the revolt. Anything less and his reputation would not have survived.

Given these considerations, the absence of Togidubnus, or indeed of any pro-Roman faction, from Tacitus' account of the uprising seems, at first, rather curious. It could of course be that the king had died just prior to the revolt, though the loyalty of his surviving family and friends in the face of a popular British uprising should still at least have been mentioned. More likely the non-appearance of Togidubnus in the story had more to do with Tacitus' feelings towards the 'quisling king' rather than any failure of his to appear during the proceedings. The contempt that Tacitus felt for Togidubnus, and indeed many other British leaders, has already been noted. Caratacus was one of the few British kings to be praised by the historian and this because Tacitus admired his sense of liberty and freedom, uncorrupted by the depravity and licentiousness of empire. The Boudiccan revolt clearly underlined all the problems of unchecked Roman imperialism whilst simultaneously providing the perfect canvas upon which Tacitus could endlessly moralise.

The true hero of the Tacitean account of the revolt is the Roman governor Gaius Suetonius Paulinus, who is presented as a classic warrior in the solid, republican mould. He is courageous, steadfast, unyielding and utterly dependable, prepared to sacrifice everything in the cause of Rome. Paulinus had, of course, been removed, both morally and geographically from the causes of the revolt, blamed on the procurator Catus Decianus, as he had been on campaign in North Wales. When news of the uprising reached him, he swiftly rode back to London to see what and whom could be saved, reaching the city without his army. Then, after making the difficult decision to abandon London, he travelled back through enemy-held territory in order to rejoin his troops for one last fight to the death. There is clearly no room in such a dramatic story for a character like Togidubnus. Tacitus would certainly not have been keen to advertise any British involvement on the side of Rome, this would not only have confused the narrative, blurring the distinction between good (Roman) and evil (British), but would also have seriously diluted the role played by Paulinus.

It is usually thought that Togidubnus received his citizenship under the emperor Claudius, perhaps for services rendered during the initial stages of the invasion, but it is just as likely, given that he 'remained loyal' that the gift was made to him after the suppression of the Boudiccan revolt. As has already been noted, the names Tiberius and Claudius could have been awarded to Togidubnus as part of his enfranchisement under either the emperors Claudius or Nero.

Given the events of AD 43 and after, not to say his unyielding dedication to Rome, Togidubnus' role in the uprising must have been critical to Roman success. As king whose territory included the Roman town of *Verulamium*, modern day St Albans, Togidubnus' people had already been targeted by Boudicca's army in an early example of ethnic cleansing. Togidubnus clearly had everything to lose and nothing to gain by the revolt of the Eceni and would have striven to ensure that the rebels were swiftly crushed. By holding the lands south of the Thames and containing the revolt to the north, Togidubnus would have ensured Roman investment in the province was saved. Given the armed forces available to the king in AD 43, it is evident we are not dealing with an effete Roman puppet, but a battle hardened veteran who enjoyed the popular support of his people. Whether he was able to deploy an army in support of Paulinus, as he had successfully done for Plautius, we will never know, but it is apparent that our understanding of the events of AD 60-1 is, if based solely on the account of Tacitus, severely flawed.

THE PEOPLE OF THE KINGDOM

Throughout the winter of AD 60/61, all traces of the Boudiccan insurgency were hunted down by the vengeful Roman administration, Tacitus noting dryly that 'any tribe that had wavered in its loyalty or had been hostile was ravaged with fire and sword' (Tacitus *Annals* XIV, 38). Only the intervention of the new procurator, Gaius Alpinus Classicianus (72), a man of continental Celtic stock, put an end to the repression, managing to get the governor, Suetonius Paulinus, recalled to Rome. Needless to say Tacitus was not impressed.

One tribe that had not wavered in its loyalty, and which indeed seems to have been deliberately targeted by Boudicca and her followers from the Eceni and Trinobantes was the Catuvellauni. As has already been noted, Togidubnus of the Catuvellauni probably played a key role during the revolt, protecting Roman (and his own) interests by holding lands to the south of the Thames. In fact Togidubnus may well have engaged the army of Boudicca on the field of battle, repeating his actions against Caratacus' army during the initial phases of the Roman expedition of AD 43, in an effort to minimise the threat to his people.

Unfortunately, Togidubnus' combat status, not to say that of his tribe, during the rebellion is unknown. Certainly the wealthy Briton buried at Folly Lane, *Verulamium*, just before the Great Revolt (around AD 55) was interred with a chain mail shirt whilst others being laid to rest at Stanway, Colchester and North Bersted, near Chichester, seemed to have possessed weapons and shields – perhaps reflecting a more general attitude of the Roman State towards the retention of

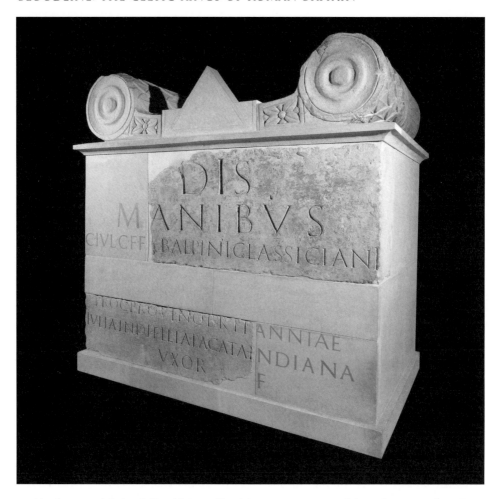

72 Tombstone of Gaius Julius Alpinus Classicianus, reconstructed from fragments found during development in London in 1852, 1885 and 1935. A second generation Roman citizen from Romano-Gallic society, Classicianus was appointed *procurator* (finance minister) to Britain following the Boudiccan Revolt. © *Trustees of the British Museum*

weapons within client states. As Tacitus notes that Togidubnus 'remained loyal' down to 'our times', it is possible that his role in helping to suppress the rebellion was a significant one. Whatever the reality of the situation in AD 60 and 61, it is interesting that within months of the revolt having been crushed, a series of wealthy civilian houses were being constructed across the coastal plain of Sussex, an area largely unaffected by the uprising. The best known, and certainly better investigated, of all the early Roman building projects of this period on the south coast is the so-called 'Proto Palace' at Fishbourne (73). This underlies the south-eastern quadrant of the later 'palace proper' which is visible today. The 'Proto Palace' comprises a substantial, stone-built courtyard house of a type familiar in the Mediterranean, but for which there is no parallel in the Iron Age of southern Britain.

Building work for the house appears to have begun in the mid AD 60s. When complete, the main phase of the first domestic building comprised a courtyard surrounded by a colonnade, a bathhouse and two separate ranges along the eastern and westernmost sides. Little is known about the use of space within the Proto Palace, with the obvious exception of the south-eastern corner. Here, a suite of rooms were designed as a bathhouse, possessing a hot range, including three *caldaria* heated by hypocausts, a *tepidarium*, a *frigidarium* and a cold immersion bath. Although the Proto Palace was incorporated into the later, larger palace structure, its building materials cannibalised for the redevelopment, much can still be said about the style and form of the early phase. Rubble from the rebuild shows that the primary building possessed an exquisite level of interior décor. No floor levels survived intact, though fragments incorporated within the building rubble of later phases, suggest a range of predominantly black and white mosaics and simple pavements composed of large pieces of cut stone (*opus sectile*). Ornamental stone, reused in the later building, further show that parts of the Proto Palace possessed columns capped with Corinthian capitals. An additional fragment of carved stone, this time of Nero as young man, further hints at the level of decoration attained by this building.

All this represents one of the earliest examples of Roman interior decoration yet recovered from a domestic site in Britain, expansive use of colour, solid decorative floors and ornate stonework were clearly all new to the province. To

73 Interpretative recreation of the Fishbourne 'proto-palace', a substantial, stone-built courtyard house of Mediterranean type, constructed in the mid 60s AD, possibly for a character such as Togidubnus. © *Sussex Archaeological Society*

someone brought up at the heart of the Roman world, such things would have appeared normal, but to the indigenous Briton, whose contact with Rome had been through trade and exchange or through a more violent form of interaction on the battlefield, such a repertoire of materials would have been mind-blowing. The total area covered by this civilian building project was evidently massive, but how can this early phase of Roman architecture in West Sussex be interpreted?

Although Nero's *Domus Aurea* in Rome and the buildings that comprise the 'Proto Palace' phase at Fishbourne are of vastly differing scale, it is clear that both possess the same date and the same central conceit: a range of buildings scattered aesthetically across a rural setting. The internal décor of the Mediterranean-style courtyard house at Fishbourne was clearly influenced by Nero's grand design in Rome, right down to the use of marble, ornate capitals, black and white tessellated floors and richly decorated wall plaster. This is, perhaps, unsurprising given the strong links between the southern British and Roman aristocracies. The Proto Palace was designed as a rural retreat, like the villas of the Roman elite and the *Domus Aurea* of Nero and it is likely that its occupant would have been an important member of the new elite whose normal daily routine was centred upon the city; in this case nearby Chichester. But whom? Was this the official residence of a Roman administrator, wanting the comforts of home or was it a well-Romanised Briton expecting to live apart from their barbarian neighbours?

It is certainly probable that Nero's delight over the defeat of Boudicca may have spilled over into rewarding those members of the native British elite who had not sided with the rebels. The extravagant levels of expenditure displayed within the first major civilian buildings at Fishbourne could easily have derived from imperial patronage. Certainly, in near by Chichester, a dedication was made by the ethnic Briton Togidubnus, to the 'Divine House' (possibly that of Nero). To this can be added a gold ring inscribed with the name Tiberius Claudius Catuarus found just to the east of Fishbourne. In the first century, only Roman citizens of the highest rank were permitted to wear gold rings, and only with the explicit permission of the emperor. We do not know who Catuarus was, but he has a Romanised Celtic name and was presumably of equivalent social standing to Togidubnus. Togidubnus and Catuarus, both ethnic Celts (if not of British descent), were of sufficient power, position and status within society, to commission and oversee the building of the Proto Palace at Fishbourne. Can we postulate that either (or both) were resident?

9

AGRICOLA AND THE NORTH: YOU CAN CARRY ON YOUR SLAUGHTER

It was late summer AD 83 and the Roman governor of Britain, Gnaeus Julius Agricola, stood on a low ridge overlooking a plain filled with the dead and the dying; the mutilated and the dismembered. Hours earlier some 10,000 Britons had been systematically slaughtered; skewered on the swords and spear points of an auxiliary Roman army. 'Everywhere there was the silence of desolation' the historian Tacitus tells us, 'deserted hills, smoking houses in the distance. Those sent out on reconnaissance met no one' (*Agricola* 38). The conquest of Britain was complete.

TACITUS AND HISTORY

We know more about Agricola's time as governor than any other person to have held the post, for his son-in-law was the Roman historian Publius Cornelius Tacitus. Tacitus' work, perhaps unsurprisingly entitled the *Agricola,* detailed the life and works of the great man, focusing upon his primary achievement: the total conquest of Britain. That the *Agricola* was not just written, but that it survives at all is reason for celebration for, as we have seen, significant texts detailing the nature of Rome's relationship with Britain have fallen victim to the passage of time. Tacitus' work covers a significant period in British history and represents the first major text relating to events in the island since Dio Cassius' and Tacitus' own accounts of the Boudiccan revolt, some 20 years before.

It is perhaps fair to say that, since its rediscovery during the European renaissance, the *Agricola* has been viewed as an unassailable literary masterpiece, the cornerstone to all studies into the history of Roman Britain. What better than a straight forward account of the final subjugation of Britain written by one of Rome's premier historians who just happened to be a close relative of the chief protagonist? Many historians have commented that it is this direct link to the hero that makes the *Agricola* such a prized resource. Perhaps Tacitus had access to private correspondence, a secret memoir, or possibly to other information held by the family that did not appear in any official document. Perhaps he had even been able to interview Agricola himself, discussing campaign strategy over wine and olives in the fading light of a long Italian afternoon. Certain sections of the

Agricola, such as the great speech made by the Roman general to his troops prior to the final battle of Mons Graupius, do certainly bear the faintest whiff of reality, although one could argue that such exhortations to the soldiery were exactly what an audience would expect a self-respecting Roman officer to have said.

Although invaluable as a (near) primary source, the *Agricola*, like Caesar's *Gallic Wars* before it, should not be treated as a wholly factual and unbiased account. Often referred to as a 'biography', the *Agricola* is far from being a well-balanced study of one man's life, for it details very little of Agricola's background, upbringing and career, a full half of the text concentrating upon the governorship in Britain (and nearly half of that describing the final battle against the Caledonians and its immediate aftermath). Instead, Tacitus' work is closer to a 'hagiography': a sanitised and overly reverential study of a saint, detailing their great works and ultimate martyrdom. A hagiography was not designed as an objective history, rather it was an inspirational tale, containing only minimal background information, detailing a key moment in the life of one imbued with the sacred or divine. Although not a religious text in any sense of the imagination, the *Agricola* is certainly uncritical when it comes to its leading man, portrayed as one of the greatest of the Romans: a keen military strategist; a humane and considerate leader; a benchmark against which the population of Rome, whether good, bad or ugly, could measure itself. As David Woolliscroft and Birgitta Hoffmann have already noted:

> Agricola's achievements can thus be expected to have been lauded to the maximum, possibly well past the point of exaggeration, whilst those of others may have been ignored or belittled, not necessarily out of malice, but simply because they were irrelevant to the writer's theme
> (Woolliscroft and Hoffman 2006, 190)

To better appreciate the full extent of the hagiography, one must first understand the context within it was written.

In AD 98 the emperor Domitian, second son and heir to the deified Vespasian, was brutally assassinated. Domitian had been disliked by the ruling aristocracy of Rome, whom he had ruthlessly persecuted and, following his death, they formally decreed that he should be erased from the collective Roman memory through a process known as *Damnatio memoriae*. Images of Domitian were overthrown, building projects rededicated, all references to him obliterated. He had, in effect, become a non-person and anyone thought to have been part of his inner circle required censure or rehabilitation (in much the same way as those accused of collaborating with the Nazis were, at the end of the Second World War, rehabilitated at the end of a rope). Amidst the general sense of euphoria at the removal of a tyrant, the senate swiftly promoted one of their own to the post of emperor: Marcus Cocceius Nerva. He was 61, childless and in ailing health.

Nerva was keen to restore order as quickly as possible, something that was relatively easy within Rome but harder to establish within the ranks of the military, most of whom had liked Domitian (he had, after all, only just granted them a significant pay rise). The solution to the unrest presented itself in the adoption of a viable successor, someone who had the backing of both the people and, rather more importantly, a significant proportion of the army. That man was Marcus Ulpius Trajanus, governor of Upper Germany.

On paper the transition of power from Domitian to Nerva to Trajan seems fairly straightforward, but the reality for those living in the city was very different. Along with the show trials, witch-hunts and general persecutions that followed Domitian's demise, there was the very real fear, amongst all levels of society, that things were descending into anarchy and chaos. A little over 20 years before, the violent death of the emperor Nero had triggered a bloody civil war in which thousands of civilians, soldiers, officials and aristocrats were butchered. The arrival of Titus Flavius Vespasianus, governor of Judea, into Italy at the head of an army in AD 69 had brought an end to the conflict, the new emperor offering stability through dynastic succession via his two sons Titus and Domitian. Now the last of this dynasty had perished and the spectre of war was once more stalking the streets of Rome. It was at this point, late in the summer of AD 98, that Publius Cornelius Tacitus chose to publish the *Agricola*.

Tacitus had served as a senator under Domitian, avoiding the reign of terror which claimed so many of his comrades. In fact his career seems to have developed relatively normally for a man of his age, a smooth progression with no obvious sign of political impediment. How complicit he had been in the deaths, censures and general seizure of property that marked the final years of Domitian's reign, we do not know. Even if, as seems likely, he had not been directly involved, his political position could be compromised by association. 'What exactly', some prominent members of the new regime may have asked 'had he been up to during this time and just how fervently did he support the new emperor Nerva?'

In part the *Agricola*, by rehabilitating a forgotten hero, may have been designed to help Tacitus and his family distance themselves from the discredited regime. This could, of course, explain the underlying theme of the work, that good men such as Agricola (and, by implication, Tacitus also) could survive and thrive under a despotic tyrant. The *Agricola* therefore is part biography, part hagiography and part apology. Agricola, a model of honesty, modesty and restraint, had accomplished many good works in his life. He had retained his principles throughout, ultimately paying dearly with his life.

AGRICOLA AND HIS STORY

The mandate for the total conquest of Britain had been given to Agricola by the emperor Vespasian (74), who was no doubt keen to see the completion of a project that he himself had been involved with, way back in AD 43. Agricola was to hold office for nearly seven years, an unusual but not unheard of posting at a time when the standard length of time given to each governor was three to four years. Perhaps the difficulty of the job, combined with the importance

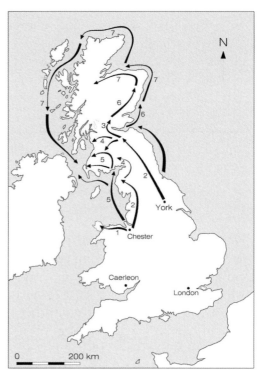

Above left: 74 Marble head of Vespasian, possibly recarved from an original portrait of Nero, from Carthage, Tunisia. © *Trustees of the British Museum*

Above right: 75 Map showing the postulated campaign seasons of the Roman governor Agricola between AD 77 and 83/4 as described by his son-in-law, the historian Tacitus. *Redrawn from Jones and Mattingly* An Atlas of Roman Britain *(1990, 75)*

of ensuring closure, necessitated an extended time period. Perhaps the rapid turnover of supreme command, Vespasian dying in June of AD 79, his son and successor Titus 27 months later, resulted in a near continual change of orders. Perhaps Agricola was simply the best man for the job.

The Established Facts of Agricola's governorship, as established by his son-in-law Tacitus, may be easily summarised (75):

AD 77:   Agricola arrives in Britain 'late in the season' and launches an attack upon the Ordovices tribe, in what is now North Wales, almost exterminating them in the process. He then directs the assault of Anglesey, left unoccupied by Rome following the Boudiccan revolt of AD 60/61 (76, 77).

AD 78:   Agricola consolidates his conquests, aiming to effectively 'eradicate the causes of war'. He pursues an aggressive policy of Romanisation across southern Britain before advancing north into what is now Yorkshire and Northumbria.

AD 79:   Agricola's army advances into what is now Scotland, reaching
            the River Tay.

AD 80:   Roman troops sweep westwards into Dumfries and Galloway.

AD 81:   Amphibious operations secure the western coast of England and
            Scotland with plans being drawn up to invade Ireland.

AD 82:   Roman infantry, cavalry and naval units advance along the eastern
            seaboard of Scotland to the north of the River Forth.

AD 83:   A final battle at *Mons Graupius* destroys native resistance.
            The Roman fleet is able to circumnavigate Britain, proving
            that it is indeed an island.

AD 83/4:   Agricola is recalled to Rome.

These, then, are the bare, immoveable facts of the final stages of the Roman
conquest; the bedrock of truth upon which all archaeological data can be hung.
Even if Agricola's exact role in the campaign has been overplayed somewhat by
Tacitus, as most historians, classicists and archaeologists now accept, the basic
sequence of events as recorded must be right – mustn't they?

The problem is that archaeological evidence recovered from northern England
and southern Scotland, rather than being subservient to the historical 'truth',
seems to want to contradict it at every stage. This is, perhaps, really not all that
surprising for we have already established that the *Agricola* was not a solidly
factual account of war in a distant province, Tacitus' work being a flattering and
wholly uncritical account of how his father-in-law came, saw and conquered
Britain through superhuman feats of endeavour and courage. Trouble is,
archaeology seems to want us to believe that Agricola may not have been the first
Roman governor of Britain to establish a garrison in Scotland. To make matters
worse, reanalysis of the *Agricola* seems to indicate that some sections of the text

76 The
amphitheatre
adjoining the
Roman fort of
Tomen-y-Mur,
Gwynedd, first
built in the late
AD 70s, probably
under Agricola
during the renewed
campaigns against
the Ordovices and
Anglesey. *Author*

77 The interior of the Roman fortress of *Segontium* (Caernarfon), Gwynedd, first constructed in the late AD 70s, probably under Agricola during the renewed campaign against the island of Anglesey, which can be seen rising up in the background. *Author*

are either untrue, or at least have been lifted (some more cynical readers might add 'plagiarised') from a variety of alternative historical sources.

The absolute certainty of Tacitus' account received its first nudge following the dendrochronological (tree-ring) dating of timbers (freshly cut rather than seasoned), found within and beneath the earthen rampart of the first Roman fort at Carlisle. These timbers generated a foundation date for the fort late in the year AD 72, a full five years *before* Agricola's arrival as governor. To be fair, Tacitus does not say that 'Agricola was the first to establish a fort at Carlisle' but then the implication in his text is that it was indeed Agricola who first moved Roman soldiery north towards the Solway Firth and who single-handedly 'marked out the encampments, and explored in person the estuaries and forests' following the general inactivity of his provincial predecessors. A date of AD 72 puts the construction of the fort at Carlisle within the remit of an earlier governor, Quintus Petillius Cerialis (AD 71-4), something that does not appear that unusual, now that similar dates have been secured 'for other forts all over the north of England'. In turn, this suggests that 'Cerialis' activities may have extended well to the north of Carlisle, and perhaps as far as Strathmore', north of the River Tay (Woolliscroft and Hoffmann 2006, 188). Further afield, artefactual evidence recovered from forts at Camelon, Castledykes, Dalswinton, Newstead and Strageath in Scotland all seem to indicate very early Vespasianic (or even pre-Vespasianic) occupation.

A tantalising glimpse of such potential pre-Agricolan activity in Scotland may be found in the *Silvae*, an occasional series of verses written by the poet Publius Papinius Statius to his friends. One, addressed to Crispinus, son of Marcus Vettius Bolanus, governor of Britain between AD 69 and 71, notes:

> What glory will extol the plains of Caledonia, when some great-aged native of that wild country tells you: 'Here it was your father's custom justice to dispense; from this mound his squadrons he addressed. Far and wide his look-out posts and

strongholds did he set (do you see them?), and with a ditch these walls he girt. These gifts, these weapons to the gods of war did he devote (you see the dedications still). This breastplate he himself put on when battle summoned; this from off a British king he seized
(Statius *Silvae* V, 2)

Poems, eulogies and congratulatory addresses are notoriously unreliable as source material and can only rarely be used in evidence, especially as the language they deloy is frequently vague, but here the mention of 'look-out posts and strongholds' set upon the 'plains of Caledonia' is intriguing.

Better still, at least in literary terms, is the fleeting reference to northern Britain made by Gaius Plinius Secundus (better known to history as Pliny the elder) in his masterwork, the *Natural History*. As an author, scientist, naturalist, geographer and friend of the emperor Vespasian, the elder Pliny was an exceptional person with a voracious appetite for learning. In Book 4 of the *Natural History*, describing the 'Sites, races, seas, towns, harbours, mountains, rivers, distances and peoples who now exist or formerly existed' he observed that:

… extensive knowledge [of Britain] was gained within 30 years of the success of Roman arms, yet even as yet they have not penetrated beyond the vicinity of the Caledonian forest
(Pliny the elder *Natural History* IV, 102)

Pliny's suggestion that 'the Caledonian forest', placed by the early second-century geographer Claudius Ptolemaeus (Ptolemy) in the region of the Great Glen, bisecting the Scottish Highlands, was reached 'within 30 years' of the Claudian invasion would, if true, indicate a campaign against the highland tribes in or before AD 73. This of course ties neatly with the observations made in the *Silvae* by Statius that governor Bolanus had committed troops to the area and was busy building forts in the early 70s AD. Pliny could not have confused any military intervention in Caledonia under Bolanus with that of Agricola, whose activities in this area, according to Tacitus, did not commence until AD 79, as this was the very year that Pliny died (during the erruption of Mount Vesuvius) and it is evident, from the dedications contained within the *Natural History*, that the book had been published at least two years before. Agricola, so it would seem, was not the first Roman governor to occupy the Scottish lowlands, whatever Tacitus has to say on the matter.

Ultimately all this should not trouble us too much, for we have already noted that the *Agricola*, although a great read, makes no pretence at being a true and objective history; no hagiography ever is. Claims that Tacitus would not have been able to stray too far from the truth in order to increase the standing of Agricola as there were likely to have been people still alive who remembered the great man or who had even served with him in Britain, are stretching credability somewhat. We have no idea what the circulation rate for published works was within the Roman world, nor how large an audience most works received so it will never be possible to say whether any such 'people' ever got to read Tacitus' words. In any case there are no critical reviews surviving for the *Agricola*, so we do not know how it was received nor whether anyone had cause to doubt its contents. Friends of the family would no doubt have praised the work, especially if they believed that Agricola had been a victim of the paranoid Domitian.

The only other surviving literary source that covers the campaigns of Agricola is, in comparison to Tacitus' work, brief, almost to the point of non-existence. Written by Dio Cassius over a century later, the *Roman History* says only that:

> War broke out again in Britain, and Gnaeus Julius Agricola overran all the enemy's territory there. He was the first Roman of whom we have any information to discover that Britain is surrounded by water. For some soldiers mutinied and, having murdered their centurions and a tribune, they took refuge in boats, put out to sea and sailed round the western part of Britain just as the current and winds took them. And they escaped detection on the other side when they put in at the forts there. As a result of this, Agricola sent others to attempt the circumnavigation, and learned from them too that it was an island. These were the events in Britain and as a result Titus was given the title Imperator for the fifteenth time. Agricola, however, lived out the rest of his life in disgrace and want since he had accomplished more than was proper for a general
> (Dio Cassius *Roman History*, LXVI, 20, 1-3)

Dio Cassius does not mention Agricola's extended office, neither does he mention the great battle of Mons Graupius, noting only that Agricola 'overran' enemy territory, presumably with some degree of success. For Dio, the most interesting aspect of Agricola's British campaign was the circumnavigation of Britain, rather bizarrely following the mutiny and attempted escape of a number of Roman troops. Intriguingly Dio places the acclamation of Titus as 'Imperator', a victory title given only to the head of state or his immediate relatives, for the fifteenth time following on from, and directly *because of*, this naval action (presumably as the conquest of the province could now officially be said to have been completed). This acclamation came in AD 79.

Now of course Dio Cassius could have made an error, truncating Agricola's period of office or confusing the order in which events actually happened. AD 79, however, marked the end of the second year of Agricola's term and Titus' acclamation, which we know *did* happen, together with the recognition that 'all Britain was conquered' should perhaps have been the cue for Agricola's return to reward, recognition or posting elsewhere. Did he actually serve a second three-year term in Britain? It seems unlikely that, if he had been recalled under Titus that Tacitus could have fabricated a further three years of military glory for the man. Perhaps Agricola was viewed as being too dangerous (or too successful) by Titus to allow him to leave Britain. Perhaps subsequent unrest and the rise of a counterinsurgency, conspired to keep him in Britain a little longer than he had hoped. Perhaps a change in leadership, Vespasian's second son Domitian taking over the reins of power late in AD 81, necessitated his continued presence in the province. That Agricola stayed in Britain after AD 79 seems reasonable enough, but the precise chronology and sequence of Tactitus' apparently unassailable account is in doubt.

From a literary perspective, a few further elements of the *Agricola* are worth noting here. First, as many have already observed, the *Agricola* is used on a number of occasions in order to make statements about the perceived morality of Rome (especially clear in the speech given by Tacitus to the Caledonian war leader Calgacus on the eve of battle) and the degenerate nature of its previous leader, Domitian. The second is that Tacitus seems to deliberately parallel aspects of Agricola's life and viewpoint with those of both Nerva and Trajan, possibly in order to curry favour or perhaps to indicate that neither Tacitus nor Agricola himself had ever willingly followed (nor been a part of) Domitian's discredited regime. Lastly, Tacitus appears to been harking back to earlier, grander times by deliberately drawing comparisons with Caesar's *magnum opus*, the *Gallic Wars*, a point already noted by Woolliscroft and Hoffmann in their book *Rome's First Frontier*. Both the *Agricola* and the *Gallic Wars* told the story of well motivated individuals who, together with their devoted troops, campaigned for seven long years beyond the frontiers of civilisation.

> Both generals reached their commands late in the season, but immediately took to the field. Both achieved two victories in quick succession. Both had to rescue a subordinate from a dangerous night attack. Both went further across the ocean than anybody before them ... Both were foiled in their attemps to conquer distant islands ... and, in the end, both had to fight a decisive battle, against an aliance of tribes, before which someone in the enemy camp supposedly gave a long speech on the value of liberty
> (Woolliscroft and Hoffmann 2006, 201)

By echoing aspects of both the style, content and basic format of the *Gallic Wars*, Tacitus may have been trying to subtly persuade his audience that Agricola had been very much the consummate politician, statesman and general. He had, in every way been 'another Caesar', albeit one that, in Tacitus' mind, had been under appreciated, unacknowledged and then quietly murdered by the state.

THE LAST BATTLE

The battle of Mons Graupius, set at the end of the summer AD 83, represents the climax of the *Agricola*. Tacitus fails to provide a detailed description of either the battlefield or an exact placement for the conflict, remaining vague throughout, something that has irritated and frustrated modern historians and archaeologists who have tried in vain to locate it on the ground. No matter. Tacitus was not interested in geography, only the human drama. Mons Graupius is presented as the culmination of the seven year campaign, the last, futile attempt by the Britons to gain their freedom. It was the final gasp of a people who did not yet realise they were beaten.

The battle is accorded significant status in the *Agricola*: it is the event that everything has been building towards and consequently takes up nearly a full fifth of Tacitus' word count. Whether the battle itself was as significant as Tacitus makes out, or whether it was merely a small skirmish that has been inflated to major status, is unclear. Certainly Dio Cassius, our only other source for the campaigns of Agricola, doesn't mention it, but then he is more interested in the Roman fleet's circumnavigation of Britain than the minor detail of war.

As the armies drew up for battle, leaders on both sides gave a rousing speech. This is Tacitus' opportunity to allow Agricola to speak for himself for the first time in the book, providing his audience with a chance to assess the man for his thoughts, rather than simply by his deeds. The 'British perspective' is given by one Calgacus ('swordsman'), a man whom Tacitus notes was 'the most distinguished for birth and valour among the chieftains' (*Agricola* 29). Interestingly, Calgacus is not presented as the leader of the Britons; he is not recognised as the genius who has single-handedly co-ordinated the British response to Rome in much the way that Cassivellaunos or Caratacus had done before. We know nothing about his origin or, contrary to much that has been said about him in recent years, anything about his tribal affiliation. He is simply a mouthpiece through which Tacitus can present an alternative perspective to that of Rome. He may not have even existed, being a literary creation: a Celtic Moriarty to the Roman Sherlock Holmes. It would certainly be difficult for Tacitus to present the barbarian viewpoint if there were no named barbarian to speak on their behalf. Whether he existed or not, and he is never mentioned again after the battle, it is clear that there is no way that Tacitus, or even Agricola for that matter, could have known precisely what he said in his pre-match pep talk, even if the Romans had later interrogated prisoners of war.

Whatever the case, seeing the contents of Calgacus' speech, it is clear that this is not a Briton speaking; the words coming from a very Roman mouth, having been formed within a peculiarly Roman mindset. Some sections, it is true, represent exactly the sort of thing that any self-respecting freedom fighter, from Spartacus to William Wallace, would be *expected* to say:

> When I reflect on the causes of the war, and the circumstances of our situation, I feel a strong persuasion that our united efforts on the present day will prove the beginning of universal liberty to Britain. For we are all undebased by slavery … (*Agricola* 30)

At other times the Roman perspective creeps in:

> We, the noblest sons of Britain, and therefore stationed in its last recesses, far from the view of servile shores, have preserved even our eyes unpolluted by the contact

of subjection. We, at the furthest limits both of land and liberty, have been protected to this day by the remoteness of our situation

(*Agricola* 30)

It is difficult to believe that any resistance leader fighting to defend their own homes from the invader would perceive themself to be at the 'furthest limits' of a landscape, their homes set remotely within the 'last recesses' of a given island. The people squaring up to face Agricola and his men were at the very centre of their world and to them the Mediterranean was a distant sea; the Roman people a remote race from a city 'far from view'.

The pre-battle speech is a standard literary device in most ancient sources, providing not only a Roman audience the opportunity to check their own moral compass, but also for the author to present something of their own perspective or viewpoint without causing offence. In this respect, Tacitus resembles a ventriloquist, someone who can use politically incorrect or sensitive material, but escape censure through the pretence that 'it's the dummy speaking'. Hence the Roman historian can have Calgacus rail against imperialism in what has become perhaps the most famous paragraph of Tacitus' work:

Robbers of the world, having by their universal plunder exhausted the land, they rifle the deep. If the enemy be rich, they are rapacious; if he be poor, they lust for dominion; neither the east nor the west has been able to satisfy them. Alone among men they covet with equal eagerness poverty and riches. To robbery, slaughter, plunder, they give the lying name of empire; they create a desolation and call it peace

(*Agricola* 30)

Against this rather damning assessment of Roman foreign policy is, of course, Agricola himself, whom Tacitus has already shown to be a humane and morally upright citizen, in contrast to the self-serving, power-abusing emperor Domitian. Julius Caesar deployed exactly the same tactics of enemy speech and comparison of values in his account of the moments before the Seige of Alesia, the last gasp of the *Gallic Wars*. Here is one Critognatus, a noble whom, although never mentioned before or again by Caesar, is noted, like Calgacus, to have been 'held in great esteem' by his people (Caesar *Gallic Wars*, VII, 77), who delivers a textbook piece of Roman rhetoric:

The Cimbri devastated our land and did us great harm, but they did in the end leave our country and move on elsewhere. They left us our freedom, with our own rights and laws and land. But what the Romans are after is quite different. They are motivated by envy. They know that we are renowned and powerful in war. So what they want is to settle on our land among our tribes and bind us in slavery forever. That has always been their reason for waging wars. You may not know what goes on in distant countries, but just look at that part of Gaul on your frontiers that has been made into a Roman province. Its laws and institutions have been changed, and the country is held in perpetual slavery, cowering under the dominion of Rome (*Gallic Wars* VII, 77)

The speech credited to Agricola at *Mons Graupius* is in turn inspiring and measured. It is, perhaps, the standard rallying call to arms that any general would make, but as already noted, it is the first time that Agricola has been allowed to speak, and its content may have been relayed to the Tacitus by the great man himself.

> In so many expeditions, in so many battles, whether you have been required to exert your courage against the enemy, or your patient labours against the very nature of the country, neither have I ever been dissatisfied with my soldiers, nor you with your general. In this mutual confidence, we have proceeded beyond the limits of former commanders and former armies; and are now become acquainted with the extremity of the island, not by uncertain rumour, but by actual possession with our arms and encampments. Britain is discovered and subdued ... As in penetrating woods and thickets, the fiercest animals boldly rush onto the hunters, while the weak and timorous fly at their very noise; so the bravest of the Britons have long since fallen: the remaining number consists solely of the cowardly and spiritless; whom you see at length within your reach, not because they have stood their ground, but because they are overtaken. Torpid with fear, their bodies are fixed and chained down in yonder field, which to you will speedily be the scene of a glorious and memorable victory
> (*Agricola* 34)

Tacitus' own account of the fighting at *Mons Graupius* represents a fairly standard account of how a set piece battle was expected to unfold, the only exception being that here Agricola did not deploy the citizen-based legions, instead using the more expendable auxilliary army. 'In the event of victory' Tacitus said, explaining Agricola's strategy, 'the engagement would be of great distinction if no Roman blood were spilled'. The auxilliary infantry, numbering around 8,000, were lined up to face the enemy, with some 3,000 cavalry placed at the wings. The British army comprised (according to Tacitus who may have inflated the numbers for effect) more than 30,000 infantry, cavalry and accompanying chariots. Battle commenced with the traditional hurling of missiles and then both sides came together, Roman troops, with their short, stabbing swords, using close quarter fighting to their advantage. Containing the charge on their shields, the auxilliaries gradually pushed the Britons back until it was all over, Tacitus observing that: 'arms and carcasses and mangled limbs, were promiscuously strewed, and the field was dyed in blood' (*Agricola* 37).

Although dramatic, Tacitus' description of the battle at *Mons Graupius* is also fairly generic. Crucially, it is also similar, in almost every detail, to the battle between Roman and Briton that Tacitus himself had used as the climax to the

Boudiccan Revolt in AD 60/1. Both sides had, in this earlier conflict, been only too aware that loosing was not an option, both leaders giving rousing, pre-battle speeches: Boudicca on liberty and the loss of freedom under Rome, Suetonius providing more practical advice on how to get the job done and go home. When battle commenced, Boudicca's army hurled themselves at the Roman line, which held, legionaries absorbing the impact upon their shields. Having broken the British charge, Suetonius' men advanced steadily, Roman steel slicing deep into the barbarian line. Finally, sensing all was lost, the Britons attempted to flee, many thousands being slaughtered in the process.

CONSEQUENCES

One particular gripe of Tacitus that runs right the way through the *Agricola* is the view that his father-in-law had been recalled at the height of his powers after defeating the last pockets of insurgency and finally brining the Claudian war in Britain to an end. 'Britain was conquered and immediately abandoned' he was later to note bitterly (Tacitus *Histories* I, 2). Agricola returned to Rome at the behest of the emperor Domitian; his victories were played down and all newly conquered territory was abandoned to the enemy. Domitian had done this, Tacitus felt, because he was jealous of Agricola's success and angered that the name of a mere governor was being 'raised above that of the emperor' (*Agricola* XXXIX, 4). There may well have been an element of truth in this, for Domitian was not the most stable of rulers, but also it could well have been felt back in Rome, that the British war was simply unwinnable; continued fighting proving too costly in terms of manpower and resources.

The *Agricola*, of course, gives none of this; Tacitus' work providing a relatively straight forward account of adventure in the far north culminating in one last, conclusively dramatic set-piece battle. The reality of the situation, a difficult advance through mountainous terrain against an enemy that possessed no large centres of population (to besiege), fixed resources (to attack) or large field armies (to fight) does not figure at all in Tacitus' story. The *Agricola* only hints at the severe difficulties faced by Roman troops when fighting a protracted campaign against a guerrilla army with nothing to loose, when it notes the reluctance of the enemy to attack secure positions, which it puts down to cowardice, and their curious strategy of moving 'their wives and children to safety' which it ascribes to arrogance. Only once does Tacitus directly acknowledge the success of the barbarian strategy, observing that, after one particular attempt at ambush was driven off, Roman troops were unable to press home the advantage, 'marshes and woodland providing cover for the fleeing enemy' (*Agricola*, 26).

A clearer idea of the difficulties faced by a well equipped professional army stuck in a hostile country with no one to fight is provided in the later accounts of the emperor Septimius Severus who launched a disastrous invasion of Caledonia in AD 208.

Once the army had crossed the rivers and earthworks on the frontier of the Roman empire, there were frequent encounters and skirmishes with the enemy in which they were put to flight. However, it was easy for them to escape and to disappear into the woods and marshes because of their knowledge of the terrain, but all this hampered the Romans and dragged out the war considerably
(Herodian *History of the Empire*, III, 14)

Were such 'underhand' barbarian tactics the reason why the Agricolan war had lasted quite so long? It is certainly possible; Agricola's unusual seven year posting perhaps being due not to his success, but because the British employed tactics that ensured that swift victory and face-saving retreat were impossible. The further Roman troops advanced into Scotland, the more isolated individual groups became, proving easy targets for a guerrilla army well acquainted with the hostile nature of both landscape and climate. Dio Cassius echoes Herodian's comments on Severus' later campaign, noting that:

He experienced untold difficulties in cutting down the forests, levelling the high ground, filling in the swamps and bridging the rivers. He fought no battles nor did he see any enemy drawn up for battle. Instead they deliberately put sheep and cattle in the Romans' way for the soldiers to seize, so that they might be lured on further still and thus be worn out. In fact the Romans suffered great hardships because of the water, any any stragglers became a prey to ambush. Then, unable to go on, they would be killed by their own men so that they might not fall into enemy hands. As a result as many as 50,000 died in all
(Dio Cassius *Roman History* LXXVI, 13)

Agricola had been given the job of finishing the conquest of Britain by Domitian's father, the emperor Vespasian, but, seven years on and with little economic gain evident from the protracted fighting, Domitian probably had a different set of priorities, not least on the Danubian frontier where barbarian hordes were threatening Roman interests. Agricola may (or may not) have smashed the Caledonian armies sent against him at the battle of *Mons Graupius*, but the campaign itself was clearly not over. Forts and roads needed to be built and garrisons initiated before northern Britain could effectively become 'Roman'. Perhaps it was better that the conquest of the north could, at least on coins, monuments and other propaganda instruments of the state, be hailed as complete, allowing the army to retreat back to a more secure position without a humiliating loss of face. After *Mons Graupius*, Domitian may have felt that the time was ripe to relieve the governor of his command and replace him with someone who better understood the Britons and could make the establishment of a Roman way of life a more permanent fixture, at least in the south. Someone who could speed up the Romanising process, stabilise the province, pump-prime the towns and hasten much-needed economic returns. The war had been won, at least in the emperor's eyes, now Agricola's successor had to win the peace.

10

LUCULLUS AND DOMITIAN: EMPIRE STATE HUMAN

Caesar Domitianus Augustus was not a well man. As emperor of Rome, he was the master of the largest empire in the ancient world; as the son of the deified Vespasian, and brother of the deified Titus, he was also convinced that he was a god. The trouble with divinity, however, was that it brought no extra form of physical protection and Domitian was almost constantly plagued with the fear of assassination. Although generally loved by both the people and military of Rome, he was unpopular with the aristocracy whom he had ruthlessly persecuted and suppressed. Paranoia had driven him to ever irrational outbursts, his behaviour increasingly bordering on the delusional. The historian and court gossip Gaius Suetonius Tranquillus noting that:

> When the anticipated danger drew near, becoming still more anxious every day, he lined the walls of the colonnades in which he used to walk with phengite stone to be able to see in its brilliant surface the reflection of all that went on behind his back (*Domitian* 14, 4)

Forever fearing the worst, Domitian is recorded as saying 'the lot of princes was most unhappy, since when they discovered a conspiracy, no one believed them unless they had been killed' (Suetonius, *Domitian* 21, 1).

Born Titus Flavius Domitianus (78), the youngest son of the emperor Vespasian, Domitian had acceded to the imperial throne in AD 81 following the death of his brother Titus. To begin with his reign had been relatively successful, Suetonius noting that 'he often gave strong proofs not merely of integrity, but even of liberality' (*Domitian* 9, 1). Towards the twelfth year of his reign, however, things were not going well. Perhaps the maxim that 'absolute power corrupts absolutely' held true or perhaps there were more deep-seated psychological issues. Whatever the case, by the beginning of AD 93 Domitian had 'turned to cruelty somewhat more speedily than to avarice' (*Domitian* 10, 1), consolidating his position of power by eradicating those whom he perceived to be a threat. Much like Joseph Stalin's 'purges' of the Communist Party in late 1930s Russia, Domitian cut a bloody swathe through the senatorial class of Rome, destroying those whom he believed guilty of treason, corruption or treachery. From the relative safety of the early second century AD, Suetonius observed that:

78 The emperor Domitian (AD 81-96).
Massingheimer Collection

He put to death many senators, among them several ex-consuls, including Civica Cerealis, at the very time when he was proconsul in Asia, Salvidienus Orfitus, Acilius Glabrio while he was in exile – these on the ground of plotting revolution, the rest on any charge, however trivial. He slew Aelius Lamia for joking remarks, which were reflections on him, it is true, but made long before and harmless ... He put to death Salvius Cocceianus, because he had kept the birthday of the emperor Otho, his paternal uncle; Mettius Pompusianus, because it was commonly reported that he ... carried about a map of the world on parchment and speeches of the kings and generals from Titus Livius, besides giving two of his slaves the names of Mago and Hannibal; Sallustius Lucullus, governor of Britain, for allowing some lances of a new pattern to be named "Lucullean," after his own name; Junius Rusticus, because he had published eulogies of Paetus Thrasea and Helvidius Priscus and called them the most upright of men; and on the occasion of this charge he banished all the philosophers from the city and from Italy. He also executed the younger Helvidius, alleging that in a farce composed for the stage he had under the characters of Paris and Oenone censured Domitian's divorce from his wife; Flavius Sabinus too, one of his cousins, because on the day of the consular elections the crier had inadvertently announced him to the people as emperor elect, instead of consul
(*Domitian* X, 2)

Eventually, convinced that his end was drawing near, Domitian began to pay very close attention to any sign or portent which seemed to suggest death, assassination or indicate a change of government. So obsessed was he of the nature and form of these predictions, that he overlooked all the evidence of a very real danger lurking within the imperial palace itself.

One day in late summer, whilst striding through the palace to his private baths, Domitian's attention was caught by Parthenius, his head valet. Parthenius informed him that a man had arrived with urgent news of a conspiracy, something that instantly grabbed Domitian's attention, and was even now waiting for a private interview in the emperor's bedroom. Once there, Domitian was greeted by Stephanus, steward to his niece Domitilla, who handed him a document listing all the names of the alleged conspirators. As Domitian hurriedly scanned the list, Stephanus quietly removed a dagger, concealed beneath a mass of woollen bandages covering a pretend wound on his left arm, and slowly moved in for the kill.

But the blade was handled clumsily; a messy strike to the groin, not the swift death-blow that Stephanus had hoped for. Surprised and no doubt howling with pain, Domitian fell forward dragging the steward with him to the floor. The freedman, now struggling to rip the dagger from his erstwhile emperor, found that his progress in this was increasingly hindered by Domitian's attempts to claw out his eyes. For a while the two of them writhed on the floor, swearing and kicking. Suetonius tells us that a boy, previously attending to the spirits of the Flavian house at the bedroom shrine, was the only witness to the fight. Upon seeing him, Domitian called for the dagger that he kept under his pillow on the couch where he slept off the effects of dinner. The boy found only the dagger handle; the conspirators having already removed the blade. By now screaming for help and bloodied by further injuries, Domitian heard the locked door to his private chamber being battered open from outside; the hinges eventually shattering in their sockets. It was not, however, the help that he had hoped for; those now entering the room, 'Clodianus, a subaltern, Maximus, a freedman of Parthenius, Satur, decurion of the chamberlains, and a gladiator from the imperial school' were there for one purpose only: to finish the job Stephanus had started.

Moments later, the assassins fled into the corridor, noisily casting their weapons aside. Behind them, in a crumpled heap of blood-stained cloth, lay Caesar Domitianus Augustus, eleventh emperor of Rome, his life force spurting out onto the cold stone floor. It was early morning on 18 September AD 96 and the Flavian dynasty was over.

GAIUS SALLUSTIUS LUCULLUS

One of the victims of Domitian's great purge was Sallustius Lucullus, governor of Britain, whom Suetonius notes had been put to death 'for allowing some lances of a new pattern to be named *Lucullean*' (*Domitian* X, 2). Lucullus fell foul of a despotic emperor for a seemingly trivial issue of naming of a new projectile weapon. Extreme though this may appear, it is clear, from the actions of many a twentieth-century dictator, that people have frequently (and sadly) died for less. It is possible that the story of the spear was one of those urban myths promulgated by people like Suetonius in order to underline the insanity of the emperor, but to some extent Domitian certainly had every right to feel insecure. People, amongst them aristocrats, senators, governors and generals, not to mention members of his own family, had indeed been plotting against him. In January AD 89, for example, Domitian had faced a revolt by the governor of Upper Germany,

Lucius Antonius Saturninus. This was finally suppressed with the help from the armies of neighbouring provinces, but it may have left the paranoid Domitian feeling uncertain about the loyalty of other governors across Western Europe. It is possible that Lucullus had conspired with Saturninus, or perhaps Domitian merely suspected that he had (which would have been reason enough in the emperor's mind to have him executed). The story of the Lucullean lance could have been a trumped up charge or a later distortion of real events. Whatever the case, Gaius Sallustius Lucullus was removed from office with extreme prejudice and presumably replaced by someone more to the emperor's liking.

In most accounts of Roman Britain Sallustius Lucullus appears as little more than a footnote: an unfortunate governor of Britannia executed by a deeply insecure emperor. We know nothing of his reign as governor, in contrast to his predecessors in the post, and his background and career structure remain unknown. Evidence recovered from a small town in West Sussex, however, suggests that Lucullus was, in fact, nothing less than the most important figure in the early years of Roman Britain. A person who had a central role in the Romanisation of the province and a man who has been almost totally airbrushed from history.

In 1658, Samuel Woodford of Wadham College Oxford, then finishing a Bachelor of Arts degree, was compiling information for a catalogue of all Roman inscriptions found in Britain entitled *Inscriptionum Romano-Britannicarum Conllectio*. Woodford's text unfortunately provides little detail concerning the nature of each discovery and rarely supplies any useful comment or interpretation. Nevertheless, though it cannot be taken entirely at face value, the *Conllectio* supplies a wealth of information relating to material since defaced, mutilated or lost. The Chichester inscription, for example, represents one such piece that, since Woodford's record, has unfortunately faded back into obscurity. We do not know where within Chichester the stone was found, nor the context for its discovery, the only source for the *Conllectio* reference being one Henry Babbington. The inscription itself originally read:

I O M

PRO SALVTE

IMP CAES DOMITIANI

AVG

C SALLVSTIVS LVCVLLVS

LEG AVG

PR PR PROV BRITANNIAE

POSVIT

V S L M Q

which may be translated as:

> To Jupiter Best and Greatest, for the Welfare of the emperor Caesar Domitianus Augustus, this was set up by Gaius Sallustius Lucullus, Legate of the emperor with

praetorian powers of the province of Britain, who willingly and deservedly fulfilled his vow.

This long forgotten and largely ignored inscription is hugely important for a number of reasons. First, dedications and images to the emperor Domitian are generally rare across the empire as, following his assassination in AD 96, Domitian was removed from memory of the Roman people through a process known as *damnatio memoriae*. Dedications made by the governor (or Propraetorian Imperial Legate) of a province are also generally rare, certainly in Britain, and, when found, usually relate to specific monumental building projects. The Legate of the emperor with praetorian powers was the most senior ranking official within any given province. Drawn from the highest level of Roman society, a governor was in control of the military organisation, civil infrastructure and judicial process of the province. His remit lasted a minimum of four years and he was directly answerable to the emperor.

Given what we have noted about the Chichester stone, it is perhaps surprising that the inscription is not cited or referred to in any of the major historical works concerning Roman Britain. In fact the only real mention of it is in *The Roman Inscriptions of Britain* produced by R. G. Collingwood and R. P. Wright in 1965. Here the dedication is consigned to a section marked *Falsa,* as both Haverfield and Wright believed it to be a forgery. No reason is ever given for this belief and, it has to be said, that on balance there is nothing in the wording, construction or phraseology of the Lucullus stone that screams 'hoax'. Given the quantity of early monumental inscriptions since recovered from Roman Chichester (including the internationally famous 'Togidubnus stone'), the likelihood is that the inscription was, in fact, utterly genuine.

A point missed by the all other writers of the period is that additional evidence has been recovered from Chichester to suggest that Woodford's stone was indeed very real. In 1823, 165 years *after* the discovery of the Lucullus stone, an inscribed altar was dug up from the area of Lion Street in the centre of the town. This stone, which also seems to date from the later years of the first century AD, read:

> Sacred to the Genius (of the place) Lucullus, son of Amminus, set this up from his own resources

It would perhaps be too heavy a strain on coincidence to have two inscriptions made at the same time in the same town citing two separate individuals with the same name, especially as the name 'Lucullus' does not appear anywhere else in the British Isles during the Roman period. The position of the altar, at the very heart of Roman Chichester, would further seem to emphasise the importance of the donor for only a major local dignitary would have had the authority to erect such a stone here. The discovery of a second inscription citing Lucullus from Chichester helps validate the first. Had the discoveries been made the other way round, Woodford's find following the recovery of the Lion Street Altar, then doubts would have certainly arisen concerning the authenticity of the latter piece, with Woodford perhaps being viewed as a hoaxer. The reality is that the dedication to Domitian was recorded *prior* to the Lion Street altar: well before Woodford or others could have made any link with an obscure governor of Roman Britain and the city of Chichester.

THE MAN

But of course Gaius Sallustius Lucullus was not an obscure governor and his association with Chichester becomes ever more interesting because of this. The Lion Street altar makes it clear that he was the son of someone with a good Celtic name: Amminus. Variants of this name occasionally crop up in Gaul, but there are only two other examples of this occurring in Britain: on Late Iron Age coins and in the writings of the Roman historian Suetonius.

Amminus (Adminius) was the Iron Age king of southern Britain (probably eastern Kent) who fled to the emperor Caligula in AD 40. The circumstances of his defection are unclear; all Suetonius tells us is that the Briton fled the wrath of his father 'Cynobellinus' and 'deserted to the Romans with a small force'. As the son of an Iron Age king in Rome, Lucullus would have required an official sponsor in order to gain Roman citizenship. Caligula could have provided this, but he was not long for this world and anyway, at least according to the imperial biographer Suetonius, had his mind on more trivial matters.

'Lucullus' itself is a good Roman name with a solid aristocratic pedigree. In historic terms it also possessed excellent historical associations, Lucius Licinius Lucullus being a former consul (and strict military disciplinarian) who as a general in the war against Mithridates, King of Pontus in the 70s BC, won a number of spectacular victories. It has been claimed that the name was chosen by the son of a Celtic king because Lucullus, whilst sounding ostensibly Roman, may disguise a Celtic name, possibly derived from the god Lug. This is an intriguing proposition, but has no clear evidence to support it. Lucullus' first names, however, recorded in full on the 1658 stone, are far more informative, for these tell us that the man was supported in his quest for citizenship by a certain Gaius Sallustius.

The only candidate of sufficient status in the imperial court with this name was Gaius Sallustius Passienus Crispus, great-great nephew of the Roman historian Sallust. Passienus Crispus was a prominent member of the imperial court and moved in powerful circles, eventually marrying Agrippina the Younger, sister of Caligula, niece to Claudius and mother of Nero. He was, in short, an ideal sponsor for a British prince. When Amminus fled to the imperial court in AD 40, he would presumably have brought close members of his family rather than leave them to the mercy of his enemies. As a citizen of Rome, the British prince would have received the Roman forenames of his sponsor and any sons that he brought with him, or whom he had later, would almost certainly inherit the same. As Lucullus was Amminus' biological heir, we would expect the king, who fled Britain in AD 40, to have reinvented himself in Rome as Gaius Sallustius Amminus.

GOVERNOR OF BRITAIN: HEIR TO CUNOBELINUS

The important issue deriving from the two Lucullus stones unearthed in Chichester is this: at some point in the 80s AD the governor of Roman Britain was a Briton. Culturally Lucullus was very Roman, but ethnically, he was a descendant of British kings. He had adopted a Roman name, was a fully paid up member of Roman society, had the patronage of one of the most important families in the capital, and had (almost certainly) been brought up within the imperial court, speaking Latin and learning the ways of empire. Gaius Sallustius Lucullus, son of Amminus and grandson of Cunobelinus, had finally made it big. His grandfather may have been recognised as 'King of the Britons' (Suetonius *Caligula* 44), and his uncle Togidubnus was officially credited as being a 'Great King of the Britons', but Lucullus had control of the whole island.

It may seem surprising that someone born a non-Roman (or whose immediate ancestors were from beyond the limits of empire) could achieve so much, becoming a Propraetorian Imperial Legate of one of the wealthiest provinces in the empire, but Lucullus' rise to prominence is not without parallel. A good example of the spectacular possibilities that promotion could bring in the Roman world is demonstrated, for instance, by the career of one Publius Helvius Pertinax. Pertinax was born in AD 126 in Alba, northwestern Italy, the son of a freed slave. Until he was 34, he worked as a *grammaticus* (teacher of grammar), before deciding on a career change and joining the army. Meteoric rise through the military command structure (including a stint as a tribune in the VI Victrix Legion stationed at York) eventually led to a variety of posts in civil administration. By the early 170s AD he was a member of the Roman senate and went on to hold the governorships of Upper and Lower Moesia (modern day Bulgaria and Serbia), Dacia (Romania), Syria and finally Britain. He served as proconsul of Africa in AD 188 and as urban prefect of Rome the following year. On 31 December AD 192 the unpopular emperor Commodus was assassinated and Pertinax found himself acclaimed as his successor. If the son of a former slave could become governor of six provinces, a senator, a Legate, a consul, an urban prefect then finally emperor of Rome, why should it seem strange that the son of a British king should become governor of Britain?

The system of bringing up the children of allied kings in Rome was an old and established one. The children in question may have gone to Rome as hostages, to ensure the loyalty of their parents, or willingly as equals to be educated in the Roman way and benefit from the patronage of the imperial court. A system of imperial protection and senatorial networking proved useful to people determined to make it good in the empire. A fine example of this is the Jewish aristocrat Marcus Julius Agrippa (Herod Agrippa), grandson of Herod the Great, who lived in the court of the emperor Tiberius, befriending both Caligula and Claudius, before returning to the east as governor Judea in the early 40s AD.

The timing of Lucullus' appointment was critical. In AD 84, Agricola, governor of Britain, was recalled to Rome by the emperor Domitian. Agricola had served in Britain for seven years and had completed the conquest of Wales, northern England and Scotland. With the armies of Caledonia smashed and with troubles elsewhere in the empire, Domitian no doubt felt that it was time to relieve Agricola of his command and replace him with someone who better understood the Britons and could make the establishment of a Roman way of life more permanent. Someone who could speed up the Romanising process, stabilise the province and hasten the much needed economic returns. The war had been won by Agricola, now Lucullus had to win the peace. Such considerations would have had no appeal to Tacitus. His father-in-law, Agricola had, in his view, been cheated of the public acknowledgement of great victories and deprived of the rewards. That an ethnic Briton was put in post after Agricola would only have made the situation worse. As it was, of course, Lucullus did not perhaps live long enough to reap the full benefits of his position, for, during his tenure as governor, he was recalled and executed by the increasingly paranoid Domitian.

QUESTION TIME

All this, of course, goes against Established Fact. When the 'Lucullean Theory' was first aired in *Roman Sussex* (2006), it generated a torrent of letters and emails, few of them positive. The letters page in Current Archaeology was twice given over to respondents, most very upset (as if I had insulted a much loved relative). Most were submitted as argument-ending rebuttals, although it is useful to respond to the worst offenders here:

> *The theory concerning Sallustius Lucullus is highly dubious. An appointment (as governor) to someone of Lucullus' supposed standing is so monumentally anomalous it could only be accepted if there was a very strong case for it.*

I'm afraid that comments like this seriously underestimate the political *probability* of the Lucullus theory. First, the situation in Britain was indeed extreme, after both the Boudiccan revolt and the final pacification of Scotland by Agricola. Native kings like Togidubnus remained in power (and 'loyal down to our times' as Tacitus says) for a lengthy period, far longer than in other provinces of the empire. In fact, looking at the archaeological evidence, Southern Britain does not seem to have been conquered by Rome at all, rather it was quietly assimilated, its client status surviving for an extended period, certainly well after Boudicca.

> *The theory is highly speculative as it all hangs on the names in the inscriptions.*

As indeed do many other less convincing theories drawn from far more fragmentary inscriptions. One only has to glance through *The Roman Inscriptions of Britain*, by R. G. Collingwood and R. P. Wright, a rather excellent tome, to see just how many strange but rather convincing theories have been generated from very little evidence.

For Sallustius Lucullus to govern Britain under Domitian, he should have been introduced into the senate, by Nero. If Claudius' introduction of senators from Gaul were an affront, senators from Britain after would have been beyond the pale.

But British aristocrats *had* been in the imperial court for over 90 years (if one takes the hostages taken by Caesar in 55 and 54 BC and later the British kings seeking an audience with Octavian) by the time of the Claudian 'invasion', well *before* Claudius' introduction of the Gauls into the senate. I would be surprised if native friendlies networking within Rome had *not* caused outrage and contempt from the more conservative elements of the system, but the Fact remains that they were there.

An appointment so monumentally anomalous would have caused of outrage in our incurably snobbish sources.

But then that's the point, it was not monumentally anomalous (especially when you consider how client and allied kings were used elsewhere in the empire) and the 'snobbish sources' (I'll avoid the obvious 'pot, kettle and sooty bottom' analogy here) are scanty to say the least. There are no surviving primary accounts of the Roman invasion and, as far as Tactitus is concerned, his interest in Britannia derives solely from the involvement of his father-in-law Agricola. Once Agricola departs, in the mid AD 80s, Tacitus' interest declines sharply. He is, in any case, pretty damning about any of the Britons who embraced Rome (e.g. Togidubnus) as opposed to those that valiantly fought against 'civilisation' (e.g. Caratacus). In any case, there does appear to be some evidence to suggest that the situation in Britain was considered 'different', for we know that, around the mid 80s AD, at least two *iuridici* were working within the province. *Iuridici*, whose 'jurisdiction' ran to the administration of a province (excluding all financial matters), were appointed to an area only when the governor was indisposed. In Britain, Gaius Salvius Liberalis Nonius Bassus was *iuridicus* before AD 84, whilst his successor, Gaius Octavius Tidius Tossianus Lucius Javolenus Priscus, may have been in post from AD 84-6. It is possible that the two were in Britain to oversee the day to day running of the province whilst Gnaeus Julius Agricola was active in the north, but given that Agricola seems to have been recalled to Rome around AD 83/4, it seems perhaps more likely that the *iuridici* were appointed to oversee the formalisation of the boundaries of the province, especially important given the abandonment of the northern territory and the possible move away from the client kingdoms of Togidubnus in the south, and the smooth transition of ultimate power to an ethnic Briton: Gaius Sallustius Lucullus.

A royal British descent embodied in Lucullus would have attracted the notice of a contemporary historian – Dio, Tacitus or Suetonius – any one of whom would have relished such a titbit.

This is a highly dubious statement to make. Tacitus is a classic(al) bigot when it comes to indigenous people like Togidubnus or Classicianus. He neglects to mention Togidubnus' role in the Boudiccan uprising (which must have been significant if he remained both 'loyal' and in power afterwards) making it a clear-cut tale of good (Roman) versus bad (British). Suetonius seldom mentions Britain at all, although he may well have visited with the emperor Hadrian early in the second century, being far more interested in the day-to-day gossip of the imperial court. Dio conflates (and garbles) a range of primary accounts, inventing lurid detail in the process. It is doubtful that any of these historians would really have cared that much about Lucullus' background.

The argument requires a dubious chain of suppositions to equate Sallustius Lucullus with Amminus Lucullus.

Why? More dubious assertions and suppositions for people in Roman Britain have been made on far more slender evidence. Two Luculli making monumental inscriptions in the same town at the same date would take far more explanation. The simple answer is that Lucullus son of Amminus and Lucullus governor of Britain are one and the same. The differing styles of message inherent in the inscription and the altar being intended for very different audiences.

That the son of a British king should become governor of Britain at a time when the province was still unstable after the Boudiccan revolt seems most unlikely.

I would think, if anything, that it was far *more* likely given the overwhelming support that Togidubnus et al must have given Rome during the revolt and the overwhelming Romanised nature of the British aristocracy of the south and east, most having been brought up in Rome as hostages – unlike the un-Romanised (and rebellious) Eceni. Nero and his advisors must have been very keen to reward those elements that had remained loyal and punish those that had stood up against him.

A sumptuous palace in Fishbourne would have been an isolated quarter for a governor to conduct his key military functions.

Not true. Given that Chichester was at the centre of Lucullus' new home territory (the Regnum) and occupied prime land by the sea (a position desired by any self-respecting Roman aristocrat) then it actually makes ideal sense. Lucullus wouldn't want to be in the north of England for every day of his governorship, especially if a key part of his remit was to oversee and accelerate the Romanising process of the south. Being stuck in York or Chester would have made no sense at all, especially once the advances and conquests of Agricola had been abandoned.

Our British prince really should, like Togidubnus and Catuarus, be a Claudius, not a Sallustius.

Why? Togidubnus and Catuarus seem to have surrendered to Claudius in AD 43/4 and benefited from his direct patronage thereafter. Lucullus' father Amminus went over to Rome *well before* the time of Claudius, when Claudius' nephew Gaius (Caligula) was emperor and would, presumably, have received patronage from one or more of the emperor's closest allies.

How do we know his name was Gaius?

Er, well because that's what it says on the inscription (well at least it says: 'C SALLVSTIVS LVCVLLVS' which ought to be expanded to *Gaius* Sallustius Lucullus).

In all probability Lucullus' real name was Lucius Sallustius Lucullus, proconsul of Baetica, mentioned by the Elder Pliny

Unfortunately 'Lucius' begins with an 'L', not a 'G'. Undoubtedly there was a *Lucius* Sallustius Lucullus in Baetica, but he is not the chap recorded from Chichester.

A man who styles himself simply N. son of M. is regularly not a Roman citizen at all.

This argument sadly misses the point of who Lucullus was and demonstrates a clear failure to understand the archaeological evidence (not to say the very nature of Roman Britain as opposed to classical Rome). The inscription citing LVCVLLVS AMMINI FIL is from a Romano British town *not* from the city of Rome. In Chichester, where it was no doubt important to win over hearts and minds, Lucullus explicitly cited his ancestry in a manner that countless other native friendlies like Tincomarus (TINCOM COMMI F) and Verica (VER COM F) had before. In other words, we have a dedication to the emperor Domitian, citing Lucullus' official name, rank and status, and a second altar outlining his blood heritage.

The Chichester inscription cannot be genuine because it is unlikely that an inscription whose honour and dedicator were both disgraced should have escaped defacement.

The stone was smashed and buried – how much defacement do you want?

It is on the other hand just the sort of thing that might have been invented by a seventeenth-century antiquary who had read Suetonius.

Well herein lies the problem, for no reason has ever been given to doubt the validity of the Lucullus inscription, other than it is 'too good to be true' (something which could be said of the Togidubnus inscription also from Chichester). The fact that it has since been lost shouldn't trouble us much as many good inscriptions from Chichester, including the famous 'Nero dedication', one of the earliest from any town in Britain, have also been consigned to oblivion. Disregarding the whole thing because 'it is too good to be true' is a case in point of hurling the baby a significant distance from both bath and bathwater. The hoax argument also fundamentally misses the point that the Lucullus inscription was found long *before* the Lucullus altar. Any forger, hoaxer or fraudster knows that that such a relationship is just not possible (or is at least very unlikely). The discovery of the later altar clearly validates the discovery of the larger, earlier inscription. End of story.

PALACES OF THE KINGDOM

There is, as already hinted above, an obvious post-script to all this. To the immediate south-west of Chichester lies one of the most imposing of all Roman sites in Britain: Fishbourne Roman Palace (79). The Palace was a major architectural achievement, a little piece of imperial Italy transposed into Britain. Ever since its discovery in the late 1960s, people have argued over what the structure means, why it was built and, rather crucially, for whom was it intended. The date of the new building work at Fishbourne is also still hotly debated. Established Fact tells us that completion was in or around AD 75, based on the observation that coins and pottery beneath the floors of the structure coalesce around the mid to late AD 70s. It is the ground plan of the new build, however, that provides our best date for its inception. Barry Cunliffe was the first to note the similarity between Fishbourne Palace and the Imperial Palace, the *Domus Flavia*, built for Domitian in Rome and it is this particular building that provides the key.

The 'business end' of the *Domus Flavia* was set around three official rooms: an entrance hall or throne room; an apsed hall or basilica; and a *lararium*, or shrine to the ancestral spirits of the Flavian family. The entrance hall was the largest of the three rooms, and possessed a throne where the emperor could greet official guests and visitors. The great basilica, to the north, was designed for more official meetings whereby delegations could seek an audience with palace officials. Behind the 'business end' lay a large open courtyard surrounded by a column-lined portico, at the centre of which was an ornate, octagonal fountain. The north wing of the palace contained two discrete, though undoubtedly lavish, guest apartments whilst the southern opened out towards the *Domus Augustana*, the older, more private areas of the complex. The west range contained areas of reception and entertainment, all focused around a monumental *triclinium* or dining room.

The main phase at Fishbourne mirrors the key architectural features of the *Domus Flavia*: central courtyard, public range containing a large entrance hall and aisled basilica, an impressive apsed triclinium, a private range and a guest wing arranged around a series of discrete apartments. As with the *Domus Flavia*, the entrance hall to Fishbourne, set centrally within the East Wing, was the single largest room in the whole complex. To the north of the main entrance, separated from it by a range of private apartments, was an aisled hall. The structured independence of the hall, combined with its relative isolation from the North and East wings, suggests that, as with the basilica in the *Domus Flavia*, this room was intended for semi-public assemblies and meetings between the outside world and representatives of the palace staff.

Two courtyards formed the central focus for three major units of accommodation in the north wing of the Fishbourne palace, each with bedrooms, living rooms / reception areas and a dining room (*80, 81*). The arrangement, creating private courtyards, largely cut off from the main building, may indicate that these discrete blocks were originally designed to accommodate important visitors or other, high status families. The western range contained areas of reception and entertainment, the focus of which was a large apsed *triclinium* or dining room. The apse may have served as a form of 'throne' or head table for the palace owner or as a curved dining couch (*stibadium*) where guests could sit and watch dancers or other forms of entertainment during more elaborate meals.

Domitian's palace was commissioned shortly after his accession to the imperial throne on the death of his brother Titus in AD 81. Although plans for an imperial residence on the Palatine may have been circulating earlier than this, foundations for the palace at Fishbourne are unlikely to have been set out before the start of construction in Rome, and probably not before the completion of works and the inauguration of the *Domus Flavia* in AD 92. Given that Domitian's palace would possess empire-wide architectural impact only on its completion, and that to commence work on a copy before the *Domus Flavia* was finished would almost certainly incur the wrath of a paranoid emperor (afterwards it could seem more a case of sincere flattery), the main phase at Fishbourne is unlikely to predate the period AD 85-90.

Who then could the Sussex palace, the *Domus Flavia* in miniature, have been built for? It is rare that an archaeological site and a historical person can be linked with any degree of certainty and attempts to do so are often fraught with difficulties. The chronology and sequence for Fishbourne, even in its revised state, does however tie in with a number of historically attested figures. Tiberius Claudius Togidubnus and Tiberius Claudius Catuarus have already been mentioned with regard to the primary phases of development at Fishbourne, the so-called 'Proto Palace'. Togidubnus is cited from an inscription in Chichester, Catuarus from a gold ring found from close to the palace. If we accept that building work for the Sussex palace did not commence before AD 90 (at the earliest) and that both men were ethnic Britons who owed their position and status to the emperor Claudius for service to Rome before and during the events of AD 43, then they would both certainly be of an advanced age by the time the foundations were being laid. If Togidubnus were in his early 20s when

79 Interpretative recreation of Fishbourne palace, based upon the *Domus Flavia*, home to the emperor Domitian in Rome, built in the early 90s AD, possibly for a character such as Lucullus. © *Sussex Archaeological Society*

80 Fragment of a late first-century mosaic in the northern wing of Fishbourne palace. © *Sussex Archaeological Society*

81 Section of a late first-century mosaic in the northern wing of Fishbourne palace. © *Sussex Archaeological Society*

first noted as a potential successor to his father, king Cunobelin, in AD 43, then he would be in his early 70s at the time of Fishbourne's dramatic redevelopment. We know next to nothing about the age or status of Catuarus, though he could conceivably have been Togidubnus' kinsman, possibly a brother, cousin or even a son. Given, however, that the main phase of building work at Fishbourne used the *Domus Flavia* as an architectural blueprint, being constructed at a time when the emperor Domitian was on the ascendant, then a third candidate for occupancy of the Sussex house appears.

Lucullus, son of Amminus and grandson to Cunobelinus, reached the pinnacle of his career when, in the mid to late 80s AD, he became Propraetorian Imperial Legate, governor of the province of Britain. Lucullus owed his position as governor to Domitian and his status as a member of the Catuvellaunian royal house to his blood ties to Cunobelinus. His family had served the emperors Caligula, Claudius and Nero well during the formative years of Rome in Britain and had no doubt forged links with the later emperor Vespasian, father of Domitian, when he had served in Britain as commander of the II Augusta during the events of AD 43 and 44. Given Lucullus' ethnic background, political history and status (holding the most important of provincial offices), then his candidature as palace owner would appear strong. If Togidubnus (and / or Catuarus) had been the owner of the Proto Palace with its links to Nero and the Julio-Claudians, then it is likely that he did not live to see the rise to power of his nephew Lucullus and the modification of his rural retreat into the palace fit for the imperial elite.

Of course Fishbourne is not alone, for the 'villa' at Southwick, also in West Sussex should also be more properly referred to as a palace for it is a smaller version of Fishbourne; another *Domus Flavia* in miniature. The main axis of entrance hall through courtyard to apsed dining room (*triclinium*) as seen at Fishbourne palace is duplicated at Southwick. To the south of the entrance hall lay what is almost certainly the remains of a large basilical hall, heavily modified during a secondary phase of development. The position of the basilica at the extreme southern margins of the palace furthermore indicates the same degree of structural independence as evidenced at Fishbourne and in the *Domus Flavia*. The North wing contained living quarters arranged into discrete areas. Given the pottery and coin evidence recorded from Southwick, a constructional date for the palace in the later half of the first century AD seems likely. Given the duplication of ground plan evident, that date can plausibly be further restricted to around, or shortly after, AD 92. Other luxurious buildings of similar date have been found, or are hinted, at Pulborough, Angmering, Eastbourne, Brighton, Arundel and Langstone (in Hampshire). As with Fishbourne, it is impossible to say with any certainty who lived at Southwick or in the other early buildings, but their chronology, sequence and structural form plausibly ties them all to the final ascendancy of Gaius Sallustius Lucullus.

The later first century AD was a time when central government went to substantial efforts so as to better Romanise key players in the province through

Above left: 82 Bronze head of a godess, probably of Sulis Minerva, from Bath (*Aquae Sulis*), Somerset. The natural hot springs here formed the centrepiece to an immense religious and bathing complex, established in the latter third of the first century AD, possibly under Togidubnus or Lucullus. *Otto Fein Collection*

Above right: 83 The 'Medusa head', from the pediment of a temple, probably belonging to Sulis Minerva, the patron deity of Bath (*Aquae Sulis*), constructed in the latter third of the first century AD, possibly under Togidubnus or Lucullus. *Otto Fein Collection*

84 The eastern wall of Caistor St Edmund (*Venta Ecenorum*), market town of the Eceni in Norfolk. The street plan of *Venta* seems to have been set out in the early 70s AD, ten years after the Boudiccan Revolt, presumably in an attempt to finally reconcile any surviving members of the tribe with the Roman government. The town does not appear to have been a great success. *Author*

the development of new civilian building projects (82, 83, 84) and (presumably) increased financial incentives. This process seems to have begun in earnest under the auspices of Lucullus' predecessor, the governor Gnaeus Julius Agricola. In fact, Tacitus specifically highlighted this process, providing an insight to the methods used when he says:

> Agricola gave private encouragement and public aid to the building of temples, courts of justice and dwelling-houses, praising the energetic, and reproving the indolent ... He likewise provided a liberal education for the sons of the chiefs, and showed such a preference for the natural powers of the Britons over the industry of the Gauls that they who lately disdained the tongue of Rome now coveted its eloquence. Hence, too, a liking sprang up for our style of dress, and the toga became fashionable. Step by step they were led to things which dispose to vice, the lounge, the bath, the elegant banquet
> (Tacitus *Agricola* 21)

The paragraph ends with a typical piece of Tactitean cynicism when he observes that: 'all this in their ignorance they called civilisation, when it was but a part of their servitude' (Tacitus *Agricola* 21).

Rather than having an obscure cameo-role in the story of Britannia, Gaius Sallustius Lucullus would seem to have been a significant player, a leading character who had a keen hand in the Romanisation of Britain and the establishment of Roman governmental systems. How the British aristocracy responded to his very public downfall at the hands of the emperor Domitian, we will probably never know, but the co-operation of the Celtic elite with the government of Rome must have suffered a very serious set back, perhaps precipitating significant troubles that occurred in Britain just prior to the construction of Hadrian's Wall in the early second century AD.

11

AFTERMATH:
A TRAIL OF THE DEAD

The death of Caesar Domitianus Augustus on 18 September AD 96 represented the end of the Flavian line but not of the concept of emperor. Republicanism, as a reality, was long past reviving; the militarily-strong monarchy had its tentacles in every aspect of the Roman State – there were too many vested interests around to allow it to die that day. Domitian's violent demise did, however, mark a key turning point in Roman political history for the emperors that followed, increasingly focusing their attentions away from the political demands of the capital and towards the ever expanding frontiers; Trajan upon Dacia (Romania) and the east; Hadrian on the provinces, especially Britain and Judea; Marcus Aurelius on the Rhine and German problem.

Nerva and Trajan, Domitian's immediate successors, seem to have been little interested in Britain. The conquest of the province had been the pet project of the Flavian dynasty, reaching its climax under the now discredited Domitian. They may have tried to distance themselves from any association with Britain, or, perhaps more realistically, as the province was now officially 'conquered' perhaps they felt their energies could be more usefully directed elsewhere. Trajan, in particular, craved military glory, and there was none to won for him in Britain (85). The energies of the emperor, as well as a large amount of the military reserves of the empire, were now to be directed against the Dacians (across the Danube) and Parthians (in the East). In Britain, following troop withdrawals to supplement these Balkan campaigns, the northern frontier appears to have stabilised along the Tyne – Solway isthmus (Newcastle – Carlisle), all of Agricola's conquered territory to the north now having been abandoned. The legionary bases at Caerleon (in South Wales), Chester and York were all rebuilt in stone, suggesting an acceptance that these were becoming more permanent, new *coloniae* were established at Gloucester and Lincoln.

Britain may have felt as if it had been cut adrift, at least politically, during the final years of the first century AD and the beginning of second. We possess little written evidence for the period recorded from the pens of Roman historians, although a wealth of information has been found from at least one British site, the frontier fort of *Vindolanda* at Chesterhom, Northumberland. Here, official documents relating to the garrison life between AD 90-105 tell us much about day-to-day activities, and have rightly been hailed as one of 'Roman Britain's

85 Large male portrait found at Hawkshaw, Scottish Borders and now in the National Museum of Scotland, Edinburgh. The head, although usually cited as being of 'unknown identity', seems to be that of the emperor Trajan and may have formed part of a triumphal monument marking the limits of the Roman province of *Britannia*, following the abandonment of territory conquered by Agricola. *Otto Fein Collection*

greatest treasures', but in truth they do not help us much in understanding what was going on in Britain beyond the walls of the fort (*86*). One document, however, is of particular interest: an incomplete writing tablet, dated 18 May (of some unknown year in the very late 80s to mid 90s AD) which records that the:

> First Cohort of Tungrians, of which Julius Verecundus, prefect, is commander [has] 752 men, among them six centurions; of those absent, as guards of the legate, 46, on the staff of Ferrox …
> (*Tabulae Vindolandeses*, ii, 154)

The fragmentary strength report seems to suggest that Ferrox, legate of a Legion (presumably the *IX Hispana* in York), was at this time also acting governor (normally legionary legates had a bodyguard drawn from their own legion), something which, it has been plausibly suggested, occurred immediately after the removal from power of Sallustius Lucullus. A further tantalising glimpse of what may have happened to Lucullus' *own* guard comes from the recorded presence of a military unit called the *pedites singulars Britannici* on the Danube, between AD 103 and 107. Pat Southern has noted, in her book *Domitian, Tragic Tyrant*, that:

> *Singulares* were bodyguard troops, and these men were probably in the bodyguard of the governor of Britain. Their removal to the Danube may have been punishment for their involvement in the supposed rebellion
> (Southern 1997, 78)

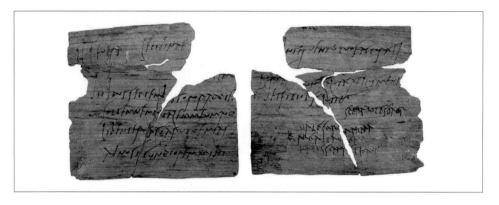

86 Part of a writing tablet, inviting to Sulpicia Lepidina to the birthday party of Claudia Severa, from Vindolanda, Northumberland and dated to between AD 93 and 107. © *Trustees of the British Museum*

The general lack of detailed, contemporary Roman information on *Britannia,* however, is frustrating, for all the later sources seem to agree that, in the early years of the second century, the province was on the verge of a catastrophic meltdown.

THE MYSTERY OF THE NINTH

> Eburacum is still, how shall I put it? – Still more than a little ghost-ridden by the ninth legion. Oh, I do not mean that their spirits have wandered back from the fields of Ra, but the place is haunted, none the less. By the altars to Spanish gods that they set up and worshipped at; by their names and numbers idly scratched on walls; by British women whom they loved and children with Spanish faces whom they fathered. All this lying, as it were, like sediment under the wine of another Legion
> (Sutcliffe 1954, 88)

Rosemary Sutcliffe's hauntingly evocative novel, *The Eagle of the Ninth*, still grips the popular imagination. Since its publication in 1954, countless children (and, dare I add, adults) have been entranced by the story of an elite unit of Roman troops disappearing into the swirling mists of Caledonia and of one young man's heroic odyssey to uncover the truth. Journeying beyond the northern frontier in disguise, Marcus Aquila, son of the Ninth Legion's Chief Centurion, hopes to find out what happened to his father, to the Legion and to its emblematic bronze eagle. The truth, as he uncovers it, proves unbearable: the Ninth, exhausted and demoralised, had became bogged down in enemy territory with no obvious hope of rescue. Surrounded and desperate, the Legion's command structure crumbled; disaffected elements became openly mutinous. Those, including Marcus' father, who had not been killed in action or joined the enemy were finally butchered whilst trying to regroup, and their eagle taken.

Two film versions of the novel are, at the time of writing, in development. This fact disturbs the British press for whom the 'Hollywoodisation' of history is a major source of concern. *The Eagle of the Ninth* although still far from completion, has already been compared, by some papers, to previous skewed celluloid takes on the past. The historical movie genre has, for example, already thrown up cases where US troops single headedly thwart Nazi ambitions in Europe (*Saving Private Ryan*: in reality they had a little help from other nations), where US commandoes single-handedly defeat the Imperial Japanese army and air force (*Objective, Burma!*: other allied forces played a more significant role), where US prisoners of war lead the way out of prison camp Stalag Luft III in *The Great Escape* (they didn't) and where US submariners capture an intact Axis Enigma code machine onboard *U571* (didn't happen). Don't even get the press started on Mel Gibson (in *Gallipoli / The Bounty / Braveheart / The Patriot / The Passion of the Christ*).

Hearing about the new version of the *Eagle of the Ninth*, the *Times* howled with predictable outrage, noting that all Romans in the movie had been 'cast as GIs in History Lesson for Iraq and Afghanistan'. The central premise of a well equipped and trained army foolishly venturing 'into a wild mountain landscape to punish an enemy that it barely understands and badly underestimates' has, in the *Times*' view 'predictably disastrous results', neatly paralleling the consequences of American foreign policy today. All popular accounts of historical events play loose and fast with the perceived Facts, however, and the British film industry is no less guilty than Hollywood (only perhaps less successful).

What seems to have upset the leader writers in the British Press, apart from the revelation that all Romans in the Eagle of the Ninth will have American accents (when in reality they all obviously spoke like Oxbridge graduates) was that the film doesn't seem to care 'that modern historical opinion suggests that the Ninth Legion survived its tour of duty in Scotland, only to be wiped out in the Middle East later in the second century'. That the fate of the Ninth was settled a long way from the windswept northern frontier of Hadrian's Wall is something which, since the 1950s, become an Established Fact so that, in 1993, Peter Salway was able to assert that:

> It is no longer thought that the unlucky Ninth disappeared from army lists while still in Britain, whether destroyed or disbanded, since there is some evidencew pointing to its continued existence beyond the present date and to its presence on the Rhine
>
> (Salway 1993, 132)

Whilst in 2006 David Mattingly could confidently state that the 'mystery disappearance' of Legio IX in the early second century appears to have been due to its strategic transfer from the province rather than its loss in an unrecorded British catastrophe' (Mattingly 2006, 90). The nature of this particular Established Fact seems so secure (not to say obvious) that few academics really feel that the point is worth mentioning. Unfortunately, as with most 'facts' in history, there is nothing secure, obvious or even definitive about this particular example. In fact all we can really say about the Ninth *Hispana* Legion is that it vanished from history in the early second century AD and, whatever ultimately happened to it, there is nothing that archaeology can do to help. Certainly there is no evidence that it was ever taken out of Britain to be anihilated elsewhere: it simply disappears.

The Legion does not seem to have been involved in the construction of Hadrian's Wall in the early 120s AD, its last testified activity in the province being in the stone rebuild of the legionary fortress at York (*Eburacum*) in AD 107-8. There is some evidence that a detatchment of the Legion was at Nijmegan (*Noviomagus*), a fortress on the Rhine frontier in what is now the esatern Netherlands, at some point after AD 121, but this is largely circumstantial. What we can say is that its place in Britain was taken by the *VI Victrix* Legion around AD 122. This unit, having been moved from Lower Germany, probably arrived with the newly appointed governor of Britain, Aulus Platorius Nepos. Whatever happened to the IX, it cetainly was no longer in existence by the mid second century as a series of army listings compiled during the reign of the emperor Marcus Aurelius (AD 161-80) fails to mention them. The idea that they were cut to pieces 'somewhere in the east' in the mid second century is based on supposition, large numbers of (unamed) units having been lost in wars against the Jews and Parthians at this time. What most people seem to forget is that large numbers of (unamed) units also seem to have been lost in Britain.

HADRIAN IN BRITAIN

Marcus Cornelius Fronto, writing in the 160s AD, consoled the emperor Marcus Aurelius, following severe Roman troop losses in the east, by reminding him of past tragedies:

> Indeed, when your grandfather Hadrian held imperial power, what great numbers
> of soldiers were killed by the Jews, what great numbers by the British
> (Fronto *Parthian War* 2, 220)

The Jewish wars we know about, thanks to numerous contemporary references, but the number and extent of British losses remain shrouded in mystery. Fronto's reference must relate to a significant event (otherwise why would he have mentioned it?) and it probably involved Legions, for auxilliary losses would not register upon the imperial radar. The action may have occurred early on in Hadrian's reign for the annomyously authored *Augustan History*, compiled in the late third century AD, notes that when Hadrian 'took over the government' (in August AD 117) he:

> immediately reverted to an earlier policy and devoted his energies to maintaining
> peace throughout the world. For at one and the same time those peoples Trajan

had subjugated were in revolt, the Moors started making attacks, the Sarmtae were waging war, the Britons could not be kept under Roman control
(*Scriptores Historiae Augustae Hadrian*, 5, 1)

The first thing to say about this reference (apart from noting its its geographical vagueness) is that the phrasing seems to make a clear distinction between the Moors (of North Africa), the Sarmate (north-east of the Danube), the Britons *and* 'those peoples Trajan had subjugated', his major spheres of conflict being against the Dacians (modern day Romania) and the Parthians (in Armenia, Iraq and the Persian Gulf). The 'Britons', therefore, do not appear to have been classed as one of 'those people'; there being little evidence that Imperator Caesar Divi Nervae filius Nerva Traianus Augustus had any real interest in the province, other than maintaining the staus quo whilst imperial ambition found its outlet elsewhere. The 'Britons' refered to in the Scriptores Historia Augustae are therefore unlikey to be those occupied by under any new Roman military initiative.

The general assumption has been that the trouble mentioned within the pages of the *Scriptores* relate to a war, possibly defensive stemming from an barbarian invasion of Roman held territory, thus precipitating Hadrian's personal visit to Britain in around AD 122 and the subsequent construction of a wall. This particular scenario was for many years, it is perhaps uneccessary to state, an Established Fact. More likely perhaps, given the phrasing that 'the Britons *could not be kept under Roman control*', that the reference is to a rebellion or uprising within existing, possibly even long-held, Roman teritory. Certainly the annoymous author of the *Scriptores* does not mention an invasion *per se* and neither does he refer to barbarian involvement (although to be fair the reference is hardly detailed). It seems reasonable then, given the phrasing, that the Britons *who could not be kept under Roman control* were operating within the province of Britannia – but where?

The tribal leaders of Northern Britain, although within the orbit of Rome for some significant time, had never been as completely infected by Mediterranean culture as had their southern colleagues. The 'Brigantes' tribal confederation, whatever their full extent and organisational nature, had, as recorded in the pages of Tactitus' *Annals* and *Histories*, always been difficult, riven as they were with multiple internal disagreements. It would seem natural to assume that, if the troubles cited by the *Scriptores* had stemmed from within the province, that it was the Brigantes, or their immediate neighbours, who were ultimately responsible.

Some evidence of this *may* be supplied by a fragmentary tombstone which was recovered from *Vindolanda*, Chesterholm in Northumberland. The critical elements of the inscription, which appeared to date to the very early second century, were missing, but enough survived to show that the man being commemorated, Titus Annius, centurion of the First Cohort of Tungrians, had been 'killed in the war' (*in bello interfectus*). Further afield, a tombstone from Ferentinum in Italy was set up to Titus Pontius Sabinus, who, amongst other things, had commanded detachments of the *VII Gemina, VIII Augusta* and *XXII Primigenia* Legions on the 'British expedition', taking much-needed

Above left: 87 Bronze head of the emperor Hadrian recovered from the River Thames, near London Bridge, in 1834. The head has been forcibly removed from a full statue, much like the head of Nero from Saxmundham (see *70*) and could similarly be the result of violent social instability. © *Trustees of the British Museum*

Above right: 88 Bronze coin of the emperor Hadrian shown (on horseback) addressing the troops of Britain issued to commemorate his visit to the province in AD 122 when restored order and 'corrected many faults'. © *Trustees of the British Museum*

89 Hadrian's Wall to the east of Housesteads (*Vercovicium*), marking the official end of Roman civilisation in Britain. *Author*

reinforcements to the island after (or even during) a major conflict. Mention of the 'deified Trajan' (*divi Traianus*) within the text of Sabinus' memorial suggests that the 'expedition' may have occurred late in Trajan's reign (AD 98-117) or early in Hadrian's (AD 117-138).

It is worth pointing out that no tribal area or geographic zone is mentioned with regard to the troubles, and, although generally placed in the north, the 'Britons' of the *Scriptores* could, in the absence of secure archaeological evidence, just as plausibly have been causing problems for the Roman administration, disrupting communication, trade, taxation and lines of supply, in the South. In this respect, the severed bronze head of the emperor Hadrian himself (*87*), recovered from the River Thames, near London Bridge, in 1834, is intriguing. The piece has been removed from a full statue with some force before being deposited (or simply dumped) in the river. This could represent a piece of later (Christian?) religious iconoclasm, or alternatively it could be representative of the troubles that affected fourth- and fifth-century Britain. It is worth noting, however, that the violent removal and subsequent deposition of the head is similar to that of the decapitated portrait of the young Nero found in the River Alde in Suffolk. The Alde piece is, of course, generally associated with the Boudiccan sack of Colchester in AD 60, but the Hadrianic portrait is unassociated with any such bloody event, unless of course there *was* a period of instability afflicting London and the south early in Hadrian's reign. Certainly, London was swept by a catastrophic fire in the early 120s AD which could, just as easily, have been the result of a native insurgency as it could be purely accidental. Were the surviving elements of the Catuvellauni, whose leader Lucullus had been violently terminated by the emperor Domitian, venting their fury against the State in a way reminiscent of the Eceni, 60 years before?

Whatever the situation in Britain, Hadrian thought it demanded his immediate presence. In the summer of AD 122, the emperor arrived in the island (*88*), whereupon 'he corrected many faults and was the first to build a wall, 80 miles long, to separate the Romans and the barbarians' (*Scriptores Historiae Augustae Hadrian* 11, 2). Hadrian and his officials set about pacifying the causes of the British troubles, whilst the emperor himself designed and set out the northernmost limits of the province in the most monumental of terms (*89*). Now, at last, the conquest of Britain could be said by the emperors of Rome to have been completed.

POSTSCRIPT

In the early years of the second century AD, the palace of Fishbourne faced an uncertain future. With the governor gone, the building would presumably have been confiscated by the State to be retained in Imperial hands, passed on to other officials or to be bought up by any surviving members of the Romano-British aristocracy untainted by the emperor Domitian's smear campaign. Alternatively, the state apartments and palatial splendour of the Fishbourne complex could have been made available at a 'knock down price' to an up and coming member of the new

90 Upton Country Park: a recreation of a Romano-British farm house, quite unlike the lavish extravagence of Fishbourne, but more typical of the sort of 'Roman' building to be found across southern Britain in the decades following the death of Lucullus. *Author*

commercial elite. Whatever the case, the basic structure and design of the palace, a range of high status apartments linked to a monumental *triclinium*, entrance hall and bath suite, seems, at the start of the second century, to have been both uneconomical and politically untenable.

Whoever finally acquired Fishbourne, they immediately initiated a major change in design. The first alterations came with the modification of the great aisled hall, one of the most prominent features of the primary phase palace. Clearly the basilica was no longer considered a necessary part of the new structure for whilst a provincial governor would require immense state apartments and assembly rooms, secondary owners would not perhaps have countenanced such a flagrant waste of floor space. The hall was remodelled, a bath suite being unceremoniously inserted through one end. Further additions to the original design of the palace, perhaps indicating an end to official or semi public functions, included the abandonment of the formal garden, parts of which were now being used to dump domestic waste.

The changes apparent at Fishbourne reflect the fact that the last prominent member of the dynasty of Tasciovanus was dead and the family itself, at least in a political sense, was finished. The primary phase of Roman Britain had run its course; the Celtic client kingdoms were over. From now on Britannia would be a province run just like any other.

FURTHER READING

As far as general works synthesising the archaeology and history of Roman Britain, the most enduring and important of all is probably still *Britannia* by S. Frere. The original text was written some time ago (1967), so be aware of what edition or reprint you are reading, but despite the occasional outdated element, this still remains the standard work on the subject. If you are serious about studying Roman Britain, then this book is essential.

Probably the best new work on the province of Britain is *Roman Britain: A New History* by G. de la Bedoyere (2006). This book synthesises and integrates the history and archaeology of the island, with a good balance of detailed, site-specific examples and more general historical interpretation. Very well illustrated throughout, *A New History* is less of an alternative take on Rome in Britain (as implied by the title) but as a thematic analysis, covering traditional subjects, such civic life, religion, trade and commerce, industrial production and the military, with more unusual topics such as slavery and the political makeup of the Roman province. There is also an up to date bibliography, chronology and full gazetteer.

The best (and certainly the first) attempt to look at Roman Britain from a largely archaeological perspective, rather than primarily from an historical one, was *The Romanization of Britain* by M. Millett (1990), even though the word 'Romanization' itself now appears to (inexplicably) be something of a dirty one within certain archaeological circles.

A wholly refreshing antidote to most dry works on the subject is *My Roman Britain* by R. Reece (1988). You will not find many references to this work in other publications, mostly because when it first came out it annoyed a lot of people due to its apparently irreverent tone. However, as something which really gets you thinking about the nature of history and archaeology, it cannot be beaten, if, of course, you can get your hands on a copy. Arguably, the most important work on the province since Frere's *Britannia*.

Two significant books that have, since their publication, really started to change people's perception of the Iron Age to Roman interface are *Britannia: the creation of a Roman Province* (2005) and *Coins and Power in Late Iron Age Britain* (2000), both by J. Creighton. They are thought provoking and well researched, but sadly also rather expensive in their original format.

Concerning the Iron Age, you can't really go wrong with anything by B. Cunliffe, whose work has been at the forefront of prehistoric studies now for the past 40 years. The most useful, recent texts are probably *Europe Between the Oceans, 9000 BC – AD 1000* (2008), *Iron Age Communities in Britain* (2004) and *Facing the Ocean: the Atlantic and its Peoples: 8000 BC to AD 1500* (2001).

The Decline and Fall of Roman Britain by N. Faulkner (2001) also represents an interesting look at the nature of Romanization, depicting the Roman Empire as a politically corrupt, warmongering machine intent on simple plunder (all of it true). This is not a particularly new take on the province, but its examination of archaeological information and interpretation of historical data is refreshing and stimulating.

An Imperial Possession: Britain in the Roman Empire, 54 BC – AD 409 by D. Mattingly (2006) is thorough and informative, but the absence of illustrations (other than the occasional plan) makes it difficult, for the non-specialist at least, to make much sense of what was going on in the Roman province. A useful book nonetheless.

For a detailed overview of what little primary historical sources there are for Roman Britain, try *Roman Britain: A Source Book* by S. Ireland (first edition 1986; third edition 2008). This contains comprehensive translations of all the main primary Latin and Greek sources for the period, especially for coins and inscriptions, with some excellent interpretation. Be warned, however, the earlier versions of this book do not contain detailed translations of Caesar's *Gallic Wars* or Tacitus' *Agricola* which are probably the most important sources for the period, an omission that is more than made up for in the most recent edition.

A Companion to Roman Britain by G. de la Bedoyere (1999) is a useful text for those new to the subject matter and cites significant numbers of primary historical sources, texts from monumental inscriptions and coins. I would certainly not suggest reading it from cover to cover, but working with it can be an extremely profitable experience.

Similarly *The Finds of Roman Britain* and *The Buildings of Roman Britain*, again by G. de la Bedoyere represent invaluable reference works if one is interested in the main types of artefact recovered from the province as well as the major architectural forms imposed by the new government and developed by the native population. Both texts are, in their original format, unfortunately now out of print. Rumours abound of reissue through another publishing company.

Roman Britain by P. Salway (1981) represents another good look at the province, though it is conducted primarily from the known historical sources and therefore provides a fair starting point to follow references. The archaeology is not covered in great detail. Updated paperback copies have been in circulation since 2005.

Anyone wishing to follow up ideas surrounding Fishbourne and the other palaces of central-southern England, should read *Roman Sussex* by M. Russell (2006). Although centring on a specific county in southern England, the book places evidence from the county within the context of events and social history of life in the Roman Empire. Early chapters contain the first discussion of the Togidubnus / Togodubus and Lucullus theories.

Excavation reports provide the primary source for studying the 'nuts and bolts' of the province. A good idea is to read these only after finding a reference in a general synthesis of the period (such as Frere's *Britannia*) so that you can see where the author got their interpretation from (and whether or not you agree with it). *Britannia* (a journal sequence not to be confused with Frere's book of the same name) is published every year by The Society for the Promotion of Roman Studies and contains all the latest theories and thoughts with a yearly update on excavation, survey and discoveries made. *The Journal of Roman Studies*, also yearly, keeps you informed about the empire as a whole whilst the *Proceedings of the Prehistoric Society* often contains significant works on the European Iron Age. Other excellent journals (requiring either subscription or a good library) include *Antiquity* and the *Oxford Journal of Archaeology*. Specific excavation reports can be found either as separate Council for British Archaeology, Society for the Promotion of Roman Studies, English Heritage, Cadw, Historic Scotland, National Trust, Society of Antiquaries etc monographs (usually very expensive), or hidden in County Journals, such as *The Wiltshire Archaeological and Natural History Magazine*, *Sussex Archaeological Collections* or *Archaeologia Cantiana*. Keep up to date with news and thoughts 'as they happen' in *British Archaeology* and *Current Archaeology*, both published monthly.

The Internet has provided a useful breaking ground for new work and theories but it goes without saying that care should be taken, for few things that appear on the net have been verified or cleared by an academic editorial panel. The sites that I have found to provide some of the most useful information are:

Bill Thayer's LacusCurtius site:
> http://penelope.uchicago.edu/Thayer/E/Roman/home.html

The Internet Classics Archive:
> http://classics.mit.edu/index.html

Paul Halsall's Internet Ancient History Sourcebook:
> www.fordham.edu/halsall/ancient/asbookfull.html

Jona Lendering's Livius – Articles on Ancient History:
> www.livius.org/

Lou Francis' de res Historiae Antiqua:
> www.reshistoriaeantiqua.co.uk/

Guy de la Bedoyere's Roman Britain:
> www.romanbritain.freeserve.co.uk/

Roman Britain.org's informative:
> www.roman-britain.org/

Chris Rudd's Celtic coin database:
> www.celticcoins.com/

The Oxford Celtic coins index:
> www.finds.org.uk/CCI/

INDEX

Addedomaros 53
Adminius (see also Amminus) 52, 80, 82, 87-8, 90, 112
Agricola 15, 33, 97-8, 109, 119, 123, 135, 141, 147-60, 167-70, 177-9, 188
Alde, river 134-5, 185
Alesia 34, 37, 54, 157
Amminus (see also Adminius) 46, 82, 87-92, 112, 165-7, 170-1, 175
Ancalites 20-1, 46
Anglesey, Isle of 11, 126-31, 135, 139, 150-2
Annius, Titus 183
Arun, river 73, 96, 99, 102-3, 108
Arverni 38
Atuatuci 36
Aquae Sulis (see also Bath) 176
Atrebates 24-6, 32, 37-9, 54-7, 63, 67, 89, 98, 108, 112, 138
Augustus 56, 60-7, 74-5, 77-84, 87-8, 91-2, 110, 117-8

Badbury Rings, Dorset 70
Bassus, Nonius 169
Batavians 101-5
Bath (see also *Aquae Sulis*) 111, 176
Beachy Head, East Sussex 40
Berikos (see also Verica) 21, 52, 82, 89, 92, 99
Belgae 17, 31, 51, 111
Bibroci 20-1, 46
Bigbury, Kent 47
Boadicea (see also Boudicca) 122
Bodunni (see also Dobunni) 28, 32, 53, 59, 96, 98, 100, 102, 108
Bodvoc 28
Boudicca (see also Boadicea) 12, 27-8, 77, 87, 116-7, 119-47, 150, 159, 168, 170, 176, 185
Brentford, London 47
Brigantes 114-4, 119, 183
Britannicus 114, 118
Burham, Kent 102-3
Caerleon, Gwent 178
Caernarfon, Gwynedd 152

Caerwent, Gwent 44
Caesar, Julius 15-23, 29-51, 54-6, 61-7, 71, 76, 79-84, 86-8, 91-4, 98, 110, 115, 127-9, 136-7, 148, 155-7, 169, 188
Caistor St Edmund, Norfolk (see also *Venta Icenorum / Ecenorum*) 27, 176
Caledonia 148, 152-5, 159-60, 168, 180
Calleva Atrebatum (see also Silchester) 25, 32, 55, 57, 75, 111
Calgacus 155-7
Caligula 46, 52, 77, 80-92, 117-8, 166-7, 171, 175
Camulodunum (see also Colchester and Colonia Claudia Victriensis) 20, 47, 57-60, 78, 81, 88, 92-4, 108, 111-112, 114, 132, 126
Canterbury, Kent (see also *Durovernum Cantiacorum*) 31, 87-8
Cantiaci (see also Cantium) 24, 26, 31, 88
Cantium (see also Cantiaci) 21, 31, 46, 63, 88, 112
Caracalla 22
Caratacus 59, 80, 87, 93-4, 99-103, 106-8, 111-5, 119, 123, 136, 142-3, 156, 169
Carlisle 152, 178
Cartimandua 114, 119
Carvilius 21, 88
Cassi 20-1, 38, 44, 46, 50
Cassius Dio (see Dio Cassius)
Cassivellaunos 21, 25, 33-5, 37-50, 58, 81, 88, 114, 123, 136-7, 156
Catuarus 146, 171, 173, 175
Catus, Decianus 124-5, 133, 135, 142
Catuvelluani 11, 21, 25, 26, 44, 46, 57-60, 63, 67, 81, 88, 100, 108, 111-2, 116-7, 119-27, 129, 131-9, 143, 175, 185
Cenimagni (see also Eceni and Iceni) 20-1, 44-6, 63, 131
Cerialis, Petilius 135, 152
Chelmsford, Essex 24
Chester 170, 178
Chesterholm, Northumberland (see *Vindolanda*)

Chichester (see also *Noviomagus*) 32, 72-4, 77-8, 89-90, 96-8, 103, 108-9. 111-2, 142-6, 164-7, 170-3
Cicero 48-9
Cingetorix 21, 38, 88
Cirencester, Gloucestershire (see also *Corinium*) 27-8, 96, 98, 100, 108
Classicianus, Alpinus 143-4, 170
Claudius 21, 23, 29, 56, 77-8, 82, 90, 91-100, 104, 107-15, 117-19, 124, 132-6, 142-3, 146, 166-7, 169, 171, 173, 175
Cleopatra 36-7, 61, 101
Colchester (see also *Camulodunum* and *Colonia Claudia Victriensis*) 12, 20, 24, 29, 47, 57-8, 73, 77-8, 81, 92-4, 98, 107-8, 111, 113-4, 132-5, 138-9, 143, 185
Colonia Claudia Victriensis (see also *Camulodunum* and Colchester) 132-5, 137-8
Commios 32, 37, 39, 54-7, 60, 64, 75, 81-2, 90
Corieltauvi 26
Corinium (see also Cirencester) 27
Coritani (see Corieltauvi)
Cornovii 32
Cranborne, Dorset 70, 76
Crispus, Passienus 166
Critognatus 157
Cunobelinus 58-60, 80, 88-9, 94, 100, 104, 108, 111-2, 167, 175

Damnatio memoriae 134, 148, 165
Deal, Kent 40-2
Dio Cassius 11, 15, 28, 41, 52, 58-9, 64-5, 80-2, 86-7, 91-108, 112, 123-5, 130-3, 136, 138-9, 147, 154, 156, 160, 169-70
Diocletian 22
Dobunni (see also Bodunni) 27-8, 53, 96, 100, 108
Domitian 96, 110, 142, 148-9, 154-60, 161-77, 178-9, 185
Domus Aurea 140-1, 146
Domus Flavia 172-5
Dorchester, Dorset 30-1
Dover, Kent 40, 85
Druids 11, 37, 126-31
Dubnovellaunos 61, 64, 75, 82, 88, 110
Durotrages (see also Durotriges) 30-1
Durotriges (see also Durotrages) 26, 28-31, 71
Durovernum Cantiacorum (see also Canterbury) 25, 31, 87-8

Eceni (see also Cenimagni and Iceni) 21, 27, 44, 46, 53, 63, 112, 116, 120-8, 130, 132, 136-9, 143, 170, 176, 185
Epaticus 60, 112
Eppillus 32, 56-7, 59

Esuprastus (see also Prastotagus) 121

Facilis, Favonius 134
Fenny Stratford, Buckinghamshire 51
Ferrox 179
Fronto 182
Fishbourne, West Sussex 12, 32, 75-9, 144-6, 170, 172-5, 185-8

Gaius (see Caligula)
Gaul 16-7, 36-8, 44, 46, 49, 54-6, 64, 71, 80, 87, 90, 94, 107, 115, 127-9, 133, 141, 157, 166, 169, 177
Gallus, Didius 119
Gosbecks, Essex 73, 77-9

Hadrian 30, 170, 177-8, 181-5
Hadrian's Wall 30, 177, 181-2, 184
Hawkshaw, Scottish Borders 179
Herodian 160
Horace 67
Housteads, Northumberland 184

Iceni (see also Cenimagni and Eceni) 21, 24, 26-7, 44, 46, 53, 116, 120-1, 124
Ilchester, Somerset 30-1
Imanuentius (see also Mannuetios) 45

Joist Fen, Suffolk 120

Kenchester, Herefordshire 27

Legio II 11, 92-3, 101-4, 107, 119, 139
Legio VI 167, 182
Legio VII 107-8, 183-5
Legio VIII 183-5
Legio IX 11, 92-3, 101-3, 107, 139, 179, 180-2
Legio X 33, 40
Legio XII 183-5
Legio XIV 11, 92-3, 101-3, 107, 135, 139
Legio XX 11, 92-3, 101-3, 107, 132, 134, 139
Lexden, Essex 73
Londinium (see also London) 132-3, 135, 137-8
London (see also *Londinium*) 12, 96, 103, 122, 132, 138-9, 142-4 184-5
Longinus 134
Lucullus 90, 162-77, 179, 185-6, 189

Maiden Castle, Dorset 29, 70
Mandubracius 20, 44-8, 50, 132, 137
Mannuetios (see also Imanuentius) 45-6
Marcus Aurelius 178, 182
Medway, river 92-3, 99, 101-2
Mons Graupius 148, 151, 154-8, 160

Nepos, Platorius 182
Nepos, Veranius 119
Nero 21, 110, 117-9, 122-4, 134-7, 140-3, 145-50, 166, 169-72, 175, 184-5
Nerva 148-9, 155, 178, 183
Newstead, Scottish Borders 152
Noviomagus (see also Chichester) 32, 34, 90, 109, 183

Octavian (see Augustus)
Old Burrow, Devon 113
Ordovices 113-4, 150-1
Orosius 21

Paulinus, Suetonius 119, 126, 138-43
Pertinax 167
Plautius, Aulus 29, 58, 80, 92-3, 96-101, 103-8, 110-1, 114, 143
Pliny 128-9, 153, 171
Portsmouth, Hampshire 95-6, 108
Prae Wood, Hertfordshire 47
Prastotagus 120-4, 137
Prasutagus (see also Prastotagus) 120-4
Priscus, Javolenus 169
Propertius 67
Ptolemy XIII 101
Ptolemy, Claudius 21-2, 26, 32, 99, 153
Ptolemy of Mauretania 90
Pulborough, West Sussex 103, 175

Regni (see also Regnum) 32
Regnum 32, 111, 120
Richborough, Kent 11, 76, 93-9, 101, 107-8

Sabinus, Pontius 183-5
St Albans (see also *Verulamium*) 12, 44, 47, 57, 74, 81, 111, 136-9, 143
Saturninus, Antonius 164
Saturninus, Sentius 98
Saxmundham, Suffolk 134-5, 184-5
Scapula, Ostorius 114, 119
Segontiaci 20-1, 46
Segontium (Caernarfon) 152
Segovax 21, 88
Severus, Septimus 159-60
Sheepen, Essex 73
Silchester, Hampshire (see also *Calleva Atrebatum*) 12, 32, 55, 73, 75, 82, 108, 111, 138-9
Silures 113-4, 119
Snettisham, Norfolk 120
Southampton, Hampshire 95-6
Southwick, West Sussex 175
Stanway, Essex 74, 143
Statius, Papinius 152-3

Strabo 18-20, 48-50, 63
Suetonius 29-30, 48, 52, 66, 80, 82-8, 90-1, 111, 117, 119, 140, 161, 163, 166-7, 169-70

Tacitus 15, 21, 33, 50, 68-9, 92, 109-110, 114-5, 119-24, 130-44, 147-59, 168-70, 177, 188
Tasciovanus 57-60, 80, 112, 186
Taximagulus 21, 88
Tay, river 151-2
Thames, river 12, 44-7, 57, 61, 80, 92-6, 98-9, 102, 104, 108, 133, 143, 184-5
Thanet, Kent 41
Thetford, Norfolk 116
Tiberius 77, 80, 83-4, 110, 128-9, 167
Tincomarus 56-7, 61, 64, 75, 79, 82, 90, 95, 110, 171
Titus 110, 149-50, 154, 161, 173
Togidubnus (see also Togodumnus) 12, 108-15, 120, 136, 139-46, 165-76, 189
Togodumnus (see also Togidubnus) 59, 80, 82, 93-6, 98-100, 104-115, 136
Tomen-y-Mur, Gwynedd 151
Trajan 22, 149, 155, 178-9, 182-5
Trinobantes (see also Trinovantes) 20-1, 44-8, 50, 57-60, 63, 81, 112, 132, 136-7, 139, 143
Trinovantes (see also Trinobantes) 11, 20-1, 26, 45, 57, 60

Venta Belgarum (see also Winchester) 31, 138
Venta Icenorum / Ecenorum (see also Caistor St Edmund) 25, 27, 176
Veneti 35
Vercassivellaunus 38
Vercingetorix 37-8, 54, 115
Verica (see also Berikos) 21, 52, 56-7, 59, 81-2, 89, 94-9, 110, 171
Verulamium (see also St Albans) 47, 57, 59-60, 81, 88, 111-112, 136-8, 143
Vespasian 29-31, 93, 101-4, 107-8, 110, 148-50, 152-3, 155, 160-1, 175
Vindolanda 178, 180, 183

Walmer, Kent 40-2
Welwyn, Hertfordshire 18
Wheathamstead, Hertfordshire 47
Wight, Isle of 29, 95
Winchester (see also *Venta Belgarum*) 12, 31, 73, 111, 138-9

York 167, 170, 178-9, 182